★ ★ ★ ★ ★

AS GOOD AS GOLD

★ ★ ★ ★ ★

GRAND PRIZE RECIPES
FROM
AMERICA'S COOKING CONTESTS

Linda Davis-O'Brien

★ ★ ★ AS GOOD AS GOLD ★ ★ ★

For additional copies, use the order blanks in the back of the book, or write directly to AS GOOD AS GOLD.

First Edition, First Printing, 10,000, September, 1993

ISBN 0-9634470-0-9

Library of Congress Catalog Card Number: 92-96945

Printed in the USA by

WIMMER
The Wimmer Companies, Inc.
Memphis • Dallas

TABLE OF CONTENTS

ACKNOWLEDGMENT

Americans love good food and thrive on competition. Put the two together and the world of recipe contests emerges — a world where, for decades, American cooks have gone for the gold in their own kitchens... where prizewinning recipes have become classics, broken new ground, and even set trends... where countless cooks have won — BIG — in contests sponsored by:

- Food manufacturers whose products are household words and pantry necessities.
- Familiar and friendly magazines, periodicals, and newspapers that have shaped and defined American lifestyles as well as educated and entertained.
- Trade associations, state fairs, and local festivals that showcase everything from apples to zucchini.
- Private organizations, companies, schools, and businesses that provide goods and services Americans would find it difficult to live without.

On behalf of America's recipe contest cooks,

THANK YOU

for the food... the fun... the fantasy and the reality. And, most of all, thank you for elevating the art of home cooking to culinary olympics status, where everyday American cooks can become gold medalists of the kitchen.

RECIPE CONTRIBUTORS

With appreciation to the following companies and organizations for the use of their recipes in AS GOOD AS GOLD:

American Egg Board, especially Kay Engelhardt, Test Kitchen Supervisor

Armour Swift-Eckrich

Baskin-Robbins Inc.

Bays English Muffins

Best Foods/CPC International Inc.

Best Foods Baking Group/CPC International Inc.

California Avocado Commission

Campbell Soup Company, very special thanks to Pat Teberg, Corporate Editor-Publications

Catfish Farmers of America

CHOCOLATIER, thank you Timothy Moriarty, Managing Editor

Churny® Athenos® Feta Cheese, special thanks to Nancy Dennis

Delmarva Poultry Industry, Inc., thank you Connie Parvis, Director, Consumer Information

Del Monte Fresh Produce Company, Inc.

Dole Food Company, Inc., very special appreciation to Joel Young and Kit Searight and to Paul J. Yoder, Manager, Industry Relations, **Dole Fresh Fruit Company**

Dow Brands L. P.

Ekco Company/Packaging Corporation of America

The Estee Corporation

FAMILY CIRCLE

Fleischmann's Specialty Brands, A Division of Burns Philp Food, Inc.

General Mills, Inc., a special thank you to Marcia K. Copeland, Director of Betty Crocker Food and Publications Center

Ghirardelli Chocolate Company, thank you Christine Fontana, Marketing Manager

Gilroy Garlic Festival Association, Inc., thanks to Richard J. Nicholls, Executive Director

GOOD HOUSEKEEPING and **GOURMET MAGAZINE**, special thanks for their roles in support of recipe contests.

Hunt-Wesson, Inc.

International Apple Institute

International Chili Society, thank you Jim West, President

The J. M. Smucker Company, special thanks to Vickie Limbach

Johnson & Wales University, thank you Linda Beaulieu

Joseph E. Seagram & Sons, Inc., special thanks to Kevin Byrne, Jon A. Lewis, Alice Bauer, and Tom McInerney

The Keebler Co., especially Steven E. Parker, Product Manager

Kellogg Company

King Arthur Flour Co., thank you Ellen Davies

KitchenAid, Inc.

Kraft General Foods, Inc., special thanks to Carol Blindauer, Group Kitchens Manager, Kraft Creative Kitchens and Linda A. Heban, Trademark Counsel

LADIES' HOME JOURNAL, special thanks to Jan T. Hazard, Food and Equipment Editor

Lamb Committee of the National Live Stock and Meat Board in cooperation with the National Lamb Feeders Association

Land O'Lakes, Inc.

Lawry's Foods, Inc., thank you Maribeth Drogosz

Maui Land & Pineapple Company, Inc.

McCALL'S

McCormick & Co., Inc., thank you Camille Appel

Memphis In May International Festival, Inc., thank you Cynthia Hamm and Ida Eleazer

Merv Griffin's Paradise Island, special thanks to Robin Busby

Nabisco Foods, Inc.

National Beef Cook-Off and the American National CattleWomen, Inc. in cooperation with the Beef Industry Council and the Beef Board, thanks especially to Anita Wehrman of the Maryland Beef Council and Nancy Burgett

National Broiler Council, thank you George B. Watts, President

National Live Stock & Meat Board, special thanks to Marlys Bielunski, Director, Test Kitchens and Editorial Services

National Oyster Cook-Off, the Maryland Department of Agriculture, Office of Seafood Marketing, and St. Mary's County Department of Economic and Community Development

National Pork Producers Council

National Turkey Federation, especially Chin Chu Moon, Consumer Affairs Specialist

Newman's Own, Inc., with special appreciation to Linda Rohr, Public Relations Director

Ocean Spray Cranberries, Inc.

Pace® Picante Sauce/Pace Foods, Inc., thank you Claudia Hueser

Pet Incorporated, special thanks to Kent M. Rapp

Pig Iron Porkers, thank you Steve McLain

The Pillsbury Company, with very special thanks to Sally Peters, Director of Consumer Service/ Publications

Pineapple Growers Association of Hawaii, special thanks go to Brian C. Nishida, Public Affairs Chairperson

Planters LifeSavers Company, thank you Chuck Wallington

PREVENTION

The Procter & Gamble Company, Inc., special thanks to Julie Northrop and Terry Koritz

Quaker Oats Company

Sara Lee Bakery, a very special thank you to Robert B. Wheatley

Sargento Cheese Company, Inc., thank you Barbara Gannon

SATURDAY EVENING POST

Sun World International, thanks to Timothy J. Dayka

Sutter Home Winery, especially B. Alexander Morgan

Thomas J. Lipton Company, with special appreciation to Mary F. Pfeil, Records Administrator and John C. Young for providing historic KNOX® recipe contest announcements and information.

Uncle Ben's, Inc.

Wailuku Agribusiness Company, Inc.

WOMAN'S DAY, Elizabeth Alston, Food Editor and Beth Richardson

THANKS TO ALL OF YOU

My husband, DENNIS, the "Master of Marinade," for your enthusiasm and encouragement... your assistance and support... your sense of adventure and willingness to explore new gustatory experiences... and for being the most fun kitchen buddy ever.

Our Friends, MARCI and DAVE SPILMAN, BETH McKNIGHT, NANCY FLETCHER, BETH SINGER, JIM BAMBERGER, for "being there"... for being frequent, willing guinea pigs and eager readers, too.

GEORGE, GIGI, and PAT O'BRIEN, MOM and DAD, My Brother, ALAN, for your inspiration, curiosity, and for being the best possible cheering section.

The HAASER FAMILY, for the good food, fun, memories, and "American Piece-A-Pie."

FREDDIE STRANGE and VICKI WADLINGTON of The Wimmer Companies, Inc., for your guidance and professional know-how.

The late HANNA FOXE, Editor of the *Blue Ribbon Cooks' Newsletter*, for her helpful assistance with many questions and requests.

NEWSLETTERS OF THE PAST:

Contest Buster Newsletter, Contest News-Letter, Shepherd Contest Bulletin,

AND NEWSLETTERS OF TODAY:

Cooking Contest Chronicle, The Cooking Contest Newsletter, for getting the recipe contest word out and reporting the news.

The RECIPE CONTESTERS OF AMERICA, for your realness and creativity, which know no bounds.

JOSEPH E. SEAGRAM & SONS, INC. and The PINEAPPLE GROWERS ASSOCIATION OF HAWAII, for hosting unforgettable, dream-come-true adventures in San Francisco and Hawaii.

Dear Recipe Contest Champions:

If you do not find your Grand Prize recipe in this collection, it may be for any of several reasons. A few organizations cited company policy that prohibited reprint permission, while a handful simply did not, or would not, respond to inquiries.

Some companies could not find "old" recipes, especially those that were pre-1990. In addition, with all of the buying and selling of companies that occurred during the 1980's, some did not keep track of contest-winning recipes and the records could not be located. In rare cases, a Grand Prize winner's name was not available. There are a few examples of these in this collection — perhaps one of them is yours.

Special effort was made to locate certain individuals' recipes, to no avail. These are the recipes of those whose names are legendary in recipe contesting circles. I sincerely hope that Roxanne Chan ("Frozen Fiesta Fantastica"), Debbie Yandric (Hanover Brands and Chex contests), and many other well-known contesters will provide their Grand Prize recipes for future editions of AS GOOD AS GOLD.

In fact, I hope that recipe contesters who have won a Grand Prize of at least $1,000 in cash and/or prizes will share their recipes with the contest information for a second edition of AS GOOD AS GOLD. In the meantime,

Happy Contesting!

Linda Davis-O'Brien

Ten percent of the profits from the sales of AS GOOD AS GOLD will benefit the Living Classrooms Foundation. As a tax exempt, non-profit organization, the Foundation provides hands-on educational programs primarily in outdoor "Living Classrooms."

These Living Classrooms feature two historic ships, a llama farm, an historic lighthouse, and the Maritime Institute, a job-training facility resembling a turn-of-the-century shipyard. All are dedicated to providing experience-based programs that involve "learning by doing."

Special emphasis is placed on at-risk youth and groups from diverse backgrounds, including the blind and physically challenged. An educational innovator, the Foundation's programs emphasize ecology and the environment, personal and career development, cultural enrichment, and the applied learning of math, science, history, and economics.

The Living Classrooms Foundation serves approximately 20,000 students annually in programs that couple teamwork and responsibility with achievable results.

LADY MARYLAND, The Ship For Kids

The tall ship <u>Lady Maryland</u> is a 104-foot replica of an 1800's pungy, an elegant Chesapeake Bay schooner that was used to haul perishable cargo quickly from port to port. The only pungy in the world today, <u>Lady Maryland</u> was built by the Foundation's shipwrights with the help of school children. She was launched in Baltimore's Inner Harbor in 1986 as a floating classroom.

Today, <u>Lady Maryland's</u> cargo is more precious than gold—our kids, tomorrow's future.

Bill McAllen ©1993

Maryland School for the Blind students deploy and haul in a 16-foot trawl net aboard <u>Lady Maryland</u>. The day's catch included crabs, a large flounder, and jellyfish.

FOREWORD

Tales of gold have long captured the imagination... stories of buried treasure and riches from Egyptian tombs... of sunken Spanish galleons brimming with doubloons and pieces of eight... of the forty-niners, gold rush days, and the Mother Lode.

We're thrilled when world class athletes earn coveted Olympic gold medals... and we're enchanted by an old Irish legend that says there's a pot o' gold to be found at rainbow's end.

In a sense, AS GOOD AS GOLD combines a little of each of these elements in weaving its tale of culinary gold — stories of treasured heirloom recipes rediscovered in the kitchens of America, where a new gold rush was sparked in 1949 when Pillsbury awarded a whopping $50,000 Grand Prize at its first Bake-Off®.

Since then, American kitchens have become one of the greatest gold districts of all — a place where everyday cooks can become gold medalists of the kitchen and where, at least in a fanciful way, food that's worth its weight in gold, and often more, transforms the lowliest casserole or cooking pot or pan into a POT O' GOLD.

INTRODUCTION

My fascination with the world of recipe contests began in 1954 when I was just a little kid still making fancy mud pies. Our family had been invited to spend the day and have dinner with another family who lived some distance away. At the time I could not have known the impact this particular dinner would have on me.

Our hostess served something called "American Piece-A-Pie," saying that it was a Junior Division winner at the Pillsbury Bake-Off®. The recipe had just been published in the newspaper and since all of us liked pizza so much, she gave it a try. I remember being intrigued with the recipe's name, it's pinkish crust (from the chili powder and tomato sauce), and today I'm still delighted with its mouth-watering taste.

As a cross between the flavors of a chili-cheeseburger and pizza, it was right in sync with the 1950's when pizza was supreme. Although "American Piece-A-Pie" did not win the Grand Prize, it's included in this collection mostly for nostalgic reasons, but also because it was the first prizewinning dish I ever tasted and it launched this cookbook.

Some years later I remember an extra special mid-morning coffee break when a co-worker presented our group with an absolutely gorgeous cake. As its lemony aroma wafted under our noses she announced, "This cake just won $10,000. I thought we'd check it out." I remember thinking that I might be able to pull something like that off since I'm often in the kitchen by choice. As it turned out, this was the experience that inspired me to enter my first recipe contest.

In 1973 Seagram's V.O. announced an International Hors d'Oeuvre Recipe Contest with GOURMET MAGAZINE. Amazingly, a recipe I created for seafood stuffed mushroom caps won me a trip to San Francisco to compete for the Grand Prize — a two-week gourmet tour of London, Paris, and Rome, plus $1,500 mad money.

Highlights of the San Francisco trip included staying at the regal Fairmont Hotel where Sarah Vaughn was headlining in the hotel's night club... a twenty-course dinner at the Empress of China (I only managed to work my way through eighteen of them) ... dinner at Ernie's, San Francisco's renowned French restaurant, followed by an academy awards-style ceremony that was punctuated by the opening of the envelope containing GOURMET's selection of the winner. Although I did not win the Grand Prize, our Seagram's V. O. hosts made each of the five finalists feel as if we had.

In 1977 I was one of 40 lucky finalists who won a trip to Hawaii to compete for a Grand Prize of $25,000 in that year's National Pineapple Cooking Classic, sponsored by the Pineapple Growers Association of

Hawaii. Although I didn't win the Grand Prize in either the Seagram's V.O. or the pineapple contest, I felt that I was the big winner — but every finalist felt that way.

It was that Hawaiian odyssey — a week in paradise — that inspired the cover for AS GOOD AS GOLD. I've included some of the memories from that trip in "A Week In The Life Of A Recipe Contest Finalist" in the "Just For Fun" section of the book.

After these wins I was hooked on recipe contesting as a hobby. Over the years I avidly entered contests and collected prizewinning recipes, storing them safely — if haphazardly — in a large suitcase. I realized I had amassed a sizeable collection the day I had to sit on my Samsonite two-suiter in order to close it. That's when I knew I would either have to invest in a three-suiter or bring some order to the chaotic collection.

I decided to share the recipes and flavor them with the fun of the contests themselves — a world where prizewinning recipes always reflect what and how America is cooking. In sifting and sorting through hundreds of top prizewinning recipes, I felt like the prospector who had struck gold. Since some recipes trace back to contests as early as 1928, 1925, and even 1904, I felt like the lucky finder of buried treasure.

No matter how dated the cooking method, the equipment required, or the ingredients themselves have become, each recipe in this collection is important to the historical reflection of food trends over the decades. It's perhaps more important to look back to see where we've been in order to understand where we are now or imagine where we might be tomorrow.

Every recipe in AS GOOD AS GOLD is the top prize winner in its competition and has won the coveted Grand Prize, earning for its creator thousands of dollars, exotic trips and cruises, luxury cars, or dream kitchen makeovers loaded with the latest in appliances. But best of all, each recipe is guaranteed for success — who could resist the temptation to prepare recipes judged to be worth $25,000... $50,000.... or a mind-boggling $100,000.

Welcome to the wonderful, colorful world of recipe contests with its broad spectrum of food fun and fun food, people and places, fantasy and reality. AS GOOD AS GOLD is your entertaining secret, your treasure trove of gold star recipes. Perhaps you'll be inspired to enter a contest or two. Regardless, when you prepare these Grand Prize recipes that have been awarded the highest possible honor — GRAND PRIZE — you'll be the winner!

So, ladies and gentlemen, start your ovens…

SWEET SUCCESSES

$2,500

APPLE-ALMOND LINZER TORTE

2 cups all-purpose flour
1 teaspoon ground cinnamon
¼ teaspoon ground nutmeg
1 cup butter or margarine, at room
  temperature
1 cup granulated sugar
2 large eggs
1 tablespoon lemon juice
1 teaspoon vanilla

½ cup finely chopped almonds
2 GRANNY SMITH OR
  GOLDEN DELICIOUS
  APPLES (6 ounces each),
  peeled, cored, and cut in thin
  wedges (2½ cups)
½ cup (6 ounces) apple jelly
½ cup sliced almonds
For garnish: confectioners' sugar

- Place oven rack at lowest position; heat oven to 350°. Grease a 9-inch springform pan. Mix flour, cinnamon, and nutmeg. In a large bowl beat butter and sugar with electric mixer until light and fluffy. Beat in eggs one at a time, then lemon juice and vanilla. Stir in flour mixture and chopped almonds until well blended. Measure out ⅔ cup batter and set aside. Spread remainder in bottom of prepared pan. Starting ¼ inch from edge of pan, arrange about 1½ cups of the apples in a circle, slightly overlapping. Form another circle on top with remaining apples, starting ½ inch from center of pan. Meanwhile, melt ¼ cup jelly and brush over apples. Drop teaspoonfuls of the reserved batter around outside edge and spread with back of spoon to make a ½-inch border (or pipe through pastry bag fitted with plain round tube with an opening of about ½ inch). Fill center of torte with remaining batter. Arrange some sliced almonds in center; sprinkle remainder over border. Bake 1 hour or until golden. Cool in pan on rack 15 minutes. Remove pan sides. Melt remaining ¼ cup jelly and brush apples again. Cool completely on rack. Sprinkle border and center with confectioners' sugar.
- Makes 12 servings.

Recipe developed by Diane Lentz of Nicholasville, Kentucky for the 1986 "Pick Apples, America" Recipe Contest. Recipe courtesy of WOMAN'S DAY Magazine, Hachette Magazines, Inc., and the International Apple Institute

$25,000

PINEAPPLE MERINGUE CAKE

1 cup sifted cake flour
2 teaspoons baking powder
⅛ teaspoon salt
4 large eggs, separated
1½ cups sugar

2 teaspoons vanilla
½ cup shortening
5 tablespoons milk
¾ cup finely chopped pecans

Pineapple Cream Filling:
1 can (13½ ounces) CRUSHED
  PINEAPPLE, well drained
1 cup whipping cream

1½ teaspoons confectioners' sugar
¼ teaspoon vanilla

- Preheat oven to 350°. Resift flour with baking powder and salt. Beat egg whites to soft peaks. Gradually beat in 1 cup sugar, continuing to beat until stiff. Fold in 1 teaspoon vanilla. Set aside. Cream shortening with remaining ½ cup sugar well. Beat in egg yolks. Blend in flour mixture alternately with milk. Stir in remaining teaspoon vanilla. Divide batter evenly between two well-greased and floured 8-inch layer cake pans. Top each with half the meringue and sprinkle with pecans. Bake about 35 to 45 minutes, until cake tests done and meringue is a light golden brown. Remove from oven and cool in pans. Loosen edges of cake and meringue with small spatula, and turn out. Place 1 layer, meringue side down, on serving plate and spread with Pineapple Cream Filling. Top with second layer, meringue side up. Refrigerate several hours or overnight before serving. (Note: Meringue will often spread or be a little crumbly in texture on baking. Press together with hands to shape, if necessary. Cake and filling will mellow on standing.)

Pineapple Cream Filling:

- Beat whipping cream with confectioners' sugar and vanilla until stiff. Fold in crushed pineapple.
- Makes one 8-inch cake, about 12 servings.

Recipe developed by Ethel Kliebert of Vacherie, Louisiana for the 1977 National Pineapple Cooking Classic. Recipe courtesy of the Pineapple Growers Association of Hawaii: Del Monte Fresh Produce Company, Inc., Dole Food Company, Inc., Maui Land & Pineapple Company, Inc., Wailuku Agribusiness Company, Inc. Look for the "100% Hawaiian" designation on canned pineapple products.

TRIP FOR TWO TO SAN FRANCISCO & $500

SUPREME CHOCOLATE CHEESECAKE

Crust:

18 chocolate sandwich cookies, crushed (1½ cups)

¼ cup (½ stick) PARKAY® Margarine, melted

Filling:

3 packages (8 ounces each) PHILADELPHIA® BRAND Cream Cheese, softened

1 can (14 ounces) sweetened condensed milk

3 eggs

1 package (12 ounces) semi-sweet chocolate chips, melted

2 teaspoons vanilla

Frosting:

⅓ cup PARKAY® Margarine

½ cup powdered sugar

1 cup semi-sweet chocolate chips, melted

2 tablespoons orange-flavored liqueur

Crust:

• Mix crushed cookies and margarine; press onto bottom of 9-inch springform pan.

Filling:

• Heat oven to 300°. Beat cream cheese and milk at medium speed with electric mixer until well blended. Add eggs, 1 at a time, mixing well after each addition. Blend in melted chocolate and vanilla; pour over crust. Bake 1 hour and 10 minutes. Loosen cake from rim of pan; cool before removing rim of pan.

Frosting:

• Beat margarine and sugar until light and fluffy. Add melted chocolate and liqueur, mixing until well blended. Frost top and sides of cheesecake. Refrigerate.

• Makes 10 to 12 servings.

1987 "Philly" Hall of Fame Recipe Contest

Four Grand Prize winners won luxurious trips to San Francisco, including first class airfare, sightseeing via limousine, an awards dinner, and $500 mad money. With her 3-D cheesecake—deep, dark, and decadent—Kim Marsden from Renton, Washington demonstrated chocolate's affinity with cream cheese.

Recipe courtesy of Kraft General Foods, Inc.

TRIP TO HAWAII

CHOCO-MYSTERIOSO

Ghirardelli chocolate is a brilliant disguise for grated carrots and zucchini. Closer investigation reveals grated orange rind and cinnamon are in on the conspiracy.

Cake:

1 cup oil
2 cups sugar
3 eggs, beaten well
3 ounces GHIRARDELLI®
  Unsweetened Chocolate,
  melted
2 teaspoons vanilla
2 teaspoons freshly grated orange
  rind

½ cup milk
1 cup finely grated, peeled
  zucchini
1 cup finely grated carrot
2½ cups unbleached flour
3 teaspoons baking powder
2 teaspoons baking soda
½ teaspoon salt
2 teaspoons cinnamon

Filling:

¼ cup water
1 tablespoon cornstarch
½ cup half-and-half
2 egg yolks
1 cup (8 ounces) unsalted
  whipped butter

2 cups confectioners' sugar, sifted
1 teaspoon vanilla
1 teaspoon orange extract
5 drops yellow food coloring
2 tablespoons grated carrot

Frosting:

1 cup (8 ounces) unsalted
  whipped butter, softened
3 egg yolks

2 cups confectioners' sugar, sifted
5 ounces GHIRARDELLI®
  Unsweetened Chocolate,
  melted and cooled

Cake:

- Preheat oven to 350°. In large mixer bowl beat together oil, sugar and eggs. Add chocolate, vanilla, orange rind and milk, beating well after each addition. Remove excess moisture from zucchini and carrots with paper towels; add to batter and mix well. Sift together flour, baking powder, soda, salt and cinnamon; add to batter and mix well.

- Spray two 9-inch cake pans with vegetable cooking spray, or grease and flour pans. Pour mixture equally into both pans. Bake for 45 to 50 minutes, or until toothpick inserted in center comes out clean. Cool 10 minutes before turning onto racks. When layers are cool, cover and chill until cold.

Filling:

- In saucepan mix water with cornstarch; add half-and-half and egg yolks. Cook over low heat, stirring constantly, until mixture thickens and coats spoon. Cover and chill about 30 minutes.

- Cream butter, adding sugar a little at a time. Add vanilla, orange extract and food color, mixing well after each addition. Gradually add the chilled cooked mixture and grated carrot, beating well. Chill until firm enough to spread.

Frosting:

- Cream butter in mixer bowl. Beat in egg yolks one at a time. Gradually beat in sugar by heaping tablespoons. Beat well. Slowly add chocolate, beating until mixture is shiny. Chill to spreading consistency. Fill and frost layers. Cake, filling and frosting are best when served chilled.

- Makes 10 to 12 servings.

1985 Great American Chocolate Layer Cake Contest

During the 1980's whole cookbooks on chocolate appeared, CHOCOLATIER Magazine was launched, and this recipe appeared in the "Chocolate News," a newsletter for chocoholics. One hundred entrants vied for the Grand Prize in this contest sponsored by Ghirardelli that was held — where else — in San Francisco. Leave it to a Californian, Carol Granaldi, to solve the mystery of how moms can get their kids to eat carrots and zucchini.

Recipe courtesy of the Ghirardelli Chocolate Company and Carol Granaldi

ONE-WEEK CANADIAN CRUISE FOR TWO
CHOCOLATE PASTILLES

Pinwheel slices of whipped cream-filled chocolate cake glazed with rich chocolate ganache. Decorative piped white icing gives each slice a pastry chef's finishing touch. (Allow at least 8 hours to freeze the roll.)

Chocolate Cake:
1¼ cups cake flour
1¼ teaspoons baking soda
¼ teaspoon salt
6 tablespoons UNSWEETENED NONALKALIZED COCOA POWDER
⅓ cup boiling water
1½ teaspoons vanilla extract

4 tablespoons (½ stick) unsalted butter, softened
¼ cup solid vegetable shortening
1 cup granulated sugar, divided
2 large eggs, at room temperature, separated
½ cup buttermilk, at room temperature

Cream Filling:
1½ cups heavy (whipping) cream
2 tablespoons granulated sugar

1½ teaspoons vanilla extract

Ganache Glaze:
1¼ pounds BITTERSWEET CHOCOLATE, coarsely chopped

10 tablespoons (1¼ sticks) unsalted butter, softened
1 cup heavy (whipping) cream

Royal Icing:
1 large egg white, at room temperature

Approximately 2 cups sifted confectioners' sugar

Cake:

- Position a rack in the center of the oven and preheat to 325°. Line the bottom of an 11½ x 17½-inch jelly roll pan with aluminum foil, leaving a 2-inch overhang on the short ends. Fold the overhang underneath the pan. Butter the aluminum foil and the sides of the pan. Lightly dust the bottom and sides of the pan with flour and tap out the excess.

- In a medium bowl, sift together the cake flour, baking soda and salt.

- In another medium bowl, whisk together the cocoa and boiling water until the mixture is smooth. Stir in the vanilla.

- In a large bowl, using a hand-held electric mixer, set at medium-high speed, beat the butter and shortening for 30 to 60 seconds, until creamy. Gradually beat in ¾ cup plus 2 tablespoons of the sugar. One at a time, add the egg yolks, beating well after each addition, and continue beating for 2 to 3 minutes, until light and fluffy, scraping down the sides of the bowl occasionally. Reduce the speed to low. In three additions, alternately mix in the flour mixture and the butter-milk, scraping the sides of the bowl after each addition. Beat in the cocoa mixture until smooth.

- In a large, grease-free bowl, using a hand-held electric mixer set at low speed, beat the egg whites until frothy. Gradually increase the speed to medium-high and continue beating the egg whites until they start to form soft peaks. One teaspoon at a time, add the remaining 2 tablespoons of sugar. Continue beating the whites until they form stiff, shiny peaks when the beaters are lifted.

- Stir one-fourth of the beaten egg white mixture into the batter to lighten. Fold the remaining whites into the batter. Scrape the batter into the prepared jelly roll pan and spread it evenly with a spatula.

- Bake 12 to 15 minutes, until the cake is just puffed and slightly underdone. The edges of the cake should not have pulled away from the sides of the pan. Cool the cake completely in the pan on a wire rack.

Cream Filling:

- In a large, chilled bowl, using a hand-held electric mixer set at medium speed, beat the cream with the sugar until stiff peaks form. Beat in the vanilla.

Assembly:

- Using a small knife, loosen the edges of the cake from the sides of the pan. Place a large flat baking sheet over the top of the cake and invert to remove the cake from the pan. Carefully peel off the aluminum foil. Re-cover the cake loosely with a new piece of aluminum foil. Place another large flat baking sheet over the foil and invert the cake again so the cake is rightside up.

- Using a flexible spatula, spread the cream filling evenly over the cake, leaving a 1-inch border around the sides. Using the aluminum foil as a guide, roll the cake starting on a long side into a tight cylinder. Wrap the roll tightly in the foil. Freeze the roll overnight or for at least 8 hours.

Ganache Glaze:

- In the top part of a double boiler over hot, not simmering, water, melt the chocolate and the butter, stirring frequently until smooth. Remove the top part of the double boiler from the bottom. Using a rubber spatula, gradually fold in the cream, until the glaze is well combined. Cool the glaze at room temperature for about 1 hour, stirring fre-quently but gently, until it is thick and almost set.

Royal Icing:

- In a small grease-free bowl, using a hand-held electric mixer set at medium-high speed, beat the egg white until soft peaks form. Gradually beat in confectioners' sugar until the icing is thick and smooth. Cover the bowl with a wet paper towel, being sure the towel is not touching the icing.

Glaze the Pastilles:

- Unwrap the roll and trim the ends. Using a sharp, heavy knife, cut the cake into fifteen 1-inch pastilles. Place the pastilles on a baking sheet and freeze until ready to glaze. Set two large wire racks on two baking sheets.

- Set the top of the double boiler over hot, not simmering, water and heat the glaze carefully, folding occasionally with a spatula, until the glaze is just melted and of a dipping consistency. Do not overwork the glaze.

- Place a pastille into the glaze. With a large two-pronged fork, such as a meat fork, press down on the top of the pastille so that it is completely submerged in the glaze and gently turn it over. Using the fork, lift the pastille out of the glaze and gently tap the fork on the side of the pot to remove any excess glaze. Place the pastille on a wire rack covered baking sheet and carefully remove the fork. Coat the remaining pastilles in the glaze.

Royal Icing:

- Transfer the royal icing to a pastry bag fitted with a coupling and a small plain tip (such as Ateco No. 2 or 3). Decorate the tops of the pastilles with the royal icing, if desired. Place the wire racks with the baking sheets containing the pastilles in the refrigerator for 15 to 20 minutes to set the glaze.

- Using a spatula, remove the pastilles from the wire racks. Serve the pastilles slightly chilled.

- Makes 15 pastilles.

1987 CHOCOLATIER's Great Chocolate Challenge

Besides demonstrating his winning recipe on "Good Morning America," the Grand Prize winner Kenneth Ayvazian of Branford, Connecticut— Yale grad and pastry chef at Robert Henry's restaurant in New Haven — won The Grand Coco Award and a seven-day Golden Autumn luxury cruise for two through the Canadian Maritime Provinces aboard Royal Cruise Line's Royal Odyssey. Chocolate connoisseurs will be "richly" rewarded with this grand prize winning recipe which rose to meet the CHOCOLATIER Challenge.

Recipe courtesy of CHOCOLATIER Magazine, Haymarket Group Ltd., New York

WINDSTAR CRUISE IN TAHITI OR THE GRENADINES

TOFFEE KAHLÚA MADNESS

CHOCOLATIER Magazine describes this spirited dessert as "a rich, fudgy bittersweet chocolate cake encased in a combination of pecans and crushed chocolate-coated toffee bars."

Crust:

Three 1⅛-ounce Heath Bars, finely chopped

½ cup pecan halves, lightly roasted and finely chopped (see Note)

Cake:

8 ounces bittersweet chocolate, coarsely chopped

8 tablespoons (1 stick) unsalted butter, cut into tablespoons

½ cup granulated sugar

3 large eggs, at room temperature, separated

1½ tablespoons Kahlúa or 1 tablespoon strong coffee

1 teaspoon vanilla extract

½ cup all-purpose flour

¼ teaspoon salt

Three 1⅛-ounce Heath Bars, coarsely chopped

Note: To roast pecans, position a rack in the center of the oven and preheat to 325°. Spread the pecan halves in a single layer on a baking sheet and roast for 5 to 8 minutes, or until the nuts are fragrant. Transfer the pecans to another baking sheet to stop the cooking process and cool completely.

Crust:

• Position a rack in the center of the oven and preheat to 350°. Lightly butter the bottom only of a 9-inch springform pan.

• In a small bowl, combine the finely chopped Heath Bars and pecans. Sprinkle the mixture over the bottom of the prepared pan. Bake the crust 9 to 11 minutes, or until softened. Cool completely on a wire rack.

Cake:

• In a heavy-bottomed, medium saucepan set over low heat, melt the chocolate and butter, stirring occasionally until smooth. Transfer the mixture to a large mixing bowl. Gradually whisk in the sugar. Add the egg yolks, one at a time. Stir in the Kahlúa and vanilla. Gradually whisk in the flour.

• In a grease-free medium bowl, using a hand-held electric mixer set at low speed, beat the egg whites until frothy. Add the salt and gradually increase the speed to medium-high and continue beating until the whites form soft peaks.

- Using a rubber spatula, fold one-third of the beaten egg whites into the batter. Scrape the remaining egg whites over the batter and fold in gently until no streaks of white remain. Scrape the batter over the cooled crust. Bake for 15 minutes.

- Gently pull the rack with the cake on it out of the oven. Sprinkle the top of the cake with the coarsely chopped Heath Bars. Return the cake to the oven and bake for 20 to 25 minutes, or until a cake tester or toothpick inserted into the center of the cake comes out clean. Set the cake in its pan on a wire rack and cool for 15 minutes. Run a thin-bladed knife around the edge to loosen. Release the sides of the springform pan and cool the cake completely.

- Makes 6 to 8 servings.

1988 CHOCOLATIER'S Great Dessert Challenge

Two Grand Prizes were awarded in this year's contest — one for the best chocolate dessert, the other for the best non-chocolate dessert. Upon being informed that her recipe had won in the chocolate category, Elaine Cooper of New Hampshire exclaimed, "I can't believe it. I've never won anything in my life." Her winnings included the choice of a one-week Windstar cruise for two in Tahiti or the Grenadines and a Litton Prestige microwave oven.

Recipe courtesy of CHOCOLATIER Magazine,
Haymarket Group Ltd., New York

$5,000 & TRIP FOR TWO TO SAN FRANCISCO

BÛCHE AUX MARRONS
(Yule Log With Chestnuts)

In France, chestnut (marron) purée is used in creating special desserts. "Marrons glacés" are glazed whole chestnuts that have been poached for hours in sugar syrup; these exotic confections are considered an extra special, if pricey, treat. Here, with a French accent, is spongecake drizzled with rum syrup, which is rolled and frosted with Chestnut Butter Cream.

3 eggs, separated, reserving
  whites
1¼ cups superfine sugar
¼ cup cold water
2 teaspoons vanilla
2¼ cups sifted flour
2 teaspoons baking powder

1 egg white
½ cup Sugar Syrup (below)
4 cups Chestnut Butter Cream
  (below)
12 marrons glacés or candied
  violets for garnish

Sugar Syrup:
½ cup sugar
¼ cup water

2 tablespoons rum

Chestnut Butter Cream:
1 pound sweet butter
1 cup superfine sugar
2 tablespoons rum

1 (15½-ounce) can unsweetened
  chestnut purée

- Preheat oven to 325°. Beat together egg yolks and sugar until light and creamy. Beat in water and vanilla. Sift together flour and baking powder and fold into egg mixture. Beat 4 egg whites stiff and fold into batter, gently but quickly.

- Butter an 11 x 16-inch baking sheet or jelly roll pan. Line with wax paper and butter again. Spread batter evenly over bottom of pan and bake 20 minutes or until sides of cake shrink away from pan. Invert warm cake onto a moist kitchen towel, peel off wax paper.

Sugar Syrup:

- Stir sugar and water in a saucepan over medium heat until sugar dissolves. Raise heat and boil syrup, stirring, 10 minutes or until a candy thermometer registers 220°. Cool syrup and stir in rum.

- Moisten cake with Sugar Syrup, roll up, and cool.

Chestnut Butter Cream:

- Cream butter until light and fluffy. Add chestnut purée, sugar, and rum and beat until mixture is smooth.

- Cut off ragged cake ends on the bias and ice with Chestnut Butter Cream to simulate the bark of a tree. Surround with marrons glacés or candied violets.

- Makes 10 to 12 servings.

1976 Seagram's V.O.® and GOURMET MAGAZINE®'s International Dessert Recipe Contest

Seagram's V.O. sought recipes with "a flavor complementary to national cuisines from the world" in this, the third in their series of three, international recipe contests. In these contests a distinctive departure from typical recipe contest rules is noticeable — recipes were not required to include the sponsor's product. Five finalists were selected by GOURMET MAGAZINE's panel of experts to receive trips for two to San Francisco where the Grand Prize winner was announced at a gala banquet.

Recipe courtesy of Joseph E. Seagram & Sons, Inc./Seagram's V.O.

$10,000

PECAN-PIE CHILLED CAKE

A richer than rich adaptation of pecan pie.

1 (13-ounce) package
  TRISCUIT® Wafers Low Salt,
  finely rolled (about 4 cups
  crumbs)
10 tablespoons BLUE
  BONNET® Sweet Unsalted
  Butter Blend

2 cups pecans, chopped
3 eggs, lightly beaten
1 teaspoon vanilla extract
1 cup light corn syrup
1 cup sugar
Whipped cream, for garnish
Pecan halves, for garnish

- Preheat oven to 350°. Line outside bottom of 8-inch springform pan with foil. In large bowl, combine wafer crumbs and ½ cup melted butter blend until well blended. Press ⅓ crumb mixture onto bottom of springform pan. Sprinkle with 1 cup pecans.

- In medium bowl, stir together remaining margarine, eggs, vanilla, corn syrup and sugar; pour ⅓ of mixture over nuts in pan. Repeat layers once. Spoon remaining crumb mixture over top, pressing lightly. Top with remaining egg mixture.

- Bake for 45 minutes. Cool in pan on wire rack. Refrigerate at least 6 hours or overnight. Remove from pan. Garnish with whipped cream and pecan halves.

- Makes 16 servings.

1986 "Top A Triscuit®" Recipe Contest

Imagine seeing your own smiling face and winning recipe on packages of Triscuit® Wafers. Grand Prize winner Diane S. Bryant and the three $1,000 First Prize winners did just that in this contest of four categories — Hot or Cold Appetizers, Savory Low Salt Snacks, Desserts, and Quick Hot Meal.

Recipe courtesy of Nabisco Foods, Inc.

$100,000 SAVINGS BOND

BERRY NUTTY PIE

Strawberry cream filling in a cookie-like meringue shell of ground pecans, crushed buttery crackers, and chopped chocolate chips.

3 egg whites, at room temperature
¾ cup granulated sugar
½ teaspoon baking powder
¾ cup semisweet chocolate chips, divided
½ cup PLANTERS® Pecan Pieces, divided

1 cup crushed butter-flavored crackers
1 teaspoon almond extract
1 cup heavy cream
2 tablespoons powdered sugar
½ teaspoon vanilla extract
1 pint strawberries, hulled and sliced, divided.

- Preheat oven to 350°. Grease a 9-inch pie plate. Beat egg whites in a small deep bowl until soft peaks form. Combine the granulated sugar and baking powder; gradually add to the egg whites, beating until stiff peaks form. Reserve 2 tablespoons of the chocolate chips; coarsely chop the remaining chips. Reserve 2 tablespoons of the pecans; grind the remaining pecans. Combine the cracker crumbs with the chopped chocolate chips and ground pecans in a small bowl; fold into the egg whites along with the almond extract. Spread the egg white mixture in the prepared pie plate. Bake for 25 minutes. Cool completely on a wire rack.

- Beat the cream with the powdered sugar and vanilla in a small deep bowl until stiff. Reserve ¾ cup of the strawberry slices for decoration; fold the remaining berries into the whipped cream. Spread the strawberry cream over the cooled baked layer. Decorate the pie with the reserved strawberries, pecans, and chocolate chips.

- Makes 8 servings.

1988 Planters® Holiday Baking Contest

Christmas wouldn't be Christmas without nuts and the barrage of baking that announces an approaching holiday season. In December, 1987 Planters® announced a contest inviting submission of favorite holiday dessert recipes and offered a truly grand Grand Prize.

Recipe developed by Bobbie C. Meyer of Chauvin, Louisiana.
Courtesy of Planters LifeSavers Company

BEST GUBERNATORIAL APPLE PIE

INDIANA CRUMB-TOP APPLE PIE

Folks from the Hoosier state are serious about their pie-making, including the Governor, with this crustless version of apple pie.

Filling:

⅔ cup sugar
½ teaspoon cinnamon
¼ teaspoon nutmeg
8 large tart apples, peeled, cored and thinly sliced (12 cups, about 4 pounds)

2 tablespoons water
2 tablespoons lemon juice
2 tablespoons butter

Crumb Topping:

½ cup firmly packed brown sugar
½ cup butter, softened

1 cup all-purpose flour

Filling:

• Preheat oven to 350°. In large bowl combine sugar, cinnamon and nutmeg. Add apples; sprinkle on water and lemon juice. Toss until evenly coated. Spoon into a 9-inch deep-dish pie pan (without pastry). Dot with butter.

Crumb Topping:

• Cream sugar and butter until light and fluffy. Add flour and stir until smooth. Daub on apples. Bake 50 to 60 minutes. Serve warm — plain or with ice cream, whipped cream or cheese.

• Makes 8 servings.

1983 LADIES' HOME JOURNAL Apple Pie Contest

LADIES' HOME JOURNAL asked the nation's Governors to enter their favorite apple pie recipes for judging. Indiana's Governor, Robert D. Orr, submitted this recipe created by his wife and, according to LADIES' HOME JOURNAL, it was the "crown of buttery crumbs" that made it outstanding. Governor John Y. Brown, Jr. of Kentucky came in second with his recipe for "Kentucky Bourbon Apple Pie" and "Tennessee Apple Pie" won third place for Governor Lamar Alexander.

$10,000

APPLE Mc'TAFFY

Break through the dessert barrier with this low-fat, zero cholesterol, minuscule-calorie caramel apple pie. You can even sneak it past the "Eat dessert first, life is uncertain" crowd or, at the very least, eliminate the guilts of chronic dieters.

4 large apples (cooking or baking)	¼ cup pecan halves, broken
⅓ cup ESTEE® Maple Breakfast Syrup	12 ESTEE® Vanilla Cookies, ground coarsely
½ teaspoon cinnamon	1 package ESTEE® Caramels, vanilla only
¼ teaspoon nutmeg	

- Preheat oven to 375°. Peel, core and slice apples. Arrange in a 9-inch pie pan. Drizzle syrup over apples evenly; sprinkle cinnamon and nutmeg on top. Bake for 20 minutes; remove and evenly top with pecans, caramels and cookie crumbs. Return to oven for 5 minutes, or until caramels are melted. Serve warm

- Makes 8 servings.

Nutrition Information Per Serving:

Calories 170	Calories from Fat 28%
Protein 1 g	Cholesterol 0
Carbohydrates 29 g	Sodium 75 mg
Fat 5 g	Potassium 135 mg

Diabetic Exchange Information:
One Serving = 1 Bread + 1 Fruit + 1 Fat exchange

1991 Estee® Delicious Desserts Recipe Contest

Estee® products are found in the diet food section of supermarkets and are especially designed to meet the needs of diabetics and those on low-salt or no table sugar diets. In this unusual contest thirteen winning recipes were selected with titles such as "Triple Chocolate Cheesecake," "Brazilian Rain Forest Torte," "Sticky Buns & Cinnamon Rolls" and "Chocolate Raspberry Cake,"...

Recipe courtesy of The Estee Corporation

$10,000 DREAM KITCHEN FROM
KitchenAid & CRISCO

HONEY CRUNCH PECAN PIE

Bourbon provides a spirited touch in this honey of a pecan pie.

Crust:
1⅓ cups all-purpose flour
½ teaspoon salt

½ cup CRISCO® Shortening
3 tablespoons cold water

Filling:
4 eggs, lightly beaten
1 cup light corn syrup
¼ cup firmly packed light brown
   sugar
¼ cup granulated sugar

2 tablespoons butter or margarine,
   melted
1 tablespoon bourbon
1 teaspoon vanilla
½ teaspoon salt
1 cup chopped pecans

Topping:
⅓ cup firmly packed light brown
   sugar
3 tablespoons butter or margarine

3 tablespoons honey
1½ cups pecan halves

Crust:

• Preheat oven to 350°. Spoon flour into measuring cup and level. Combine flour and salt in a medium bowl. Cut in Crisco using pastry blender (or 2 knives) until all flour is blended to form pea-size chunks. Sprinkle with water, one tablespoon at a time. Toss lightly with fork until dough will form a ball. Press dough between hands to form a 5- to 6-inch "pancake." Flour rolling surface and rolling pin lightly. Roll dough into circle. Trim one inch larger than upside-down pie plate. Loosen dough carefully. Fold dough into quarters. Unfold and press into pie plate. Fold edge under. Flute.

Filling:

• Combine eggs, corn syrup, ¼ cup light brown sugar, granulated sugar, 2 tablespoons butter, bourbon, vanilla and salt in large bowl. Stir in chopped nuts. Mix well. Spoon into unbaked pie crust. Bake for 15 minutes. Cover edge with foil to prevent overbrowning. Bake 20 minutes. Remove from oven. Remove foil and save.

Topping:

- Combine ⅓ cup light brown sugar, 3 tablespoons butter, and honey in medium saucepan. Cook about 2 minutes or until sugar dissolves. Add pecan halves. Stir until coated. Spoon over pie. Re-cover edge with foil. Bake 10 to 20 minutes or until topping is bubbly and crust is golden brown. Cool to room temperature before serving. Refrigerate leftover pie.

- Makes one 9-inch pie.

1989 Crisco® American Pie Celebration

Procter & Gamble began the American Pie Celebration in 1986 to commemorate its 75th anniversary. Since then the annual event has grown in popularity, becoming a much anticipated event in which the search is on for the best pies in America. Beginning with contests in State and County fairs in all fifty states, competitors enter in pie categories that are geared to include the state's native ingredients.

All entries are judged on the quality of the crust, filling, appearance and originality. The winning pie maker from each state goes on to compete in a national competition for the "Silver Rolling Pin" trophy, the title of "Baker of The American Pie" and an exciting $10,000 prize package. Rosalie Seebeck of Bethany, Oklahoma took top honors in 1989 with her version of a perennial favorite using pecans picked from trees in her backyard and honey from her own beehive.

Recipe courtesy of The Procter & Gamble Company, Inc.

$15,000 PRIZE PACKAGE

MAUI PINE CREAM PIE

The pie from paradise...Not one, but two fillings go into the buttery macadamia nut crust — a layer of cream cheese with toasted macadamia nuts and a hint of pineapple, then a pineapple cream filling. A topping of whipped cream garnished with grated lemon peel, more chopped macadamia nuts and nontoxic tropical flowers are the finishing touches.

Pineapple Cream Filling:
1 can (20 ounces) crushed pineapple (juice pack or light syrup)
4 egg yolks, lightly beaten
1 tablespoon water
⅓ cup firmly packed cornstarch

1 cup sugar
¼ teaspoon salt
2 cups milk
2 tablespoons butter or margarine
1 teaspoon vanilla

Crust:
1½ cups all-purpose flour
2 tablespoons granulated sugar
½ teaspoon salt
½ cup Butter Flavor CRISCO®

2 tablespoons finely chopped unsalted macadamia nuts, toasted*
2 teaspoons grated lemon peel
3 to 4 tablespoons cold milk

Cream Cheese Filling:
1 package (8 ounces) cream cheese, softened
½ cup confectioners' sugar
½ teaspoon vanilla

⅓ cup finely chopped unsalted macadamia nuts, toasted
Reserved ⅓ cup drained pineapple

Topping:
1 cup whipping cream, whipped
1 teaspoon grated lemon peel

1 tablespoon finely chopped unsalted macadamia nuts, toasted*
Nontoxic flowers for garnish

Or substitute toasted finely chopped pecans or walnuts. To toast, place about ½ cup chopped nuts in baking pan in 350° oven. Stir every 2 minutes until browned. Cool.

Pineapple Cream Filling:
• Drain pineapple, reserving ⅓ cup for cream cheese layer. Combine egg yolks and water in small bowl; stir in cornstarch. Combine sugar, salt, milk, and remaining drained pineapple in medium saucepan. Cook and stir on medium heat until mixture almost comes to a boil.

Reduce heat to low. Add egg yolk mixture slowly, stirring constantly. Cook and stir until thickened. Add butter and vanilla. Remove from heat. Cover surface of mixture with waxed paper. Refrigerate 30 minutes, stirring once or twice.

Crust:

• Combine flour, sugar, and salt in medium bowl. Cut in Butter Flavor Crisco using pastry blender (or 2 knives) until all flour is blended in to form pea-sized chunks. Add nuts and lemon peel. Add milk. Toss lightly with fork until dough forms a ball. Press between hands to form 5- to 6-inch "pancake." Wrap in waxed paper. Refrigerate 15 minutes.

• Preheat oven to 350°. Flour rolling surface and rolling pin lightly. Roll dough into circle. Trim one inch larger than inverted 9-inch pie plate. Loosen dough carefully. Fold into quarters. Unfold and press into pie plate. Fold edge under. Flute. Prick bottom and sides thoroughly with fork (50 times) to prevent shrinkage. Bake for 15 to 20 minutes or until golden brown. Cool completely.

Cream Cheese Filling:

• Combine cream cheese and confectioners' sugar in medium bowl. Beat with fork until blended and smooth. Add vanilla. Add nuts and reserved ⅓ cup drained pineapple. Mix well. Spread cream cheese filling over bottom of cooled baked pie shell. Cover with Pineapple Cream Filling.

Topping:

• Spread ½ cup whipped cream on top center of pie. Spoon remaining cream into pastry bag with large rosette tip; pipe a border around pie. Garnish with lemon peel, nuts, and flowers. Serve or refrigerate until ready to serve.

• Makes one 9-inch pie, 10 servings.

1992 Crisco®'s American Pie Celebration

Pie contests were held at 50 state fairs, then 10 of the 50 were selected to compete at the finals held at the GOOD HOUSEKEEPING Institute kitchens in New York. The panel of judges was headed up by GOOD HOUSEKEEPING's Food Editor, Mildred Ying. In winning the Grand Prize, Marian Ching of Maui, Hawaii received $7,000 in KitchenAid appliances, $3,000 from Crisco for kitchen remodeling, and an assortment of kitchenware, plus the "Crissie" award — a silver rolling pin.

Recipe courtesy of The Procter & Gamble Co., Inc.

TRIP FOR TWO TO MAUI
WAIKIKI PINEAPPLE PIE

Crust:

¼ cup (½ stick) butter or margarine

¾ cup flaked coconut, toasted
¾ cup vanilla wafer crumbs

Filling:

1 package (3½-ounce or 4⅛-ounce size) vanilla pudding and pie filling mix
1 can (15-ounces) crushed pineapple in syrup, undrained

1 cup sour cream
¼ cup milk
½ teaspoon rum extract

Meringue:

3 large egg whites at room temperature
¼ teaspoon cream of tartar

½ teaspoon vanilla extract
6 tablespoons sugar

Crust:

- Place butter in 9-inch microwave-safe pie plate; microwave on HIGH 45 seconds to 1 minutes, or until melted. Blend in all but 1 tablespoon coconut and the crumbs. Press mixture firmly against bottom and side of pie plate. Microwave on HIGH 1 minute, rotating dish a half turn after 30 seconds.

Filling:

- In medium, microwave-safe mixing bowl, combine pudding mix and pineapple. Stir in sour cream and milk. Microwave on HIGH 6 to 8 minutes, or until mixture boils, stirring after 2 minutes and then every minute. Blend in rum extract. Let stand 5 minutes. Pour into crust.

Meringue:

- In small bowl, beat egg whites with cream of tartar and vanilla until foamy. Add sugar, a tablespoon at a time, beating until stiff peaks form. Spread meringue over filling, carefully sealing to edge of crust and swirling top decoratively. Microwave on HIGH 1½ to 2½ minutes, or until meringue is set. Chill 3 hours before serving. Sprinkle with remaining toasted coconut.

- Makes 8 servings.

Recipe developed by Carolyn Reif of Dubuque, Iowa for the 1986 McCALL'S Microwave Recipe Contest. Recipe courtesy of McCALL'S/The New York Times Company Women's Magazines

$5,000

PUMPKIN MALLOW PARFAIT PIE

*Yo-ho-ho, please **don't** leave out the rum.*

Crust:

2 cups gingersnap cookie crumbs

⅓ cup PARKAY® Margarine, melted

Filling:

1½ cups canned pumpkin
1 jar (7 ounces) KRAFT®
   Marshmallow Creme
1 teaspoon rum extract (optional)

1 container (8 ounces) COOL
   WHIP® Non-Dairy Whipped
   Topping, thawed (3½ cups)
Pecan halves (optional)

Crust:

• Mix crumbs and margarine. Reserve ¼ cup crumb mixture; press remaining mixture onto bottom and sides of 9-inch pie plate. Refrigerate.

Filling:

• Mix pumpkin, marshmallow creme and extract at medium speed with electric mixer or wire whisk until well blended.

• Fold in whipped topping; pour into crust. Sprinkle with reserved ¼ cup crumb mixture; cover. Freeze.

• Top with additional whipped topping and pecan halves, if desired.

• Makes 8 servings.

1984 Kraft® Marshmallow Creme "Easy Secret Ingredient" Recipe Contest

"Easy" is the catchword of the many Marshmallow Creme contests sponsored by Kraft during the 1980's. In this one, recipes were submitted in three categories: "Frozen Favorites," "Festive Fruits," or "Chocolate Challenge" (excluding fudge). This Grand Prize recipe from Helen Julian of Brooklyn, New York features a new approach to pumpkin pie that is... easy as pie.

Recipe courtesy of Kraft General Foods, Inc.

TRIP FOR TWO TO SAN FRANCISCO & $500

CARAMELIZED GINGERSNAP PEAR TART

Crust:

1½ cups gingersnap cookie crumbs

½ cup finely chopped nuts

⅓ cup PARKAY® Margarine, melted

Filling:

2 packages (8 ounces each) PHILADELPHIA® BRAND Cream Cheese, softened

¼ cup granulated sugar

2 tablespoons pear nectar *or* pear brandy

½ teaspoon vanilla

Topping:

3 ripe pears, peeled, thinly sliced*

¼ cup firmly packed dark brown sugar

¼ teaspoon ground ginger

Strawberries, for garnish (optional)

Crust:

- Preheat oven to 350°. Mix crumbs, nuts and margarine; press onto bottom and sides of 10-inch quiche dish or 9-inch pie plate. Bake 5 minutes. Cool.

Filling:

- Beat cream cheese and granulated sugar at medium speed with electric mixer until well blended. Blend in nectar and vanilla; pour into crust. Refrigerate several hours or overnight.

Topping:

- Heat broiler. Arrange pears over cream cheese mixture. Sprinkle with combined brown sugar and ginger. Broil 3 to 5 minutes or until sugar is melted and bubbly. Garnish with strawberries, if desired. Serve immediately.

- Makes 6 to 8 servings.

* Variation: Substitute 1 can (16 ounces) pear halves, drained, thinly sliced, for fresh pears.

Recipe developed by Jan Exline of Milwaukee, Wisconsin for the 1987 "Philly" Hall of Fame Recipe Contest. Recipe courtesy of Kraft General Foods, Inc.

TRIP FOR FOUR TO DISNEY WORLD

CHOCOLATE TRUFFLES

With a name like truffles, these have got to be great. They are, and they make an impressive gift if you can keep them around long enough. Place individual truffles in metallic gold fluted candy papers and arrange in decorative tins or boxes. But beware, these are so professional looking (but easy) that your friends will think you bought them. Try them with SMUCKER'S® Raspberry Preserves too.

1 package (18.5-ounces) chocolate cake mix
½ cup (1 stick) butter or margarine, softened
½ cup unsweetened cocoa
½ cup confectioners' sugar
½ cup SMUCKER'S® Apricot Preserves
1 teaspoon vanilla extract
2 packages (8 ounces each) semisweet chocolate squares

- Prepare cake as package directs; cool.

- In 3-quart saucepan over medium heat, melt butter; add cocoa and sugar; stir until smooth. Add apricot preserves and vanilla; stir until smooth and glossy. Remove saucepan from heat; crumble cake into mixture in saucepan; mix until well blended and moist. Roll into 1½-inch balls.

- In small heavy saucepan over low heat, melt semisweet chocolate, stirring until smooth. Dip truffles into melted chocolate, one by one, completely coating each with chocolate. Place on jelly roll pan lined with waxed paper or aluminum foil; let stand at least 1 hour.

- Makes about 45 truffles.

1985 Smucker's® Great American Recipe Contest

One of the rules in this contest forbade the use of wine, liquor flavoring, and alcoholic beverages as ingredients. Considering that chocolate truffles, which originated in the Flanders region of Belgium, always have one form or another of alcoholic flavoring as an ingredient, Grand Prize winner Jeannine Navratil of Syracuse, New York earned high marks for creativity with her version, a serious chocolate experience.

Recipe courtesy of The J. M. Smucker Company

$5,000

CREMEDOODLES

Supreme binge food and absolutely goof proof.

1 jar (7 ounces) KRAFT®
  Marshmallow Creme
1 cup peanut butter
½ cup honey

2 bars (1.65 ounces each) milk
  chocolate candy, chopped
1½ cups raisins
1 cup chopped walnuts
2 cups shredded coconut

- Mix marshmallow creme, peanut butter and honey at medium speed with electric mixer or wire whisk until well blended.
- Add chopped chocolate, raisins and walnuts; mix well.
- Shape rounded teaspoonfuls of mixture into 1-inch balls; roll in coconut. Refrigerate or freeze.
- Makes 6 dozen.

**1981 Kraft® Marshmallow Creme "Easy Secret Ingredient"
Recipe Contest**

Nothing could be easier or yummier than these delectable doodles of richness, the creation of Hilda Borri from Mark, Illinois who entered them in the "Easy Recipe for Kids" category.

Recipe courtesy of Kraft General Foods, Inc.

$10,000 PLUS HOTPOINT APPLIANCES

PRALINE UNIQUES

Treat your sweet tooth to these creamy brown sugar and pecan confections that whip up lickety-split.

54 TRISCUIT® Wafers
½ cup BLUE BONNET®
   Margarine or Butter Blend
1 package (16 ounces) light brown
   sugar

1 large egg
1 cup unsifted all-purpose flour
2 tablespoons vanilla extract
2 cups pecan pieces

- Preheat oven to 325°. Arrange Triscuit wafers in single layer, trimming to fit if necessary, on bottom of well-greased 15½ x 10½ x 1-inch baking pan; set aside.

- In saucepan, over medium heat, melt Blue Bonnet margarine. Remove from heat; stir in brown sugar, egg, flour and vanilla until well blended. Pour over Triscuit wafers, spreading to cover wafers; sprinkle with pecan pieces.

- Bake 20 minutes. Cool. Cut into squares, following outline of Triscuits.

- Makes 54 squares.

1985 Triscuit® 10's Recipe Contest

Wondering what the "10's" part of this contest is? According to the contest announcement, "Triscuit 10's are quick and easy recipes using Nabisco Triscuit Wafers." One of the rules specified that recipe preparation time could only take from 10 to 20 minutes, not including cooking time. Five finalists, one in each of five categories, each received an array of five major Hotpoint household appliances including dishwasher, trash compactor, refrigerator/freezer, microwave oven and self-cleaning oven range. Ella Rita Helfrich from Houston, Texas received the $10,000 bonus as Grand Prize winner for her unique praline-inspired treats.

Recipe courtesy of Nabisco Foods, Inc.

SUB-ZERO REFRIGERATOR-FREEZER & $500

ITALIAN BISCOTTI CRESCENTS

Nobody doesn't like cookies, and that's a fact. By popular vote — through public voting via 1-900 numbers — these cookies were voted the best.

1(10¾-ounce) SARA LEE®
Pound Cake, thawed
½ cup cinnamon graham cracker
crumbs (approximately 6
squares, crushed)
½ cup unblanched almonds

⅓ cup butter or margarine, melted
¼ cup finely chopped red and
green candied cherries (2
tablespoons *each*)
1½ teaspoons anise extract
Powdered sugar, as needed

- Preheat oven to 350°. Place pound cake pieces in a food processor or blender container; cover and process or blend until pieces are coarse crumbs. Add graham cracker crumbs and almonds; cover and process or blend again until the texture of sand. Transfer Crumbs to a medium bowl; stir in butter, candied cherries, and anise extract, blending well until mixture holds together.

- Shape rounded tablespoons of mixture into crescent shapes on an ungreased 15 x 10 x 1-inch baking pan. Bake for 20 to 25 minutes or until lightly browned. Cool on baking sheets until firm. Cookies harden as they cool. Remove and roll each cookie in powdered sugar, coating well.

- Makes about 2 dozen cookies.

Variations: Dip one end of baked biscotti into melted white or dark chocolate and sprinkle with finely chopped almonds.

1992 Sara Lee Bakery's "America's Best Dessert" Recipe Contest

In the first recipe contest of its kind, the Grand Prize winner was chosen by popular vote. As it turned out, America's favorite dessert was really Italian, the creation of Marie Serena of Campbell, California. After 17 semi-finalists were selected from thousands of entries, the top pastry chefs in the country narrowed the field to the 5 best. In its June issue, HOUSE BEAUTIFUL presented the five recipes with edible-looking photographs and readers were invited to vote via 1-900 numbers.

Recipe courtesy of Sara Lee Bakery

$10,000

DOUBLE NUT CHOCOLATE CHIP COOKIES

These chocolate chip cookies are doubly good with ground and chopped pecans and sliced almonds in the rich dough; the tops are pressed into even more sliced almonds before baking.

1⅓ cups Butter Flavor CRISCO®
1½ cups firmly packed brown sugar
½ cup granulated sugar
2 eggs
2 teaspoons vanilla
2¾ cups all-purpose flour

½ cup finely ground or chopped pecans
1 teaspoon baking soda
1 teaspoon salt
2 tablespoons milk
2 cups semisweet chocolate chips
½ cup coarsely chopped pecans
1½ cups sliced almonds, divided

- Preheat oven to 375°. Combine Butter Flavor Crisco, brown sugar, granulated sugar, eggs and vanilla in large bowl. Beat at medium speed until well blended. Combine flour, ground pecans, baking soda and salt. Add alternately with milk to creamed mixture, blending at low speed. Stir in chocolate chips, coarsely chopped pecans and ½ cup sliced almonds.

- Form rounded tablespoonfuls of dough into balls. Press top of cookies into remaining almonds. Place 2 inches apart on greased baking sheet. Bake for 10 to 12 minutes or until set. Cool 2 minutes on baking sheet.

- Makes about 4 dozen cookies.

1990 Butter Flavor Crisco®'s "Great American Cookie Challenge"

Crisco awarded three $10,000 Grand Prizes in this contest — one each in the three classic cookie categories of Chocolate Chip, Peanut Butter and Oatmeal. Although Ruth Wakefield's original 1930 recipe for "Toll House Cookies" (chocolate chip) did not call for nuts, Jan Rexrode of Harrisburg, Pennsylvania found them to be a winning addition.

Recipe courtesy of The Procter & Gamble Co., Inc.

$10,000

OATMEAL SCOTCH CHIPPERS

Massive amounts of crunchy peanut butter, chocolate and butterscotch chips, and walnuts make these oatmeal cookies exceptional.

1¼ cups Butter Flavor CRISCO®
1½ cups firmly packed brown
  sugar
1 cup granulated sugar
3 eggs
1¼ cups JIF® Extra Crunchy
  Peanut Butter

4½ cups old fashioned oats
2 teaspoons baking soda
1 cup semisweet chocolate chips
1 cup butterscotch-flavored chips
1 cup chopped walnuts

- Preheat oven to 350°. Combine Butter Flavor Crisco, brown sugar and granulated sugar in large bowl and beat at medium speed until well blended. Beat in eggs. Add Jif Extra Crunchy Peanut Butter and beat until blended.

- Combine oats and baking soda. Stir into creamed mixture with spoon. Stir in chips and nuts. Drop rounded teaspoonfuls of dough 2 inches apart onto ungreased baking sheet. Bake 10 to 11 minutes or until browned. Cool 2 minutes on baking sheet. Remove to cooling rack.

- Makes 6 dozen cookies.

**1990 Butter Flavor Crisco®'s
"Great American Cookie Challenge"**

It must have been a wonderful challenge to judge cookies that are proven favorites. As Grand Prize winner in the Oatmeal category, Jennifer Nystrom of Woodinville, Washington shows how to turn an old-fashioned favorite into a new-fashioned treat.

Recipe courtesy of The Procter & Gamble Co., Inc.

$10,000

PEANUT BUTTER CRUNCH COOKIES

It's the "crunch" that makes these cookies notable — crunchy peanut butter, crispy rice cereal and chopped peanuts combined with oatmeal and flaked coconut.

1 cup Butter Flavor CRISCO®
2 cups firmly packed brown sugar
1 cup JIF® Extra Crunchy Peanut Butter
4 egg whites, slightly beaten
1 teaspoon vanilla
2 cups all-purpose flour

1 teaspoon baking soda
½ teaspoon baking powder
2 cups crisp rice cereal
1½ cups chopped peanuts
1 cup quick oats (not instant or old fashioned)
1 cup flaked coconut

- Preheat oven to 350°. Combine Butter Flavor Crisco, sugar and Jif Extra Crunchy Peanut Butter in bowl and beat at medium speed until well blended. Beat in egg whites and vanilla. Combine flour, baking soda and baking powder. Mix into creamed mixture at low speed until just blended. Stir in, one at a time, rice cereal, peanuts, oats and coconut with spoon.

- Drop rounded tablespoonfuls of dough 2 inches apart onto ungreased baking sheet. Bake 8 to 10 minutes or until set. Remove immediately to cooling rack.

- Makes about 4 dozen cookies.

**1990 Butter Flavor Crisco®'s
"Great American Cookie Challenge"**

Darlene Brown of La Cañada, California was the Grand Prize winner in the Peanut Butter cookie category with this masterpiece, a marvelous munchie for any cookie monster.

Recipe courtesy of The Procter & Gamble Co., Inc.

$5,000

FROSTED PEANUT BUTTER BRITTLE COOKIES

Beautiful to look at, better to eat. Half of the tops of these peanut butter cookies are frosted with melted peanut butter chips, then sprinkled with crushed peanut brittle.

Peanut Brittle:

¾ cup sugar
¾ cup shelled unroasted peanuts
　(¼ pound)
⅓ cup light corn syrup
¼ teaspoon salt

1½ teaspoons Butter Flavor
　CRISCO®
¾ teaspoon vanilla
¾ teaspoon baking soda

Cookies:

½ cup Butter Flavor CRISCO®
½ cup sugar
½ cup firmly packed light brown
　sugar
½ cup JIF® Creamy Peanut Butter
1 tablespoon milk

1 egg
1⅓ cups all-purpose flour
¾ teaspoon baking soda
½ teaspoon baking powder
¼ teaspoon salt

Frosting:

1¼ cups peanut-butter chips

1 cup crushed peanut brittle

Peanut Brittle:

• Grease a 15½ x 12-inch baking sheet. Combine sugar, peanuts, syrup, and salt in 3-quart saucepan. Cook and stir on medium-low heat until 240° on candy thermometer. Add Butter Flavor Crisco and vanilla; cook and stir until 300°. Remove from heat. Stir in soda. Spread ¼-inch thick on baking sheet. Cool. Crush enough to measure one cup.

Cookies:

• Preheat oven to 375°. Combine Butter Flavor Crisco, sugar, brown sugar, Jif Creamy peanut butter, and milk in large bowl. Beat at medium speed of mixer until blended. Beat in egg. Combine flour, soda, baking powder, and salt. Add gradually at low speed. Shape dough into 1¼-inch balls. Place 3½ inches apart on ungreased baking sheet. Flatten to 3-inch circles. Bake 8 to 10 minutes or until brown. Cool 2 minutes; remove to rack; cool completely.

Frosting:

- Melt peanut butter chips in double boiler over boiling water. Frost half of each cookie; sprinkle with crushed peanut brittle.

- Makes about 2 dozen cookies.

1991 Crisco® Parent-Child Cookie Contest

In celebration of its 80th birthday and to promote family baking, Crisco added this family affair contest to its state fair pie competitions. Recipes were required to use Butter Flavor Crisco. The Grand Prize was won by the team of Claudia Cysensky and her eleven-year-old son, Verne, of Tacoma, Washington, who surely must have received coaching from Dad who works in a peanut butter factory.

Recipe courtesy of The Procter & Gamble Co., Inc.

ONE-WEEK TRIP FOR TWO TO ENGLAND

CHUNK WILD COOKIES

King-size cookies chock-full of delectable morsels of richness.

1 cup butter
1 cup white sugar
1 cup light brown sugar
2 eggs
1 teaspoon vanilla extract
2½ cups oatmeal
2 cups KING ARTHUR®
  Unbleached Flour

1 teaspoon baking powder
1 teaspoon baking soda
6 ounces peanut butter chips
6 ounces chocolate chips
4 ounces grated white chocolate
1½ cups chopped walnuts

- Preheat oven to 375°. Cream together butter and sugars. Add eggs and vanilla. Using a blender or food processor, grind the oatmeal until it turns to powder. In a separate bowl, mix the oatmeal, flour, baking powder, and baking soda. Add peanut butter chips, chocolate chips, white chocolate, and chopped walnuts. Stir into creamed mixture.

- Drop by tablespoonfuls, 2 inches apart, onto an ungreased baking sheet. Bake for approximately 7 minutes.

- Makes about 4 dozen cookies.

1991 King Arthur® Flour WinterBake

The King Arthur Flour Co. of Norwich, Vermont hosts its WinterBake competitions in February at the Inn at Essex in Essex, Vermont, home of the New England Culinary Institute. Finalists' recipes are first prepared at the Institute and then are judged by a group of food experts. Sarah Nist of Montpelier, Vermont won Grand Prize in the Junior Division (for ages 7 to 18) with her recipe for these wildly unrestrained chunky, chocolatey, nutty cookies.

Recipe courtesy of the King Arthur Flour Co.

TRIP FOR TWO TO OAHU, MAUI, & KAUAI

LEMON CUSTARD ICE CREAM PIE

Dip into a dream of a dessert — glide through the whipped cream into two luscious lemon layers down to a buttery shortbread crust.

6 tablespoons butter, softened
1 cup flour
¼ cup powdered sugar
2 eggs, beaten
¾ cup sugar
2 tablespoons flour
3 tablespoons lemon juice
1 teaspoon grated lemon peel

1 quart BASKIN-ROBBINS®
    Lemon Custard Ice Cream (or
    other Baskin-Robbins lemon
    flavored ice cream), slightly
    softened
1 cup whipping (heavy) cream
2 tablespoons sugar
1 teaspoon vanilla
8 thin slices of lemon

- Preheat oven to 350°, or 325° for a glass plate. Make a shortbread crust by blending the butter, flour, and powdered sugar. Press mixture into the bottom and up sides of a 9-inch greased pie pan. Bake for 15 minutes.

- Mix eggs, sugar, flour, lemon juice and grated peel. Pour over hot crust; bake 20 minutes longer. Remove from oven; let cool completely. Fill cooled crust with ice cream. Freeze.

- Beat cream, sugar, and vanilla until stiff peaks form. Swirl whipped cream over top of pie. Garnish with twisted lemon slices. Freeze at least 3 hours. Remove from freezer about 10 minutes before serving to mellow.

- Makes 8 servings.

1975 Baskin-Robbins® Ice Cream Show-Off Recipe Contest

Mr. Baskin and Mr. Robbins opened their first "dipping store" in 1945. By 1970 there were 1,000 Baskin-Robbins franchises nationwide; now there are more than 3,000, one third of them outside the United States. Jeanne Randall of Corning, New York must have been delighted with her triple-dip Grand Prize, a two-week trip to three Hawaiian islands.

Recipe courtesy of Baskin-Robbins Inc.

1973 CHEVY VEGA HATCHBACK COUPE

HEAVENLY ICE CREAM PUFF FONDUE

Paradise found — These mini ice cream stuffed puffs swirled in chocolate sauce are divine indeed.

36 Miniature Cream Puffs *(homemade recipe follows; puffs can also be ordered in advance from many bakeries):*

½ cup water
¼ cup butter or margarine
¼ teaspoon salt

½ cup all-purpose flour
2 eggs

Ice Cream Filling:

1 pint BASKIN-ROBBINS®
  Burgundy Cherry Ice Cream *
1 pint BASKIN-ROBBINS®
  Chocolate Mint Ice Cream *

1 pint BASKIN-ROBBINS®
  JAMOCA® Ice Cream
* or any 3 or more of your favorite
  Baskin-Robbins flavors

2 cups Chocolate Fondue Sauce:

1 (14-ounce) can sweetened
  condensed milk
1 (12-ounce) package semisweet
  chocolate bits
½ cup milk

1 (7-ounce) jar marshmallow
  creme or 1 (6¼-ounce) package
  miniature marshmallows
  (3¾ cups)
1 teaspoon vanilla

Optional:
Flaked coconut
Chopped pecans

Sprinkles

Miniature Cream Puffs:

• Preheat oven to 375°. In a small saucepan slowly bring water, butter or margarine, and salt to a boil. Turn heat to low, stir in flour all at once. Beat with a wooden spoon until mixture leaves sides of pan and forms a small compact ball. Remove from heat, add eggs, beating until smooth. Drop dough by half teaspoonfuls, the size of a nickel, 2 inches apart, onto an ungreased baking sheet. Bake 25 to 30 minutes or until puffed and golden. Cool away from draft.

• Makes about 36 Miniature Cream Puffs, 1½ inches in diameter. Cut top off puffs; pull out any filaments of dough to form hollow shells.

Ice Cream Filling:

• Fill and mound six puffs (using a melon ball cutter or teaspoon) with one flavor of ice cream. Press tops into ice cream and place in freezer. Fill six more puffs with first flavor. Freeze. Repeat with second and third flavors. Continue until desired number of puffs are filled, allowing 6 to a serving. When all are frozen, place in a plastic bag and freeze until serving time.

Chocolate Fondue Sauce:

• Combine all ingredients in saucepan. Heat over medium heat, stirring just until mixture is smooth and warmed through. Sauce can be made ahead, refrigerated, and reheated. (It will keep indefinitely in the refrigerator.) Add a little milk if sauce becomes too thick. (Makes 4 cups sauce.)

To Serve:

• Gently heat Chocolate Fondue Sauce in a fondue pot or decorative skillet; arrange frozen filled puffs on plates. Each guest spears a puff with fondue fork, dips into the sauce and swirls to coat.

• If desired, small bowls of flaked coconut, chopped pecans, and sprinkles can arranged around sauce in which to dip the chocolate-coated puffs.

• Makes 6 servings.

1973 Baskin-Robbins® Ice Cream Show-Off Recipe Contest

During the 1970's and 1980's Baskin-Robbins sponsored a number of "Show-Off" contests which produced thousands of entries. Although Baskin-Robbins has developed more than 600 flavors of ice cream, a-flavor-a-day-for-a-month has been sold in their dipping stores on any given day, thus the magic "31" flavors. If you still own a fondue pot, dust it off, select three favorite Baskin-Robbins flavors, and give this show-off dessert from Laurie H. Freedman of Brooklyn, New York a try.

Recipe courtesy of Baskin-Robbins Inc.

TWO-WEEK TRIP FOR TWO TO LONDON

PRESIDENTIAL ICE CREAM PIE

As Baskin-Robbins describes it, "The pie has a crisp peanut butter cookie crust, a center of delectable Pralines 'n Cream Ice Cream, a layer of richer-than-rich peanut butter date sauce, and — talk about lily gilding! — a topping of whipped cream and peanuts."

1 roll (15-ounces) refrigerated
   peanut butter cookies
1 cup dates, chopped
⅔ cup water
¼ cup sugar
3 tablespoons peanut butter

1½ quarts BASKIN-ROBBINS®
   Pralines 'n Cream Ice Cream,
   slightly softened
1 cup whipping cream
1 tablespoon sugar
1 teaspoon vanilla
3 tablespoons chopped peanuts

- Preheat oven to 350°. Cut cookie roll in half crosswise. Cut half roll into about 30 ⅛-inch slices; refrigerate remaining half roll. Lightly butter bottom and sides of a 9-inch pie pan. Line bottom of pan with cookie slices, pressing to form a solid crust. Overlap remaining slices on side (not edge) of pan to complete crust. Bake for 10 minutes; cool, chill.

- In a small saucepan cook dates, water and sugar until thick, about 7 minutes, stirring constantly. Remove from heat, stir in peanut butter; cool.

- Fill pie shell with ice cream, mounding in center. Spoon date mixture over ice cream. Freeze at least 3 hours.

- To serve, beat whipping cream with sugar and vanilla until it holds its shape. Swirl over pie, sprinkle with peanuts.

- Makes 8 to 10 servings.

1977 Baskin-Robbins® Ice Cream Show-Off Recipe Contest

Peanuts enjoyed a culinary spotlight when Plains, Georgia's main claim-to-fame Jimmy Carter occupied the White House. Baskin-Robbins noted that "an unusual amount of peanuts were called for" in this year's contest when Marguerite Balbach of La Crescenta, California was awarded the Grand Prize for a Very Important Pie.

Recipe courtesy of Baskin-Robbins Inc.

$5,000

PEANUT CRUNCH PIE

Pronounced "one of the all-time best desserts" by an anonymous dessert expert.

6 ounces peanut brittle, coarsely chopped
5 cups (2½ pints) vanilla ice cream, slightly softened
1 6-ounce KEEBLER® READY-CRUST® Butter-Flavored Pie Crust

⅔ cup milk chocolate chips or one 3-ounce bar milk chocolate, chopped
½ cup heavy (whipping) cream
¼ cup confectioners' sugar
¼ cup smooth peanut butter, at room temperature

- Reserve some chopped peanut brittle for decoration. Mix remaining brittle with the ice cream in a large bowl. Spoon into pie crust, mounding it in center. Smooth with a metal spatula, cover with foil and freeze at least 6 hours or overnight.

- Stir chocolate chips and heavy cream in a medium-size saucepan over low heat until chocolate melts and mixture is smooth. Stir in confectioners' sugar and peanut butter until well blended.

- Put pie on waxed paper to catch drips. Pour chocolate mixture evenly over filling, spreading it quickly with a thin metal spatula (topping may flow over edge of pie). Freeze 1 hour or until topping is firm. Just before serving, decorate with reserved brittle.

- Makes 8 servings.

1991 WOMAN'S DAY/Keebler® Ready-Crust® No-Bake Pie Recipe Contest

The challenge of this competition was filling Keebler Ready-Crust pie shells with yummy no-bake concoctions. Eleanor J. Froelich's no-bake ice cream pie is as easy as no-make pie crust. The $2,000 Second Prize recipe was for "Cinnamon Sticky-Bun Pie" and the $1,000 Third Prize was awarded for "Caramel Pecan Turtle Pie." Oh, to have been a judge...

Recipe courtesy of WOMAN'S DAY Magazine, Hachette Magazines, Inc., and The Keebler Co.

$5,000

IRRESISTIBLE ICE CREAM PIE

Chocolate and coffee lovers especially will revel in three layers of bliss — a thick fudgy sauce separates the coffee ice cream base from a Kahlúa and cream topping, all in a chocolate crust.

1 6-ounce KEEBLER® READY-
CRUST® Chocolate Flavored
Pie Crust
1 pint coffee ice cream, slightly
softened
¾ cup evaporated milk

¼ cup butter
2 ounces unsweetened chocolate
½ cup sugar
½ cup heavy cream
¼ cup Kahlúa liqueur
¼ cup chopped pecans

- Press the ice cream into the crust and freeze.

- In a small saucepan combine evaporated milk, butter, chocolate and sugar. Cook over medium heat stirring constantly until thickened (about 10 to 15 minutes). Cool sauce completely and then pour over ice cream, spreading evenly. Freeze.

- Whip cream until stiff. Blend Kahlúa into cream and spread over frozen pie. Sprinkle with chopped pecans and freeze until solid.

- Makes 8 servings.

1992 WOMAN'S DAY/Keebler® Ready-Crust®
Recipe Contest

This year's competition required filling Keebler Ready-Crust pie shells with ice cream, ice milk, frozen yogurt, sherbet, or sorbet. Notice that the new-for-the-'90's-no-fat rules did not apply to this Grand Prize win, offering proof that when it comes to desserts, we simply can't resist. Regina Albright from Alton, Illinois proved the point with this high-spirited masterpiece.

Recipe courtesy of WOMAN'S DAY Magazine, Hachette Magazines, Inc., and The Keebler Co.

TRIP FOR TWO TO SOUTH AMERICA

ELEGANT MAI TAI MOUSSE

Refreshing flavors of the exotic Hawaiian Mai Tai are blended into this creamy, custardy pineapple mousse.

18 ladyfingers, split
2 envelopes unflavored gelatin
½ cup pineapple juice (from crushed, drained pineapple below)
5 egg yolks (reserve whites)
¾ cup sugar
¼ teaspoon salt
1 cup milk, scalded

⅓ cup lime juice
⅓ cup white rum
1 can (20 ounces) crushed pineapple, well drained
5 egg whites
½ cup sugar
1 cup heavy cream, whipped
¼ cup chopped macadamia nuts (or walnuts)

- Line sides and bottom of a 9-inch springform pan with split ladyfingers. Soften gelatin in pineapple juice. Beat egg yolks in top of double boiler. Stir in sugar and salt. Blend in milk, cook over boiling water, stirring for 5 minutes or until thickened. Blend in lime juice and rum. Add well-drained pineapple. Chill until thickened but not set.

- Beat egg whites, adding sugar. Fold pineapple custard and whipped cream into egg whites. Pour into lined pan. Sprinkle nuts on top. Chill several hours or overnight. To serve, remove pan rim.

- Makes 12 servings.

1974 SATURDAY EVENING POST's
Big Mixing Bowl Game Cooking Contest

Editors of the SATURDAY EVENING POST judged this contest with assistance from the kitchens of Purdue University's Department of Restaurant, Hotel and Institutional Management. Mrs. Michael W. Nagy of Cleveland Heights, Ohio was awarded the Grand Prize, a 15-day trip for two to Argentina, Chile, Brazil and Peru.

Recipe courtesy of the SATURDAY EVENING POST

WINDSTAR CRUISE IN TAHITI OR THE GRENADINES

FROZEN GRAND MARNIER SOUFFLÉ

"Light, creamy, and refreshing — sort of a cross between a mousse, a soufflé and ice cream," according to the sponsor, CHOCOLATIER Magazine. (Allow at least 8 hours for the soufflé to freeze.)

Tasteless vegetable oil
8 large egg yolks
¾ cup water
1½ cups granulated sugar
½ to ¾ cup Grand Marnier (see Note)

1 quart (4 cups) heavy (whipping) cream
Mandarin orange sections, strawberries and mint leaves, for garnish (optional)

Note: For a non-alcoholic variation, substitute ½ cup fresh orange juice plus 2 teaspoons vanilla extract for the Grand Marnier, and beat in 2 to 3 teaspoons of freshly grated orange zest with the egg yolks.

- Fold a 12 x 29-inch piece of aluminum foil in fourths lengthwise to form a quadruple-thickness 3 x 29-inch piece of foil. Tape the foil tightly around the outside of a 2-quart soufflé dish, making sure it extends at least 2 inches above the rim of the dish. Oil the inside of the foil collar lightly with tasteless vegetable oil.

- In a very large bowl, using a hand-held electric mixer set at medium-high speed, beat the egg yolks for 9 to 10 minutes, or until a thick yellow ribbon forms when the beaters are lifted.

- In a heavy, small saucepan, combine the water and sugar. Stirring constantly with a wooden spoon, cook the mixture over medium-low heat for 5 to 10 minutes, or until the sugar crystals are completely dissolved. Dip a clean pastry brush in water and wash down the side of the pan to remove any sugar crystals clinging to the side of the pan. Raise the heat to medium-high and bring the syrup to a boil without stirring. Remove the pan from the heat.

- Using a hand-held electric mixer set at medium speed, beat the egg yolks, while pouring in the hot sugar syrup in a slow, steady stream. Continue beating for 8 to 10 minutes, or until the mixture is cool to the touch and has a thick, smooth consistency. Beat in the Grand Marnier.

- In a chilled, large bowl, using a hand-held electric mixer set at medium speed, beat the cream until soft peaks begin to form. Gently whisk one-third of the whipped cream into the yolk mixture to lighten. Using a rubber spatula, gently fold in the remaining whipped cream.

- Transfer the cream mixture to the prepared soufflé dish. Loosely cover the top of the soufflé with plastic wrap. Freeze the soufflé for at least 8 hours, or overnight, until firm.

- Carefully remove the foil collar from the frozen soufflé. Garnish with mandarin orange sections, strawberries and mint leaves, if desired.

- Makes 8 servings.

1988 CHOCOLATIER'S Great Dessert Challenge

Astronaut Marsha Ivins of the Johnson Space Center in Houston, Texas won the Grand Prize in the non-chocolate category with her soufflé judged "out of this world" by CHOCOLATIER. The Grand Prize was the winner's choice of a Windstar cruise for two in the Grenadines or Tahiti and a Litton Prestige microwave oven.

Recipe courtesy of CHOCOLATIER Magazine,
Haymarket Group Ltd., New York

$2,000

BAVARIAN CUSTARD

Feeling deprived? With only 150 calories per serving, 1 gram of fat, and 5 milligrams of cholesterol, this rich custard is fit for the '90's.

1 (3.4-ounce) package instant vanilla flavor pudding and pie filling (see Note)
1 cup skim milk
1 cup LAND O LAKES® No-Fat Sour Cream

1 (8-ounce) carton (1 cup) low-fat vanilla-flavored yogurt
Fresh (or thawed frozen) strawberries, raspberries, blueberries or blackberries

Note: 1 (0.9-ounce) package sugar-free instant vanilla pudding and pie filling can be substituted for the regular pudding and pie filling.

- In a medium bowl place instant pudding. With wire whisk, stir in milk until mixture is smooth and slightly thickened. Add the sour cream and yogurt; whisk until smooth. Cover; refrigerate at least 2 hours.

- Spoon custard into 6 individual dessert dishes; top with assorted berries.

- Makes 6 servings.

1992 Land O Lakes® No-Fat Sour Cream Family Recipe Contest

Originally her recipe was high in fat and calories but Grand Prize winner Lois Lowe of Ellicott City, Maryland altered it without compromising the custardy richness. Entering the contest on a whim, the sixth-grade math teacher commented, "Not since my 4-H days have I ever done anything like that."

Recipe courtesy of Land O'Lakes, Inc.

$25,000

MOLDED SANGRIA

Sangria became popular in this country after its debut at the Spanish pavilion of the 1964 New York World's Fair. This shimmering jewel-like dessert is best if served in sherbet glasses to inspire midsummer night reveries of Spanish castles, flamenco dancers, Don Quixote...

1 cup sectioned navel oranges, peeled
½ cup very thinly sliced tart apples, peeled and cored
¼ cup brandy
1 tablespoon Cointreau
2 cups dry red wine

3 whole cloves
1 cinnamon stick
1 (6-ounce) package JELL-O® Brand Gelatin, Lemon Flavor
Juice of 1 lime
1 (12-ounce) bottle club soda, chilled

- Marinate orange sections and apple slices in brandy and Cointreau for 30 minutes at room temperature. Bring wine, cloves, and cinnamon to a boil. Strain to remove spices, pour wine over gelatin, and stir until dissolved. Add lime juice and chilled soda.

- Chill until slightly thickened. Stir in fruit and marinade. Spoon into sherbet glasses. Chill until firm.

- Makes 5¼ cups or 8 to 10 servings.

1972 Great Jell-O® Brand Gelatin Recipe Swap Contest

Molded gelatin desserts became fashionable during the 1940's. By the '50's elaborate shapes, towers, and multi-layered spectaculars vied for center-piece position on buffet tables — a covered dish supper without a variety of gelatin salads was unimaginable... Remember Strawberry-Pretzel Molded Dessert and 7-Up Salad? For Virginia T. Smith of Los Angeles, California this sangria gelatin was elevated to a Grand win indeed.

Recipe courtesy of Kraft General Foods, Inc.

$1,000

CRANBERRY BREAD PUDDING

The tang of cranberries comes through in this hearty whole wheat bread pudding that should be served warm from the oven with vanilla ice cream or frozen yogurt.

6 cups toasted whole wheat bread cubes, packed
1 cup OCEAN SPRAY® Fresh or Fresh Frozen Cranberries
2 cups OCEAN SPRAY CRAN•RASPBERRY® Raspberry Cranberry Drink

1 cup honey
½ cup butter
1 teaspoon cinnamon
½ teaspoon nutmeg
1 cup raisins

• Preheat oven to 350°. Grease a 2-quart casserole dish or pudding pan. Pour bread cubes into prepared pan. Set aside.

• Combine all remaining ingredients in a large saucepan. Bring to a boil over medium heat. Boil gently just until the cranberries begin to pop. Pour cranberry mixture over bread cubes, mixing gently. Let sit 15 minutes. Bake pudding 45 minutes. Serve warm with vanilla ice cream.

• Makes 10 servings.

1991 Ocean Spray® Distinctive Taste Recipe Contest

Considering all the good stuff in the ingredients list and the fact that cranberries are loaded with Vitamin C, this "dessert" could revolutionize the breakfast table as a buffer against harsh winter mornings — thanks to Diane Halferty from Seattle, Washington.

Recipe courtesy of Ocean Spray Cranberries, Inc.

$26,000 WINNEBAGO
APPLE AMERICANA

Apples star in this healthful cobbler-like dessert.

4 cups finely chopped red
  delicious apples, unpeeled
1 cup fresh Michigan cultured
  blueberries
2 tablespoons fresh lime juice
½ cup chopped, dried figs
¼ cup currants

½ cup flake coconut or shredded
  fresh coconut, if available
⅓ cup wheat germ
¼ teaspoon curry powder
1 cup white grape juice
½ cup clover honey

Topping:
½ cup sesame seed
½ cup wheat germ

½ cup slivered almonds

- Preheat oven to 350°. In a large mixing bowl combine apples, blue-berries and lime juice. Toss gently to mix. Stir in figs, currants and coconut, mixing well. Lightly rub bottom of 9 x 13 x 2-inch baking dish with oil. Sprinkle ⅓ of the fruit on bottom of dish. Combine wheat germ and curry powder and sprinkle half over fruit. Top with second ⅓ of fruit; sprinkle with remaining wheat germ/curry mixture. Spread remaining fruit over all. Combine grape juice and honey, mixing well, and pour over fruit.

- Combine topping ingredients and sprinkle over fruit. Bake for 30 minutes. Reduce heat to 325°. Bake another 15 to 20 minutes, then remove from oven. Place baking dish on wire rack to cool. Serve while still warm.

- Makes 12 servings.

1983 SATURDAY EVENING POST Health Recipe Contest

Apples have long been a symbol of good health, attributed as they are to putting roses on cheeks and keeping doctors away. How appropriate that the Grand Prize recipe in this health-focused contest features them. Ann Borth from Michigan and Florida no doubt made good use of her grand new motor home.

Recipe courtesy of the SATURDAY EVENING POST

$25,000

PINEAPPLE-CHEESE BAKLAVA

1 (1-pound, 4-ounce) can
CRUSHED PINEAPPLE in
syrup
1 (8-ounce) package cream
cheese, softened
1 cup ricotta
1 cup sugar

2 egg yolks
1 teaspoon grated lemon peel
1 teaspoon vanilla
½ pound frozen phyllo pastry
leaves, thawed (8 leaves)
½ cup butter, melted
1 teaspoon lemon juice

- Preheat oven to 350°. Turn pineapple into wire strainer and drain, saving syrup. In mixer bowl, combine cream cheese, ricotta, ½ cup sugar, egg yolks, lemon peel and vanilla. Blend together on medium speed. Stir in drained pineapple. Place phyllo leaves between damp towels to keep moist. Place a sheet of pastry in well greased pan (9 x 13 x 2-inches). Brush with melted butter. Repeat with three more leaves. Spoon on the pineapple-cheese mixture, and spread level. Top with remaining phyllo, brushing each sheet with butter as it is layered. Mark pastry into diamonds with point of sharp knife. Bake about 50 minutes, or until golden brown.

- Combine ½ cup reserved pineapple syrup, remaining ½ cup sugar, and lemon juice, and cook to a thick syrup. When baklava is baked, spoon the hot syrup evenly over the top. Cool, then cut into diamonds at markings.

- Makes 1 large baklava.

1979 National Pineapple Cooking Classic

Forty finalists enjoyed a week of festivities in Honolulu, highlighted by an intense cook-off and a glittering awards ceremony that was capped by fireworks. Sales of phyllo dough shot up, too, after this recipe was announced the winner; Annette Erbeck from Mason, Ohio developed this innovative Hawaiian twist on a classic Greek dessert.

Recipe courtesy of the Pineapple Growers Association of Hawaii: Del Monte Fresh Produce Company, Inc., Dole Food Company, Inc., Maui Land & Pineapple Company, Inc. and Wailuku Agribusiness Company, Inc. Look for the "100% Hawaiian" designation on canned pineapple products.

MAIN DISH MEDALS

THE NATIONAL CHICKEN COOKING CONTEST

AND THE

DELMARVA CHICKEN COOKING CONTEST

But first a riddle...

Gastronomically speaking, what bird:

- fries better than it flies
- is often broiled, oiled, or foiled... but never ever boiled

and is most:

- promoted, coated, and table d'hôted
- favored, flavored, savored
- propagated, celebrated, highly rated, not to mention marinated
- basted, tasted
- roasted, broasted
- grilled, frilled
- delicious and nutritious?

Answer: BROILER-FRYER CHICKEN

Always In Good Taste

Ever since these sister chicken cooking contests began in 1949, broiler-fryer chicken has been dressed for success. Whether garbed in Sunday dinner best or in picnic and barbecue casual; whether glossed and sauced or varnished and garnished, chicken has been consistently rated a favorite American main course.

Just as fashion fads come and go, what's "in" today in cooking tastes and trends may be out tomorrow. Despite the whims of the times, chicken will continue to hold its place at the top of the "Best Dressed" list. The seven recipes that follow are examples of Grand Prize chicken dishes that have been in vogue from the more than 40 years of chicken cooking contests.

KINDRED CONTESTS

Originally the Delmarva Chicken Festival was an idea hatched in 1948 to spotlight the burgeoning poultry industry on Delmarva Peninsula, the birthplace of the commercial broiler industry. In 1949 the first annual Delmarva Chicken Festival was held in Salisbury, Maryland. Over the years, these events have become real wing dingers, complete with parades, beauty queens, and vintage cars. And the highlight, of course, is the chicken cooking contest.

That first year Mrs. A. L. Karlik of Salisbury won the $250 Grand Prize with her recipe for "Broiled Chicken Deluxe." But it wasn't until a decade later in 1959 that Governor J. Millard Tawes presented a Citation to Mrs. Karlik in recognition of being the first winner of the chicken cooking contest.

In the early years these festivals were regional events sponsored by the Delmarva Poultry Industry and were concentrated in Delmarva's broiler market consisting of northeastern states and the District of Columbia. In 1972, with the soaring popularity of chicken and the national attention the events themselves were receiving, the National Broiler Council took on nationwide sponsorship of the National Chicken Cooking Contest.

The Delmarva Chicken Cooking Contest is still a regional event sponsored by the Delmarva Poultry Industry. Two finalists are selected from the states of Maine, New Hampshire, Vermont, Connecticut, Massachusetts, Rhode Island, New York, New Jersey, Pennsylvania, Delaware, Maryland, Virginia, and the District of Columbia. In recent years the 3-day event has attracted a crowd of 40,000 who consume 12,000 pounds of chicken from more than 20 chicken concessions. Besides the cooking contest, there is the Giant Frying Pan (read about it with the recipe for "Olympic Seoul Chicken"), antique car and trade show exhibits, jugglers, rides and games, and musical groups offering a full menu of entertainment from Bluegrass, to Dixieland and barbershop, jazz, rock 'n' roll, pipers, and sacred music on Sunday.

Today, the National Chicken Cooking Contests and the Delmarva Chicken Cooking Contests are held biennially in alternating years. Among recipe contesters, both competitions are much anticipated events... and the prizes aren't exactly chicken feed.

$10,000

DIPPER'S NUGGETS CHICKEN

These are THE golden fried chicken nuggets with dipping sauces that are credited with starting the 1970's fast food trend.

2 whole BROILER-FRYER
　CHICKEN BREASTS, halved,
　skinned, boned and cut into
　1 x 1 x ½-inch pieces
2 cups corn oil
1 egg, beaten

⅓ cup water
⅓ cup flour
2 teaspoons sesame seed
1½ teaspoons salt
Sauces: recipes follow

- In deep fryer place corn oil, filling to no more than ⅓ full. Heat to medium temperature. In large bowl mix egg and water. Add flour, sesame seeds and salt, stirring until smooth batter is formed. Dip chicken nuggets into batter, draining off excess. Carefully add nuggets, a few at a time. Fry about 4 minutes or until golden brown and fork can be inserted with ease. Drain on paper towels. Serve with sauces as desired.

- Makes 4 servings.

Nippy Pineapple Sauce:

- In saucepan mix (12-ounce) jar pineapple preserves, ¼ cup prepared mustard, and ¼ cup prepared horseradish. Cook over low heat, stirring, for about 5 minutes.

Dill Sauce:

- In bowl mix together ½ cup sour cream, ½ cup mayonnaise, 1 teaspoon dried dill weed, and 2 tablespoons finely chopped dill pickle. Let stand at room temperature about 1 hour allowing flavors to blend.

Royalty Sauce:

- In saucepan mix together 1 cup catsup, ½ teaspoon dry mustard, 1 tablespoon brown sugar, 2 tablespoons vinegar, and 6 tablespoons margarine. Cook over low heat for 5 minutes, stirring constantly.

1971 — 23rd National Chicken Cooking Contest

Bound for stardom, this recipe's fame reached all the way to McDonald's' golden arches and beyond. The Midas-like golden touch belongs to Norma Young of Searcy, Arkansas.

Recipe courtesy of the National Broiler Council

$10,000

CURRIED CHICKEN ROLLS

Curry powder imparts unmistakable aroma, pungency and golden color to the stuffing of these rolled chicken breasts.

2 WHOLE BROILER-FRYER
  CHICKEN BREASTS, halved,
  boned, skinned
½ teaspoon salt
⅛ teaspoon pepper
1 tablespoon margarine
½ onion, finely chopped
¾ cup cooked rice
¼ cup raisins

1 tablespoon chopped parsley
1 teaspoon curry powder
½ teaspoon poultry seasoning
1 teaspoon brown sugar
1/16 teaspoon garlic powder
1 tablespoon cooking oil
½ cup white wine
1 teaspoon granulated chicken
  bouillon

- On hard surface with meat mallet or similar flattening utensil, pound chicken to ⅜-inch thickness. Sprinkle salt and pepper on chicken.

- In medium frypan, make stuffing by placing margarine and melting over medium heat. Add onion and sauté about 3 minutes or until soft. Add rice, raisins, parsley, curry powder, poultry seasoning, brown sugar and garlic powder. Stir until well mixed. Divide stuffing in 4 portions. Place one portion on each piece of chicken. Roll, jelly roll fashion; fasten with wooden picks.

- In another frypan, place oil and heat to medium temperature. Add chicken rolls and cook, turning, about 15 minutes or until brown on all sides. Add wine and bouillon. Cover and simmer about 30 minutes or until fork can be inserted in chicken with ease.

- Makes 4 servings.

1979 — 31st National Chicken Cooking Contest

At the time Barbara Long of Laramie, Wyoming won, she commented that she knew she had a winner when her husband "ate it without adding ketchup which he automatically puts on everything."

Recipe courtesy of the National Broiler Council

$10,000

BAKED CHICKEN REUBEN

One of the best of the numerous Reuben clones.

4 WHOLE BROILER-FRYER
  CHICKEN BREASTS, halved
  and boned
¼ teaspoon salt
⅛ teaspoon pepper
1 can (16-ounces) sauerkraut,
  drained (press out excess liquid)

4 slices (each about 4 x 6 inches)
  natural Swiss cheese
1¼ cups bottled Thousand Island
  salad dressing
1 tablespoon chopped fresh
  parsley

- Preheat oven to 325°.

- In greased baking pan, place chicken. Sprinkle with salt and pepper.
  Place sauerkraut over chicken; top with Swiss cheese. Pour dressing
  evenly over cheese. Cover with foil and bake for about 1½ hours or
  until fork can be inserted in chicken with ease. Sprinkle with chopped
  parsley to serve.

- Makes 4 servings

1982 — 34th National Chicken Cooking Contest

*Ever since 1956 when the original Reuben sandwich won the National
Sandwich Idea of the Year contest, "Reuben" has inspired many other
contest-winning recipes. For this competition held in Dallas, Texas,
Marcia Adams of Ft. Wayne, Indiana can take the credit for a dream team
combination of traditional Reuben ingredients and chicken breasts.*

Recipe courtesy of the National Broiler Council

TRIP FOR TWO TO HAWAII

STUFFED CHICKEN WITH APPLE GLAZE

1 WHOLE BROILER-FRYER
 CHICKEN
½ teaspoon salt

¼ teaspoon pepper
2 tablespoons cooking oil

Stuffing:
1 package (6-ounces) chicken
 flavor stuffing mix
1 cup grated apple
¼ cup chopped walnuts

¼ cup raisins
¼ cup finely chopped celery
½ teaspoon grated lemon peel

Apple Glaze:
½ cup apple jelly
1 tablespoon lemon juice

½ teaspoon ground cinnamon

- Preheat oven to 350°. Sprinkle inside of chicken with salt and pepper; rub outside of chicken with oil.

Stuffing:

- In bowl, mix stuffing mix according to package directions. Add apple, walnuts, raisins, celery and lemon peel; mix thoroughly. Place stuffing in cavity of chicken. Place chicken in baking pan; cover loosely with foil. Roast about 1 hour.

Apple Glaze:

- In small saucepan, place apple jelly, lemon juice and cinnamon. Simmer, stirring, 3 minutes or until blended. Brush chicken with glaze. Roast, uncovered, 30 minutes longer or until leg moves freely when lifted or twisted, brushing frequently with glaze.

- Makes 4 servings.

1984 Delmarva Chicken Cooking Contest

Besides winning the 10-day Hawaiian vacation, Ruth E. Dykes of Beltsville, Maryland won $1,000 spending money, a microwave oven, gas grill, and other household gifts. Among the competitors was a member of the House of Representatives.

Recipe courtesy of the Delmarva Poultry Industry, Inc.

TRIP FOR TWO TO HAWAII

OLYMPIC SEOUL CHICKEN

Robust Korean flavors dominate this chicken dish, developed the year the Olympics were held in Seoul.

¼ cup white vinegar
3 tablespoons soy sauce
2 tablespoons honey
¼ teaspoon ground ginger
2 tablespoons peanut oil
8 BROILER-FRYER CHICKEN THIGHS, skinned

10 cloves garlic, coarsely chopped (when cooked, the garlic becomes mellow and is not overpowering)
1 teaspoon crushed red pepper
Hot cooked rice

- Combine the vinegar, soy sauce, honey and ginger in a small bowl and set aside.
- Heat the oil in a large skillet over medium-high heat. Add the chicken and cook about 10 minutes or until evenly browned on all sides. Add the garlic and red pepper and cook, stirring, for 2 to 3 minutes. Drain off excess fat. Add the vinegar mixture. Cover the skillet, reduce heat and simmer about 15 minutes or until the chicken is fork-tender. Uncover and cook for about 2 minutes or until the sauce has reduced and thickened. Serve with hot rice.

1988 Delmarva Chicken Cooking Contest

For its 40th anniversary the Delmarva Chicken Festival returned to its roots in Salisbury, Maryland. Muriel Brody of Cumberland, Rhode Island won the Grand Prize — a 10-day stay in Hawaii for two, $1,000 in cash, plus an assortment of appliances and kitchen equipment. The trademark of the three-day festival is the

GIANT FRYING PAN:

Weighing 650 pounds, it is 10 feet in diameter, has an 8-foot-long handle, is 8 inches deep, holds 180 gallons of cooking oil which is changed daily during the festival, can cook 800 chicken quarters at a time, is mounted on a concrete block base, and requires 15 cooks and 60 gallons of LP gas to operate.

Recipe courtesy of the Delmarva Poultry Industry, Inc.

$10,000

SUMMER ITALIAN STUFFED CHICKEN

4 BROILER-FRYER CHICKEN BREAST HALVES, boned, skinned
½ cup, plus ⅓ cup bottled oil-vinegar dressing
1 small head radicchio, torn into bite-size pieces
1 small bunch watercress, cut into bite-size pieces
¼ cup fresh basil
2 plum tomatoes, thinly sliced
1 tablespoon water
1 egg
⅔ cup Italian seasoned breadcrumbs
½ cup Parmesan cheese
4 tablespoons olive oil
Tomato rosettes

- With meat mallet or similar flattening utensil, pound chicken to ¼-inch thickness; place in large baking pan. Add ½ cup of the oil-vinegar dressing; turn to coat, cover, and refrigerate 30 minutes.

- In medium bowl, place radicchio and watercress; add remaining ⅓ cup oil-vinegar dressing; toss to mix. Arrange radicchio mixture on platter; refrigerate.

- Remove chicken from dressing; drain. Cut each chicken breast in half crosswise. Place an even portion of basil and tomatoes on each of 4 pieces of chicken; top each piece with remaining half of breast. With textured side of mallet, pound edges together to seal.

- In a shallow dish, beat water and egg. On wax paper, mix breadcrumbs and Parmesan cheese. Dip chicken, one piece at a time, in egg mixture and then in breadcrumb mixture. In a large frypan, place oil; heat over medium-high temperature. Add chicken and cook about 10 minutes or until brown and fork can be inserted with ease. Arrange chicken on radicchio mixture. Garnish with tomato rosettes.

- Makes 4 servings.

1989 — 38th National Chicken Cooking Contest

Great taste and good nutrition with an Italian flair ensured the win for Melissa Mathie of Michigan at this year's competition held in Hershey, Pennsylvania.

Recipe courtesy of the National Broiler Council

CARIBBEAN TRIP FOR TWO

CHICKEN ROYALE

Raspberry vinaigrette sauce and vivid stuffing ingredients give this chicken technicolor and techniflavor qualities.

2 WHOLE BROILER-FRYER CHICKEN BREASTS, halved, boned, skinned
1 package (4-ounces) Boursin or other herb-flavored cheese, quartered
½ cup English walnuts, finely chopped

4 large spinach leaves, steamed slightly
½ teaspoon salt
½ teaspoon pepper
½ cup dry white wine
½ cup bottled reduced-calorie raspberry vinaigrette dressing*
2 tablespoons margarine
Cooked rice

*If raspberry vinaigrette dressing is not available, substitute ¼ cup bottled reduced-calorie red wine vinegar and oil dressing and ¼ cup seedless raspberry jam. Omit the margarine.

- Preheat oven to 350°. On hard surface with meat mallet or similar flattening utensil, pound chicken to ¼-inch thickness. Roll the cheese quarters in walnuts. Place one spinach leaf on each breast; top with a cheese quarter. Fold chicken around spinach and cheese to form a mound. Sprinkle salt and pepper over chicken. Place chicken in baking pan. Cover and bake 30 minutes or until chicken is fork tender.

- In small frypan, mix together wine and raspberry vinaigrette dressing. Cook over medium heat until sauce is reduced by one-half; stir in margarine. Pour sauce over chicken. Serve with rice.

- Makes 4 servings.

1992 Delmarva Chicken Cooking Contest

Dwight Dewsnap, a computer programmer from Brockton, Massachusetts, cooked his way to the Caribbean with his "chicken cordon rouge" recipe. His winnings included an extra $1,000 and a variety of kitchen gear and gadgets. Five men and 21 women participated in the cooking contest at this year's 44th Annual Delmarva Chicken Festival held once again in Salisbury, Maryland.

Recipe courtesy of the Delmarva Poultry Industry, Inc.

HILLARY RODHAM CLINTON'S HERBED CHICKEN BREASTS

The secret's in the sauce; try it with triple the amount of fresh herbs too.

Herb Basting Sauce:

3½ tablespoons melted butter or margarine
1 tablespoon finely grated onion
1 large clove garlic, crushed
1 teaspoon crumbled thyme
½ teaspoon salt

½ teaspoon freshly ground pepper
½ teaspoon crumbled rosemary
¼ teaspoon ground sage
⅛ teaspoon crumbled marjoram
Dash of hot pepper sauce

2 WHOLE LARGE BROILER-FRYER CHICKEN BREASTS, halved and boned

1½ tablespoons minced parsley, for garnish

Herb Basting Sauce:

- Preheat oven to 425°. Stir all Herb Basting Sauce ingredients together until well blended. Wipe each breast piece dry. Place chicken in sauce and turn to coat thoroughly. Tuck edges under, forming a compact shape about 1½ inches thick. Place chicken, skin side up, in shallow baking dish. Bake, basting occasionally with pan juices, just until chicken is opaque almost to center, about 14 minutes. Remove to warm plates. Spoon pan juices over chicken and sprinkle with parsley.
- Makes 4 servings.

1991 — 39th National Chicken Cooking Contest

One finalist from each state and the District of Columbia gathered for the competition in Little Rock, Arkansas. Judith Markiewicz of Canton, Ohio won the $25,000 Grand Prize with a recipe for "Southwestern Oven-Fried Chicken."

Since Arkansas is the Nation's top broiler-producing state, its First Lady and the wives of its two senators were invited to share their favorite chicken recipes. Above is the recipe offered by Hillary Rodham Clinton, wife of then-Governor Bill Clinton. Together, the Clintons won the biggest contest of all in 1992 and, don't forget, Hillary's chocolate chip cookies won FAMILY CIRCLE's Bipartisan Bake-Off just prior to the election.

Recipe courtesy of the National Broiler Council

TRIP FOR TWO TO LONDON, PARIS, ROME

COMIN' THROUGH THE RYE

In the best of Northern Italian culinary tradition, the style is tasty, aromatic and refined.

1 broiler-fryer chicken (3½ pounds)
1 teaspoon salt
Pepper
2 tablespoons butter
2 tablespoons olive oil
¼ cup Seagram's V.O.®
3 links sweet Italian sausage
1 cup coarsely chopped onion
2 chicken gizzards, coarsely chopped

2 chicken hearts, coarsely chopped
2 chicken livers, coarsely chopped
1 cup sliced mushrooms
1 cup converted rice
3 tablespoons grated Parmesan cheese
3 chicken bouillon cubes
2½ cups boiling water

- Cut chicken into 8 pieces, sprinkle with salt and pepper. Heat butter and oil in flameproof casserole, brown chicken, skin down first, about 16 minutes. Remove chicken to platter, sprinkle with Seagram's V.O. Let stand, turning occasionally to season evenly. Pour off all but 4 tablespoons fat from casserole. Discard sausage casings, cut sausage into small chunks. Cook in casserole with onion until onion is wilted, stirring briskly. Add gizzards and hearts, cook, stirring, 5 minutes. Add chicken livers and mushrooms, cook 3 minutes, stirring. Stir in rice. Push rice to sides of casserole, return chicken to center, pour juices from platter over chicken. Cover with rice, sprinkle with cheese. Dissolve bouillon cubes in boiling water, add. Bring to a boil, cover, simmer 25 minutes.

- Makes 4 servings.

**1974 Seagram's V.O.® & GOURMET MAGAZINE®'s
International One Dish Supper Recipe Contest**

From more than 10,000 entries, five finalists selected by GOURMET MAGAZINE participated in a week-long dining and sightseeing experience in Montreal, Canada. The Grand Prize winner was announced at a banquet at Desjardins, one of Canada's most famous restaurants.

Recipe courtesy of Joseph E. Seagram & Sons, Inc./Seagram's V.O.

$50,000 FOR HABITAT FOR HUMANITY

"THE DEVIL MADE ME DO IT" CHICKEN BREASTS DIAVOLO

Devilishly delicious — These rolled chicken breasts and artichokes with Chianti-spiked Diavolo Sauce are topped with Mozzarella cheese and croutons, then served over pasta or rice.

6 chicken breast halves, boned, skinned, and slightly flattened
½ cup finely minced fresh parsley
1 teaspoon lemon-pepper spice
Dash each of salt and garlic powder
3 tablespoons olive oil
3 (6-ounce) jars marinated artichoke hearts
1 tablespoon fresh lemon juice

1 (26-ounce) jar NEWMAN'S OWN® Diavolo Sauce
½ cup red wine (preferably Chianti)
1½ cups shredded Mozzarella cheese
1½ cups onion-garlic flavor croutons tossed with 1 tablespoon olive oil
6 cups cooked pasta or rice

- Preheat oven to 350°. Sprinkle chicken breasts with minced parsley, lemon-pepper spice, salt and garlic powder. Roll each breast, seasoned-side in; secure with wooden toothpicks, and sauté in olive oil in large skillet until golden brown. Remove from pan with tongs and place in a 9 x 13-inch casserole. Carefully remove toothpicks.

- Drain artichoke hearts, sprinkle with lemon juice and distribute among rolled chicken breasts.

- Combine Newman's Own Diavolo Sauce with wine and pour over chicken and artichokes. Spread the shredded mozzarella cheese evenly over top. Sprinkle with crouton mixture as topping. Bake 30 to 40 minutes, until golden brown and bubbly.

- While casserole is baking, prepare pasta or rice. Spoon "Chicken Breasts Diavolo" over pasta or rice, and serve with crusty Italian bread or rolls, a green salad with Newman's Own Olive Oil & Vinegar Salad Dressing, and the rest of the good bottle of red wine.

- Makes 6 servings.

1991 Newman's Own® & GOOD HOUSEKEEPING's
Spicy Diavolo Sauce Recipe Contest

To introduce the latest member of his ever-growing family of food products, Paul Newman invited submission of recipes using Spicy Diavolo Sauce. Staff from the GOOD HOUSEKEEPING Institute kitchens selected the finalists from six regions in this special competition that introduced a whole new dimension to contest cooking—the huge cash awards were made to the winners' favorite charities, befitting the philosophy of the Newman's Own company. As models for social change in creating a more caring world, Paul Newman and his long-time friend and partner, author A. E. Hotchner, created a booming food business from which all profits go to charitable causes.

Finalists won a trip to New York, a stay at the Waldorf Astoria, and lunch at the Rainbow Room with Paul Newman who judged the dishes himself. His favorite was the recipe of Geraldine Kirkpatrick from Huntington Beach, California, whose winning recipe was a favorite cream soup-based recipe which she transformed into this lively, delicious creation.

The other winners' recipes and charitable prizes were:

"Cool Hand Luke's Brunch Burrito"
Timothy Conrad, Columbus, Ohio
$10,000 — Columbus Children's Hospital

"Diavolo Seafood Loaves"
Christine Loughridge, Felton, California
$10,000 — Crohns & Colitis Foundation of America

"Garden Party Pasta Salad"
Chris Kissel, Denver, Colorado
$10,000 — American Cancer Society

"Mediterranean Shrimp Diavolo"
Tali Ann Katz, Annapolis, Maryland
$10,000 — AIDS Health Education Resource Organization,
The Annapolis Chapter of Hadassah & The Baltimore City Child Care
Resource Center

"Spicy-Sweet Brisket"
Edda Bickler, Coral Springs, Florida
$10,000 — Crohns & Colitis Foundation of America

"Bandito Vegetables"
The "Wild Dream Team" * from Ms. Teri Lindner's and Sharon Pearson's
Special Education/Learning Support Class, State College, PA
$10,000 — Easter Seal Society

*The "Wild Dream Team," as this special education class is known, admitted to not knowing who Paul Newman was when they entered the contest. One student became interested in meeting him when he learned of Newman's sports car racing hobby. Another student knew him only as a guy who made a movie with Tom Cruise ("The Color of Money"). Following their win, the "Wild Dream Team" acquired some fame of their own with an appearance on Charles Kuralt's "CBS Sunday Morning" program.

Recipe courtesy of Newman's Own, Inc.

$1,000 & MICROWAVE OVEN FOR HOME EC DEPARTMENT

CHICKEN MEXICANA

Once the chopping is done, this south-of-the-border style chicken and rice dish passes the taste test with ease to earn an A+.

2 whole chicken breasts, split, boned and skinned
¼ teaspoon garlic salt
2 tablespoons butter or margarine
½ cup sliced green onions with tops (½-inch pieces)
½ cup chopped green pepper

1 cup PACE® Picante Sauce
4 ounces pasteurized process cheese spread, diced
2 to 3 cups hot cooked rice, as desired
¼ cup chopped cilantro

- Sprinkle chicken with garlic salt. Heat butter in a 10-inch skillet over medium heat. Add chicken and cook 5 minutes. Turn chicken over. Add onion and green pepper around edges of chicken. Cook 5 minutes or until chicken is tender.

- Place rice on serving platter. Remove chicken from skillet and place over rice; keep warm.

- Add picante sauce and cheese to skillet. Cook and stir until cheese is melted and sauce is hot. Pour over chicken and rice; sprinkle with cilantro. Serve with additional Pace Picante Sauce.

- Makes 4 servings.

1989 Pace® Picante Sauce Young Cooks Recipe Contest

Thirteen-year-old Junior High School student Adrienne Sloboden of Puyallup, Washington added $1,000 to her pocket and a microwave oven to her school's Home Economics department with her Grand Prize win in this contest for cooks aged 12 to 18.

Recipe courtesy of Pace® Picante Sauce and Pace Foods, Inc.

TRIP FOR FOUR TO DISNEY WORLD
SAUCY CHICKEN KIEV OLÉ

The perfect example of America's great mixing bowl of tastes, combining ever-popular Mexican flavors with a chicken Kiev-style preparation method. But the real secret is in the sauce.

⅓ cup butter or margarine, softened
1 envelope (1.24 to 1.3 ounces) taco seasoning mix
1 cup (4 ounces) shredded Cheddar cheese
4 whole chicken breasts, halved, skinned, boned

1 jar (12 ounces) SMUCKER'S® Tomato Preserves (see Note)
1 jar (8 ounces) taco sauce
½ cup pitted ripe olives, sliced
2 cups shredded iceberg lettuce
2 medium tomatoes, cut into wedges

Note: If tomato preserves are not available, combine a 6-ounce can of tomato paste, a 10-ounce jar of Smucker's® Apple Jelly and the taco sauce in a small saucepan. Stir over low heat until jelly melts. Proceed as directed.

- Preheat oven to 350°. Combine butter, taco seasoning mix and ¼ cup Cheddar until blended. With meat mallet or dull edge of French knife, pound chicken breasts to ¼-inch thickness. Place equal amounts of butter mixture in centers of chicken; fold sides over center; secure with wooden picks. Put chicken smooth side up in a 12 x 8-inch baking dish.

- Mix tomato preserves and taco sauce. Set aside 1 cup sauce mixture; pour remaining mixture over chicken. Cover with foil; bake 25 minutes. Remove foil; top chicken with ¾ cup Cheddar and the olives. Bake 5 minutes more, or until cheese is bubbly.

- To serve, arrange lettuce on platter; top with chicken; garnish with tomato wedges. Pass remaining tomato-preserve sauce.

- Makes 8 servings.

1985 Smucker's® Great American Recipe Contest

Veteran recipe contest winner Jean W. Sanderson from Shawnee Mission, Kansas went beyond the traditional in featuring tomato preserves in a tangy sauce. Two Grand Prizes were awarded in this contest; the other was awarded to "Chocolate Truffles."

Recipe courtesy of The J. M. Smucker Company

$3,000

STUFFED CHICKEN BREASTS EL CALVADOR

SARAN WRAP® for the
Microwave
2 tablespoons fine dry bread
crumbs
1 tablespoon finely chopped
parsley
1 teaspoon paprika
4 skinned, boneless chicken
breast halves (about 1¼ pounds)

3 tablespoons margarine, melted
1 cup finely chopped, pared tart
apple (1 large)
1 cup chopped pecans
½ cup (2 ounces) shredded Swiss
cheese
½ teaspoon onion salt
1 egg, slightly beaten

Apple Sauce:
¾ cup apple juice
1 tablespoon apple brandy or
apple jack

2 teaspoons cornstarch
Apple wedges for garnish
(optional)

• Combine bread crumbs, parsley and paprika in small bowl; reserve.
Pound chicken breasts between 2 sheets of microwave-safe Saran
Wrap to thickness of ⅜ inch. Remove top sheet. Brush top surfaces of
chicken with 1 tablespoon of the margarine. Sprinkle with bread
crumbs. Lift chicken pieces carefully and place into four 10-ounce
microwave-safe custard cups, crumbed-side against cup and allowing
sides to overlap top edge if necessary. Combine apple, pecans, cheese,
onion salt, egg and the remaining 2 tablespoons margarine in medium-
size bowl; mix lightly. Spoon stuffing into prepared custard cups; fold
any overhanging chicken over tops. Cover each with microwave-safe
Saran Wrap, venting each at one side. Place custard cups in circle in
microwave oven. Microwave at full power 6 to 8 minutes, rotating each
cup one-quarter turn every 3 minutes. Let stand, covered on solid
surface 5 minutes.

• Combine apple juice, apple brandy and cornstarch in 2-cup microwave-safe measure; mix until smooth. Microwave, uncovered, at full
power 3 to 5 minutes until mixture thickens and boils, stirring once.
Remove from microwave; whisk until smooth. To serve, unmold
chicken onto plate. Serve with Sauce; garnish with apple wedges.

• Makes 4 servings.

Recipe developed by Diane Bryant of Texas for the 1986 FAMILY CIRCLE/
Saran Wrap® Microwave Cooking Recipe Contest. Recipe courtesy of Dow
Brands L.P. and FAMILY CIRCLE/The New York Times Company

TRIP FOR TWO TO SAN FRANCISCO & $500

SAUTÉED CHICKEN BREASTS IN CREAM SAUCE

Subtly seasoned strips of chicken with vegetables in a rich cream cheese sauce served on tri-color pasta.

4 boneless skinless chicken breast halves (about 1¼ pounds)
2 tablespoons PARKAY® Margarine
1½ cups sliced mushrooms
1 cup sliced celery
1 small onion, thinly sliced
½ teaspoon pepper
½ teaspoon dried basil leaves, crushed
¼ teaspoon dried chervil, crushed

⅛ teaspoon dried thyme leaves, crushed
¼ cup dry white wine or sherry, divided
1 package (8 ounces) PHILADELPHIA® BRAND Cream Cheese, cubed
⅓ cup milk
8 ounces tri-color rotini, cooked, drained

- Cut chicken crosswise into ¼-inch strips. Melt margarine in large skillet over medium heat. Add chicken, vegetables and seasonings; cook 10 minutes or until chicken is tender, stirring occasionally.
- Add 2 tablespoons of the wine; simmer 5 minutes.
- Stir cream cheese, milk and remaining 2 tablespoons wine in saucepan over low heat until smooth.
- Place rotini on serving platter; top with chicken mixture and cream cheese mixture.
- Makes 4 to 6 servings.

1987 "Philly" Hall of Fame Recipe Contest

As one of the four Grand Prize winners — one in each category — Stephen Thomas of Bethlehem, Pennsylvania enjoyed luxurious accommodations, sightseeing by limousine, an awards dinner, plus $500 spending money while he and a guest were in San Francisco.

Recipe courtesy of Kraft General Foods, Inc.

$2,000

GINGER SPICY CHICKEN

Another example of cross-cultural cooking at its best. East meets west as picante sauce spices up an oriental-style chicken stir-fry.

Salt
2 whole chicken breasts, split, skinned, and boned
2 tablespoons vegetable oil
1 medium-size red bell pepper, cut into 2 x ¼-inch strips (about 1½ cups)
1 medium-size green bell pepper, cut into 2 x ¼-inch strips (about 1½ cups)

1 (8-ounce) can pineapple chunks in juice, undrained
½ cup PACE® Picante Sauce
2 tablespoons chopped cilantro or parsley
2 to 3 teaspoons grated fresh ginger or ¾ to 1 teaspoon ground ginger

• Lightly salt the chicken breasts. Heat the oil in a large skillet over medium heat. Add the chicken breasts and cook for about 5 minutes or until lightly browned and cooked through. Remove the chicken and reserve.

• Add the pepper strips, pineapple, picante sauce, cilantro and ginger to the skillet; cook, stirring frequently, for 5 to 7 minutes or until the peppers are tender and the sauce is thickened. Return the chicken to the skillet and heat through.

• Makes 4 servings.

1987 Pace® Picante Sauce 40th Anniversary Recipe Contest

To celebrate its 40th anniversary, Pace sponsored this contest with an eligibility twist: "Open to residents of all states west of the Mississippi River." Besides the Best-of-Contest cash award, Priscilla Yee of Concord, California received a case of Pace® Picante Sauce; four category prizes of $1,000 each were awarded, and 100 runners-up received Pace's 40th Anniversary Recipe Collection Cookbook.

Recipe courtesy of Pace® Picante Sauce and Pace Foods, Inc.

$2,000

LEMON TURKEY STIR-FRY WITH PASTA

Teenage Mutant Ninja Turkey? Well-l-l-l-l, this was a contest for teens, the dish does have an Oriental preparation method, and we are talking turkey here — the pasta's the mutant part.

1½ pounds TURKEY CUTLETS OR SLICES, cut into ½-inch strips
1 tablespoon soy sauce
1 tablespoon white wine vinegar
2 teaspoons cornstarch
1 teaspoon lemon pepper
2 tablespoons olive oil
6 medium green onions, sliced

1 medium fresh lemon, cut into 10 thin slices and finely slivered
1 clove garlic, finely minced
1 bag (10 ounces) fresh spinach, washed, drained and chopped
1 pound linguine, prepared according to package directions and drained
Parsley sprigs and lemon slices, for garnish (optional)

- In self-closing plastic bag combine turkey, soy sauce, vinegar, cornstarch and lemon pepper; shake bag to coat turkey thoroughly. Refrigerate 30 minutes to allow flavors to blend.

- In large skillet, over medium heat, sauté turkey and marinade in oil 2 to 3 minutes or until turkey is no longer pink. Add onions, lemon slivers and garlic; continue to cook until onions are translucent. Stir in spinach and cook until just wilted. To serve, combine turkey mixture with hot linguine and garnish with parsley and lemon slices, if desired.

- Makes 6 servings.

1992 National Turkey Lovers' Recipe Contest for Teens

In a triple-challenge contest for ages 12 to 18, not only did teens have to come up with a tasty turkey recipe, but they were required to accompany it with two short essays, one describing the nutritional aspects of their recipe, the other describing the safe food handling techniques they use while cooking. Fifteen-year-old winner Matt McHargue of Richmond, Kentucky closed one of his essays by saying, "Turkey is good tasting health food. I gobble it up." Wonder how many adults would enter recipe contests if they had to send in two essays with each recipe...

Recipe courtesy of the National Turkey Federation

$5,000

ORIENTAL ENHANCED TURKEY

The accent is on leftovers, turkey that is. Here's a quick and easy microwave main course featuring turkey and chopped apple topped with a curried chutney sauce and served with rice, couscous or basmati.

4 (¼-inch thick) slices cooked turkey breast (about 1 pound)

1 medium tart green apple, peeled, cored, and cut into ¼-inch dice

¼ cup *each*, nonfat plain yogurt, mayonnaise, prepared fruit chutney

1 tablespoon lemon juice

1 teaspoon *each* curry powder, grated fresh ginger root

½ teaspoon AC'CENT® Brand Flavor Enhancer

¼ cup *each* sliced green onions, unsalted roasted whole cashews or peanuts

Cooked rice, couscous or basmati

- Arrange turkey in shallow 2-quart microwave-safe casserole. Scatter apple evenly over turkey.

- In small bowl, combine yogurt, mayonnaise, chutney, lemon juice, curry, ginger and Ac'cent. Spoon mixture evenly over turkey and apples. Cover and microwave on HIGH for 5 minutes, rotating half-way through heating time. Sprinkle with green onions. Cover and microwave on HIGH for 2 minutes. Top with cashews. Serve over rice.

- Makes 4 servings.

1991 Ac'cent® "Day After Delicacies" Recipe Contest

What to do with leftover turkey — that was the challenge of this three-category contest. Recipes for Sandwiches, Microwaveable dishes, or Casseroles required using at least ½ teaspoon of Ac'cent® Brand Flavor Enhancer per 4 to 6 servings of cooked turkey. Scoring high in taste and ease of preparation was this Grand Prize recipe submitted by Danielle Bergmooser of Rockland, California.

Recipe courtesy of Pet Incorporated

$10,000

BLACK BEAN TAMALE PIE

Sure to become a permanent part of your cantina's menu.

Filling:
1 tablespoon vegetable oil
½ cup chopped onion
⅓ cup chopped green pepper
8 ounces ground turkey
1 cup cooked black beans,
  drained (1 cup cooked pinto
  beans, drained, can be
  substituted)

1 (8-ounce) can tomato sauce
1 (1¼-ounce) package taco
  seasoning mix

Crust:
1 cup cornmeal
2 teaspoons sugar
½ teaspoon salt
⅓ cup milk
1 egg, slightly beaten

2 tablespoons vegetable oil
1 cup whole kernel corn, drained
1 cup (4 ounces) shredded LAND
  0 LAKES® CHEDARELLA®
  Cheese

Dairy sour cream
Salsa

- Preheat oven to 350°. In 10-inch skillet heat oil over medium heat; add onion and green pepper. Cook, stirring occasionally, until vege–tables are crisply tender (2 to 3 minutes). Add turkey. Continue cooking, stirring occasionally, until turkey is no longer pink (5 to 7 minutes). Stir in beans, tomato sauce, and seasoning mix; set aside.

- In medium bowl combine cornmeal, sugar, and salt. Stir milk, egg, and oil into cornmeal mixture just until moistened. Stir in corn. Press mixture on bottom and up sides of greased 9-inch pie pan. Spoon bean mixture into cornmeal crust. Bake 20 to 30 minutes or until set. Remove from oven; sprinkle with cheese. Continue baking for 2 to 5 minutes or until cheese begins to melt. Let stand 5 minutes before serving. Serve with sour cream and salsa.

- Makes 6 servings.

Recipe developed by Greta Weingast from Benicia, California for the 1991 Land 0' Lakes/Lake To Lake® Chedarella® Cheese Recipe Contest. Recipe courtesy of Land 0'Lakes, Inc.

$10,000

SMOKED TURKEY & BLACKEYED PEAS

High-impact flavor, no-impact fat. As a member of the '90's "in" crowd (legumes and grains), blackeyed peas and turkey drumsticks are infused with an enticing combination of seasonings, then served on rice.

2 cans (16-ounces each)
  blackeyed peas
1 can (14½-ounces) stewed
  tomatoes, broken up
1 medium onion, sliced
2 teaspoons SEASON-ALL®
  Seasoned Salt
1½ teaspoon Basil Leaves

½ teaspoon Oregano
½ teaspoon Thyme Leaves
½ teaspoon Black Pepper
¼ teaspoon ground (Cayenne)
  Red Pepper
3 pounds smoked turkey
  drumsticks
Cooked white rice

• Combine first 9 ingredients in a 6-quart stock pot. Add smoked turkey. Bring to a boil. Cover, reduce heat and simmer 30 minutes. Uncover and simmer 30 minutes.

• Remove turkey drumsticks and slice meat from bones. Stir turkey meat back into pea mixture and serve over rice.

• Makes 6 servings.

1992 McCormick/Schilling Spice Up Your Life Recipe Contest

At the McCormick/Schilling Company, life is the variety of spice and its products harmonize perfectly with the culinary chorus of the '90's — "Flavor, Not Fat." After sponsoring this four-category contest featuring McCormick/Schilling spices, seasonings, and extracts, a spokesperson commented, "We learn so much from seeing how other cooks use our spices and flavorings"... three of the top five winners had their roots in Louisiana-style cooking.

---

*Recipe developed by Janat Davis of Milwaukee, Wisconsin.
Courtesy of McCormick & Co., Inc.*

$5,000

APPLE-GLAZED BEEF BRISKET

4 to 5-pound BONELESS BEEF
  BRISKET
1 medium onion, quartered
2 large garlic cloves, halved
10 whole cloves
1 jar (10-ounces) apple jelly
⅓ cup dry white wine
3 tablespoons Dijon-style or spicy
  brown mustard

3 tablespoons minced green
  onions, including tops
1½ teaspoons salt
¾ teaspoon curry powder
¾ teaspoon cracked black
  peppercorns
Parsley
Tomato roses

- Place brisket, onion, garlic and cloves in large Dutch oven. Add water to cover. Bring to a boil, reduce heat, cover and simmer 2½ to 3 hours or until tender. Drain brisket, cover and refrigerate up to 24 hours.

- To prepare glaze, combine apple jelly, wine, mustard, green onions, salt, curry powder and pepper in small saucepan and heat until jelly melts, stirring occasionally. Place brisket in shallow roasting pan. Brush with glaze and roast in slow oven (325°) 45 minutes, basting frequently with glaze. (Brisket may also be cooked on charcoal grill for 30 minutes, basting often with glaze.) Place brisket on heated serving platter and garnish with parsley and tomato roses. Carve brisket into thin slices and serve with remaining glaze.

- Makes 8 servings.

1984 — 11th Annual National Beef Cook-Off

The National Beef Cook-Offs began in 1974 for the purpose of featuring beef recipes, understanding the various cuts of beef and their preparation, and for promoting the beef cattle industry. Competitions are first conducted on a state by state basis with finalists competing at the National Cook-Off in a different location each year. Representing Tennessee, Vicki Wadlington won the "Best of Beef" Grand Prize at the Cook-Off held in Albuquerque, New Mexico.

Recipe courtesy of the National Beef Cook-Off and the American National CattleWomen, Inc. in cooperation with the Beef Industry Council and the Beef Board and Vicki Wadlington

$5,000

CHEESY BEEF 'N SPINACH CASSATA

Of her recipe the winner said, "I'm Italian and I think Italian. I baked my recipe in a springform pan and it was high like a cake so I called it 'cassata.' Cassata is the Italian word for cake."

2 pounds GROUND BEEF
½ cup chopped green pepper
½ cup chopped onion
2 cloves garlic, minced
2 tablespoons olive oil (optional)
¾ teaspoon salt
1 can (8-ounces) tomato sauce
1 can (6-ounces) tomato paste
⅓ cup white wine
2 teaspoons dried oregano leaves, crushed
¼ teaspoon ground pepper
¼ cup seasoned dry bread crumbs
½ cup plus 2 tablespoons grated Parmesan cheese

⅓ cup butter or margarine, melted
1 package (10-ounces) frozen chopped spinach, thawed, well drained
2 large eggs, beaten
1 cup ricotta cheese
1 cup (4 ounces) shredded mozzarella cheese
8 (14 x 18-inch) or 10 (12 x 15-inch) frozen phyllo pastry leaves, thawed
Parsley (optional)
Ripe olives (optional)
Cherry tomatoes (optional)

- Brown ground beef with green pepper, onion and 1 clove garlic in oil over medium heat; pour off drippings. Sprinkle salt over beef mixture. Add tomato sauce, tomato paste, wine, oregano and pepper, stirring to combine; simmer 5 minutes. Stir in bread crumbs and ¼ cup Parmesan cheese; reserve.

- Lightly brown remaining clove garlic in 1 tablespoon butter. Add spinach; cover, and simmer 3 minutes; remove from heat. Stir in eggs, ricotta, mozzarella and ¼ cup Parmesan cheese; mix well.

- Preheat oven to 350°. Line a 9-inch springform pan with 6 phyllo leaves, overlapping edges. Brush top with butter. Spoon beef mixture into pan, pressing lightly; top with spinach mixture. Fold phyllo edges over top. Cut out four 9-inch circles from remaining phyllo leaves. Place one circle over filling; brush with butter. Repeat 3 times. Cut through top leaves to form 8 wedges. Brush with remaining butter.

- Place springform pan in shallow baking pan (to catch drippings). Bake 35 minutes. Sprinkle remaining 2 tablespoons Parmesan on top; bake 10 minutes more, or until golden brown. Let stand 10 minutes. Re-

move side of pan; cut into wedges. Garnish with parsley, olives and tomatoes if desired.

• Makes 8 servings.

1985 — 12th Annual National Beef Cook-Off

Gloria Bove of Bethlehem, Pennsylvania won the "Best of Beef" award at the Cook-Off held in Wichita, Kansas with her ethnically inspired beef cassata. When the Cook-Offs began in 1974, top prize was $800. Since then, the beef stakes have increased substantially. For the 1993 20th Anniversary Cook-Off in Cheyenne, Wyoming, the Grand Prize award soared to a bullish $20,000.

Recipe courtesy of the National Beef Cook-Off and the American National CattleWomen, Inc. in cooperation with the Beef Industry Council and the Beef Board

$15,000

SPANISH STEAK ROLL WITH SAUTÉED VEGETABLES

Our sights were on Barcelona in preparation for the Olympics when these flavors of Spain hit the bull's eye right here in America.

1 pound trimmed BONELESS BEEF TOP SIRLOIN STEAK, cut ¾-inch thick (or 1-pound top round steak, cut ¾-inch thick)
1 teaspoon garlic powder, divided
¼ teaspoon freshly ground black pepper
2 teaspoons vegetable oil, divided
1 teaspoon butter
¾ teaspoon salt, divided

1 *each*, medium red and green bell pepper, cut lengthwise into thin strips (approximately 3 cups)
1 small white onion, thinly sliced
1 cup sliced fresh mushrooms
⅓ cup chopped walnuts
¼ teaspoon chili powder
1 tablespoon dairy sour cream
2 tablespoons drained, chopped canned green chilies
Lemon slices
Cilantro sprigs

- Pound boneless beef top sirloin steak with flat side of meat mallet to about ¼-inch thickness. Combine ½ teaspoon garlic powder and pepper; sprinkle over steak. Heat 1 teaspoon oil and butter in 12-inch heavy frying pan over medium-high heat until hot. Panfry steak 5 to 7 minutes for medium-rare (150°) or to desired doneness, turning once. Remove steak to heated platter; sprinkle with ½ teaspoon salt. Keep warm.

- Add remaining 1 teaspoon oil to frying pan. Add red and green peppers, onion, mushrooms and walnuts. Cook 2 minutes, stirring frequently. Combine remaining ½ teaspoon garlic powder, ¼ teaspoon salt and chili powder; sprinkle over vegetables and continue cooking 2 minutes, stirring frequently. Spread steak with sour cream; top with chilies. Starting at short side, roll up steak jelly roll fashion; secure with four wooden picks. Spoon vegetables around steak roll; garnish with lemon slices and cilantro sprigs. To serve, carve steak roll between wooden picks; remove and discard wooden picks.

- Makes 4 servings.

Recipe developed by Sandy Collins of Wheat Ridge, Colorado for the 1991, 18th Annual National Beef Cook-Off. Recipe courtesy of the National Beef Cook-Off and the American National CattleWomen, Inc. in cooperation with the Beef Industry Council and the Beef Board

$15,000

MARGARITA BEEF WITH ORANGE SALSA

1½-pound well-trimmed
BONELESS BEEF TOP
ROUND STEAK, cut 1-inch
thick
⅔ cup frozen orange juice
concentrate, thawed
½ cup tequila
⅓ cup fresh lime juice

2 tablespoons olive oil
2 tablespoons chopped fresh
ginger
2 medium cloves garlic, crushed
1 teaspoon each salt and dried
oregano leaves
¼ teaspoon ground red pepper

Orange Salsa:

2 oranges, peeled and cut into
½-inch pieces
1 small red or white onion,
chopped
1 jalapeño pepper, seeded and
finely chopped
¼ cup chopped fresh cilantro

2 to 3 tablespoons fresh lime juice
2 tablespoons olive oil
½ teaspoon *each* salt and dried
oregano leaves
Cilantro sprigs and lime wedges,
for garnish

- Combine orange juice concentrate, tequila, lime juice, oil, ginger, garlic, salt, oregano and red pepper. Place steak in plastic bag; add marinade, turning to coat. Close bag securely and marinate in refrigerator 4 hours or overnight, as desired.

- Prepare Orange Salsa. Combine all ingredients in non-metallic bowl and refrigerate at least one hour. Makes 1½ cups.

- Remove steak from marinade; discard marinade. Place steak on grid over medium coals (test about 4 inches above coals for medium with 4-second hand count). Grill 22 to 26 minutes for medium rare (150°) to medium (160°) doneness, turning once. Remove steak to carving board; let stand 10 minutes. Carve steak crosswise into thin slices; arrange on serving platter. Garnish with cilantro sprigs and lime wedges. Serve with Orange Salsa.

- Makes 5 to 6 servings.

Recipe developed by John W. Hund from San Francisco, California for the 1992, 19th Annual National Beef Cook-Off. Recipe courtesy of the National Beef Cook-Off and the American National CattleWomen, Inc. in cooperation with the Beef Industry Council and the Beef Board

$10,000 DREAM KITCHEN FROM
KitchenAid & CRISCO

FIESTA BEEF POT PIE

Celebrate! A hearty and satisfying Mexican beef pot pie with a cornmeal-wheat germ-Cheddar cheese crust. Can be baked ahead and refrigerated or frozen; if preparing in advance, sprinkle cheese on top just before serving for a more freshly baked appearance.

Crust:
1⅔ cups all-purpose flour
⅓ cup yellow cornmeal
2 tablespoons toasted wheat germ
1 teaspoon salt

⅓ cup shredded Cheddar cheese
¾ cup CRISCO® Shortening
5 to 7 tablespoons cold water

Filling:
1 pound lean boneless beef chuck, cut into ¼- to ½-inch chunks
1 tablespoon CRISCO® Shortening
½ cup chopped green pepper *
½ cup chopped onion *
1 can (14½ ounces) Mexican style stewed tomatoes *
½ cup water
⅓ cup tomato paste

2 teaspoons sugar
1 teaspoon chili powder
½ teaspoon ground cumin
¼ teaspoon salt
⅛ teaspoon crushed red pepper (optional)
1 can (8½ ounces) whole kernel corn, drained
1 can (4 ounces) sliced mushrooms, drained
⅓ cup sliced black olives

Glaze:
1 egg, beaten

¼ teaspoon salt

Topping:
⅓ cup shredded Cheddar cheese

Use plain stewed tomatoes if Mexican style is not available. Increase green pepper and onion to ⅔ cup each. Add one tablespoon diced jalapeño pepper and ¼ teaspoon garlic powder.

Crust:
- Preheat oven to 425°. Combine flour, cornmeal, wheat germ and salt in bowl. Cut in cheese and Crisco with pastry blender (or 2 knives) until all flour is just blended in to form pea-size chunks. ·

- Sprinkle with water, one tablespoon at a time. Toss lightly with fork until dough forms ball. Divide dough into 2 parts. Press between hands to form two 5 to 6-inch "pancakes".

- Flour rolling surface and pin lightly. Roll dough for bottom crust into circle. Trim one inch larger than upside-down 9-inch pie plate. Loosen dough carefully. Fold into quarters. Unfold. Press into pie plate. Trim edge even with pie plate.

Filling:

- Brown beef in shortening in large skillet. Remove beef with slotted spoon. Cook green pepper and onion in drippings until tender. Add beef, undrained tomatoes, water, tomato paste, sugar, chili powder, cumin, salt, red pepper (if used), corn and mushrooms. Cover. Heat to boiling. Reduce heat. Simmer 30 minutes, stirring occasionally. Remove from heat. Stir in olives. Spoon hot filling into unbaked pie shell.

- Roll top crust same as bottom. Lift onto filled pie. Trim ½-inch beyond edge of pie plate. Fold top edge under bottom crust. Flute. Cut slits or designs in top of crust or prick with fork for escape of steam.

Glaze:

- Combine egg and salt. Brush lightly over top crust.

- Bake for 30 to 40 minutes or until crust is golden brown.

- Sprinkle with cheese. Serve hot or warm.

- Makes one 9-inch pie.

1990 Crisco®'s American Pie Celebration

Americans' love of Mexican food is evident in this main dish pie, the inspiration of Mary King from Concordia, Kansas. Mary was awarded an array of appliances from KitchenAid, a check from Crisco for kitchen remodeling and the contest's keepsake medal, a silver rolling pin.

Recipe courtesy of The Procter & Gamble Co., Inc.

$25,000

BEAN BURRITO BAKE

Long on flavor, short on effort.

1 can (16 ounces) refried beans
1 cup BISQUICK® Baking Mix
¼ cup water
1 pound browned hamburger,
 drained

1 sliced avocado (optional)
1 cup thick salsa
1½ cups shredded Cheddar
 cheese
Sour cream

- Preheat oven to 375°. Mix refried beans, Bisquick and water and spread in bottom and half-way up side of a greased 10-inch pie plate.
- Layer in order: hamburger, avocado, salsa and cheese. Bake 30 minutes. Serve with dollops of sour cream.
- Makes 8 servings.

1985 Bisquick® Creations Recipe Contest

At the time of her win, Lois DePiesse from Wichita, Kansas said, "This sounds funny, but I knew I had a winner. It's a good recipe. It only has a few ingredients, and it's ready in minutes. Besides, Mexican food is Seth's (her son's) favorite." There were more than 23,000 entries in this contest; besides the $25,000 Grand Prize, two First Place winners received $10,000 each, nine Second Place winners received $5,000 each, and 96 Third Place winners received Hamilton Beach food processors.

Recipe courtesy of General Mills, Inc.

$5,000

REUBEN CROQUETTES

Another member of Reuben's big family.

½ cup UNCLE BEN'S®
  CONVERTED® Brand Rice
1 (1 pound) can sauerkraut
1 (12-ounce) can corned beef
¼ cup chopped onion
3 eggs
1 cup shredded Swiss cheese
1 teaspoon salt

¼ teaspoon pepper
2 tablespoons water
1½ cups fine dry bread crumbs
1 cup mayonnaise
⅓ cup milk
¼ cup prepared mustard
4 teaspoons lemon juice
Oil for frying

- Cook rice according to package directions for half the basic recipe. Drain sauerkraut very well, pressing out as much liquid as possible. Chop sauerkraut and corned beef very fine. Add onion, 2 eggs, cooked rice, cheese, salt and pepper; mix well. Shape into 18 croquettes or balls using ¼ cup of mixture for each.

- Combine remaining egg and water; beat slightly. Roll each croquette in crumbs, then egg mixture, and in crumbs. Let dry 10 minutes. Combine and mix mayonnaise, milk, mustard and lemon juice. Fry croquettes in hot shallow oil, 5 to 7 minutes, turning once, or bake at 450° 10 minutes, turn and bake 10 minutes longer. Serve with sauce.

- Makes 18 croquettes or 6 servings.

1976 Uncle Ben's® "Cook & Tell" Recipe Contest

Reuben has been the star of many prizewinning recipes since winning the title "Sandwich Idea of the Year" in 1956. Two decades later, the popular combination of ingredients were featured in these croquettes for yet another big win. James Beard was among the distinguished panel of judges in this contest of more than 20,000 entries when this recipe entered by Sarah Paul from Philadelphia, Pennsylvania was declared the best.

Recipe courtesy of Uncle Ben's, Inc.

$25,000

SWEET & SOUR PORK ROAST
WITH GINGERED PINEAPPLE
& SWEET POTATOES

Add a mini-luau to your menu.

1 rolled pork roast (5 pounds)
3 tablespoons flour
2 tablespoons salad oil
2 cups canned pineapple juice
1 (8¼-ounce) can CRUSHED
   PINEAPPLE, undrained

½ cup cider vinegar
¼ cup dark brown sugar
¼ cup soy sauce
½ cup sliced celery
6 sweet potatoes
¼ cup cornstarch

Gingered Pineapple Slices:

1 (1-pound, 13-ounce) can
   PINEAPPLE SLICES
½ cup sugar

2 tablespoons white wine vinegar
¼ cup dry white wine
1 large piece crystallized ginger

- Preheat oven to 300°. Coat meat with flour. Heat salad oil and brown meat on all sides. Place in a roasting pan. Mix together the pineapple juice, crushed pineapple, vinegar, brown sugar, soy sauce, and celery. Spoon pineapple mixture over the browned pork roast. Cover and bake about 3 hours, basting frequently with pineapple mixture while roasting.

- Meanwhile, pare sweet potatoes. Cook potatoes in lightly salted water for 30 minutes, or just until tender. Drain; keep warm.

Gingered Pineapple Slices:

- Drain pineapple, saving syrup. Mix drained syrup, sugar, vinegar and wine in saucepan. Cut ginger into 3 pieces lengthwise and add to syrup. Bring to boil; reduce heat and simmer for 5 minutes. Add pineapple slices and continue to simmer for 5 minutes longer, basting frequently.

- When meat is tender, remove and place on heated platter and keep warm. Mix cornstarch with a little water to make a thin paste. Stir into pan liquid and cook, stirring, until gravy has thickened. Pour over roast. Garnish platter with sweet potatoes alternating with spiced pineapple slices.

- Makes 6 to 8 servings.

1972 National Pineapple Cooking Classic

Surrounding the Hawaiian islands is a golden aura that might well be attributed to the sun's rays as they touch each pineapple. The first pineapple canning plant was established in Hawaii in 1892 and, since much of the islands' succulent pineapples are sold in canned form, the Pineapple Growers Association of Hawaii sponsored a number of cooking "classics" during the 1970's to promote the industry.

*In a traditional luau, a whole roast pig is cooked with sweet potatoes in an **imu**, an in-the-ground roasting pit. The inspiration of Virginia F. Harrison from Clatskanie, Oregon, this winning recipe features pork roast enhanced by a sweet and sour pineapple sauce, with sweet potatoes and gingered pineapple slices on the side.*

Recipe courtesy of the Pineapple Growers Association of Hawaii:
Del Monte Fresh Produce Company, Inc.
Dole Food Company, Inc.
Maui Land & Pineapple Company, Inc.
Wailuku Agribusiness Company, Inc.

Look for the "100% Hawaiian" designation on canned pineapple products.

95

TRIP FOR TWO TO ITALY

ITALIAN SAUSAGE SPAGHETTI SAUCE

Sweet Italian sausage and Cheddar cheese are two secret ingredients.

3 tablespoons olive oil
3 cloves garlic, chopped
4½ pounds sweet Italian sausage
3 cans (28-ounces each)
  HUNT'S® Whole Tomatoes
3 cans (8-ounces each) HUNT'S®
  Tomato Sauce
3 cans (6-ounces each) HUNT'S®
  Tomato Paste
3 whole onions, peeled

1½ green bell peppers
¾ pound fresh mushrooms, sliced
1½ cups chopped fresh parsley
1 tablespoon sugar
1½ teaspoons dried oregano
  leaves
1½ teaspoons dried basil leaves
¾ teaspoon fennel seeds
¾ pound Cheddar cheese, grated
Salt

- In a large Dutch oven, heat oil; sauté garlic in oil until lightly browned. Add sausage, removing casing, and crumble. Brown sausage. Drain fat; remove sausage from Dutch oven; set aside. Add undrained whole tomatoes, tomato sauce and tomato paste to Dutch oven. Cook over medium heat 15 minutes, stirring occasionally. Return sausage to pan. Add remaining ingredients except cheese and salt; simmer 15 minutes. Add cheese a little at a time; stir until cheese is blended. Simmer, covered, 1½ hours more. Remove and discard onions and peppers. Add salt to taste.

- Serve over cooked pasta.

- Makes 18 (1-cup) servings of sauce.

1985 Hunt's® Great Spaghetti Hunt Recipe Contest

Sixty finalists competed in five regional cook-offs; then each regional winner won a trip for two to Los Angeles to compete for the Grand Prize — a one-week dream trip for two to Italy. Rita Futral of Ocean Springs, Mississippi won the first cooking contest she ever entered with the spaghetti sauce she had always made.

Recipe courtesy of Hunt-Wesson, Inc.

$5,000

PIG IRON PORKERS

In the "Whole Hog" category, everything is cooked except the oink.

WHOLE HOG (85 pounds or
    more)

Seasoning Spice:

14 ounces chili powder
5 pounds salt

5 ounces onion powder
3 ounces garlic

Glazing Sauce:

2 cups hot water
1 tablespoon seasoning salt
3 tablespoons MSG

½ cup honey
Add cornstarch to thicken

- Establish fire and cooking temperature of 240° to 260°. Place hog on rack and cook for 12 to 16 hours (depending on size of hog and stability of temperature).

Seasoning Spice:

- In large bowl mix all ingredients thoroughly. Place in sealed container. Cut and remove skin from hog and season with Seasoning Spice after initial 12 to 16 hour cooking period, and return to cooker and cook at 210° until golden brown (heavy smoke in cooker during this period), about 4 to 6 hours.

Glazing Sauce:

- Combine all ingredients in container and bring to a boil. Mixture should have medium thickness. One hour before serving, cover entire pig with Glazing Sauce and cook at 170° to 180°. Serve and enjoy pig and compliments.

**1986 Memphis in May World Championship
Barbecue Cooking Contest**

Memphis in May is "America's largest month-long celebration of international culture, business and fun. Each May a different country is honored with over 100 events..." One of the main attractions is the barbecue cooking contest in which cooking teams compete in three categories. According to the **1990 Guinness Book of World Records***, this big pig gig is the largest barbecue contest in the world.*

---

*Recipe courtesy of Memphis in May International Festival, Inc. &
Steve McLain from Memphis, Tennessee and the Pig Iron Porkers*

$1,000

PORK TENDERLOIN DIANE

For the epicure, a classic revisited.

1 pound PORK TENDERLOIN, cut into 8 crosswise pieces
2 teaspoons lemon pepper
2 tablespoons butter
2 tablespoons lemon juice

1 tablespoon Worcestershire sauce
1 teaspoon Dijon-style mustard
1 tablespoon minced parsley **or** chives

- Press each tenderloin slice to a 1-inch thickness. Sprinkle surfaces of medallions with lemon pepper. Heat butter in a heavy skillet; cook tenderloin medallions 3 to 4 minutes on each side. Remove medallions to serving platter; keep warm.

- Add lemon juice, Worcestershire sauce, and mustard to skillet. Cook, stirring with pan juices, until heated through. Pour sauce over medallions, sprinkle with parsley and serve.

- Makes 4 servings.

1986 "Good Ideas with Boneless Pork" Recipe Contest

Entries required using one pound of boneless fresh pork in four categories: "Fast and Fantastic Pork," "Calorie Conscious Pork," "New Favorites with Fresh Ham," and "Texas Cookout Recipes." With the touch of a true gourmet, Janice Elder of Spartanburg, South Carolina turned her skillet into a magic pan.

Recipe courtesy of the National Pork Producers Council

$2,500

MOROCCAN LAMB WITH CURRIED CARROT SPINACH SALAD

1½ to 2-pound BONELESS LAMB LOIN (DOUBLE) ROAST, tied
1 cup plain yogurt, divided
¼ cup thinly sliced onion
2 tablespoons fresh orange juice
2 tablespoons chopped cilantro
2 garlic cloves
½ teaspoon *each* ground cardamom and cumin

¼ teaspoon *each* ground cinnamon and ginger
¼ teaspoon coarsely ground black pepper
8 cups mixed greens, such as spinach and romaine, thinly sliced
3 cups diagonally sliced carrots
Cilantro and oranges for garnish

Vinaigrette:
2 tablespoons olive oil
1 tablespoon fresh orange juice
1 teaspoon minced fresh ginger

¼ teaspoon curry powder
¼ teaspoon sugar
Salt and pepper to taste

- Combine ⅔ cup yogurt, onion, orange juice, cilantro, garlic and spices in blender container; process until smooth. Add salt to taste. Combine ½ cup yogurt mixture with remaining plain yogurt for sauce; refrigerate until serving.

- Place lamb loin roast in plastic bag; pour remaining yogurt mixture from blender over roast, turning to coat. Close bag securely and marinate in refrigerator 2 hours or overnight, turning occasionally.

- Remove lamb from marinade and place on grid over medium coals. Grill about 20 minutes for rare (140°), turning ¼ turn every 5 minutes. Let stand 10 minutes. Meanwhile, whisk together Vinaigrette ingredients. Season to taste with salt and pepper. Toss Vinaigrette with carrots and greens; place on large serving platter. Carve roast into slices and arrange over salad. Garnish as desired. Serve with reserved sauce.

- Makes 6 to 8 servings.

Recipe developed by Jan Hill of Sacramento, California for the 1991 "Sizzlin' Lamb Barbecue Contest." Recipe courtesy of the Lamb Committee of the National Live Stock and Meat Board in cooperation with the National Lamb Feeders Association

$10,000

GRILLED IMPERIAL CROWN MEAT LOAF

Meat loaf goes Hawaiian in a savory ground lamb mixture with a stuffing of mushroom "crowns" and pineapple chunks.

2 pounds ground lamb
2 eggs, beaten
1 cup cracker crumbs
⅓ cup chopped parsley
3 tablespoons soy sauce
1 clove garlic, pressed
1 teaspoon cumin

½ teaspoon seasoned pepper
1 cup catsup
10 mushrooms, medium size
½ cup pineapple chunks, drained
KAISER QUILTED
   ALUMINUM FOIL, 18-inch
   heavy-duty

- Line firebox with quilted foil; let coals burn down until coated with gray ashes.

- In large mixing bowl, combine lamb, eggs, cracker crumbs, parsley, soy sauce, garlic, cumin, pepper, and ½ cup catsup. Mix thoroughly. Place half of mixture on an 18-inch sheet of foil; shape into lower half of loaf. Place mushrooms in a row down center of meat; arrange pineapple chunks beside each mushroom "crown." Top with remaining meat mixture, sealing edges together. Wrap foil around loaf, sealing securely.

- Grill loaf about 1 hour, turning a quarter turn every 15 minutes. Open foil and fold back to make a pan. Brush meat with remainder of catsup and continue cooking and turning loaf about 15 minutes longer.

- Makes 8 servings.

1963 Kaiser Foil Championship Cookout (For Men Only!)

Although thousands of men entered their favorite cookout recipes, only 25 were selected for the competition in Honolulu, Hawaii. For North Hollywood, California attorney Thomas J. McDermott, Jr., this was quite a win. In addition to the $10,000 Grand Prize and trip to Hawaii, the title "All-American Cookout Champion" was conferred on him, along with a kiss from Joan Crawford who presented the awards; four runners-up received station wagons.

Recipe courtesy of the Ekco Company and Packaging Corporation of America

$3,000

FARM RAISED CATFISH SERENDIPITY WITH MASON/DIXON STUFFING

Sweet white-fleshed catfish with cornbread-apple-walnut-raisin stuffing.

6 (5-7 ounce) FARM RAISED
CATFISH FILLETS *or* 3 (13-
15 ounce) whole IQF FARM
RAISED CATFISH
2½ cups cornbread stuffing mix
½ cup diced cooking apples
½ cup finely chopped walnuts
½ cup raisins

⅓ cup evaporated milk
2 tablespoons brown sugar
1 large egg
½ cup French-style salad dressing
8 tablespoons (1 stick) butter
3 tablespoons lemon juice
6 lemon slices, for garnish

- Preheat oven to 350°. Thaw fish if frozen. Combine cornbread mix, diced apples, walnuts, raisins, milk, brown sugar and egg. Heat on low 10 minutes.

- Combine French dressing, butter and lemon juice in saucepan and heat on low for 15 minutes. Add half of mixture to stuffing ingredients. Set remainder aside for basting.

- Stuff cavity of whole fish, or place stuffing in middle of fillets, roll, secure with toothpicks and place seam side down on baking sheet. Bake for 15 minutes. Remove and baste fish with remaining mixture. Garnish with lemon slices.

- Makes 6 servings.

1987 — 13th Annual National Farm Raised Catfish Cooking Contest

Although an ancient art, catfish farming in the U.S. didn't begin in earnest until the 1960's and '70's. With demand for fresh fish on the rise, the industry has gone far in educating the public on the merits of catfish. From the 1,119 recipes entered, 20 semi-finalists were selected; then 5 finalists prepared their entries for a panel of famous New Orleans chefs. Bruce Michael Shiffler of Carlisle, Pennsylvania was awarded the Grand Prize in a cook-off held at the famous Riverwalk in New Orleans.

Recipe courtesy of the Catfish Farmers of America

$1,125

GRILLED OYSTERS MORNAY

2 dozen MARYLAND
OYSTERS
2 tablespoons butter
1 clove garlic, minced

1 shallot, minced
½ pound Smithfield ham, finely
chopped
1 pound Maryland lump crabmeat

Mornay Sauce:
2 tablespoons butter
2 tablespoons all-purpose flour
1 cup milk
2 ounces (½ cup) Swiss cheese,
grated

2 ounces (½ cup) Cheddar cheese,
grated
2 ounces (½ cup) Parmesan
cheese, grated

- Shuck oysters leaving them in the deep half of the shell; set aside. In a pan, melt butter, add minced garlic and shallot. Sauté about 2 minutes. Add Smithfield ham, cook another 2 minutes.

Mornay Sauce:

- Melt butter in small saucepan, remove from heat, add flour and stir with a whisk. Return to moderate heat, add milk gradually, stirring constantly until thickened. Add remaining ingredients, stirring constantly.

- On each oyster on the half shell put some of the butter, garlic, shallot and Smithfield ham mixture. Add several crabmeat lumps to the top of the mixture and then add a spoon of the Mornay Sauce to cover. Cook over hot coals until bubbly and serve piping hot.

- Makes 2 dozen oysters on the half shell.

1987 — 8th Annual National Oyster Cook-Off

Since 1980 an oyster cook-off has been held in conjunction with the Oyster Festival in Leonardtown, Maryland. The event has grown into a national cook-off attracting people from all over the country, but this Grand Prize winner, Roland S. Ormrod hails from Towson, Maryland.

Recipe courtesy of the National Oyster Cook-Off, the Maryland Department of Agriculture, Office of Seafood Marketing, and St. Mary's County Department of Economic and Community Development

TRIP FOR TWO TO PARADISE ISLAND, BAHAMAS

SEXY SHRIMP, SHIITAKES, & CILANTRO

X-rated for X-cellent. With its lusty seasonings and wine recommendation, this dish signals X-citement for two.

2 tablespoons butter
1 tablespoon shallot, chopped
2 cloves garlic, minced
1 small jalapeño pepper, seeded and chopped fine
12 large SHRIMP, peeled, butterflied, uncooked
¼ pound fresh shiitake mushrooms, trimmed and quartered, or 2 ounces dried shiitakes or French cepes (If using dried, soak in the wine for 30 minutes; drain, reserving wine. Chop coarsely.)

Salt and freshly ground black pepper
½ cup dry white wine
½ cup heavy cream
1 ounce (¼ cup) cilantro leaves, chopped coarsely
1 tablespoon fresh lime juice
8 grinds black pepper
4 tablespoons butter, cut into four pieces
Garnish: 6 toast triangles per serving, sautéed in 2 tablespoons olive oil and 2 tablespoons chopped cilantro

- Heat butter in a large skillet over medium heat. Add shallot, garlic and jalapeño; stir two minutes. Add shrimp, mushrooms, salt and pepper; sauté until shrimp turn pink, about 3 minutes. Remove shrimp and mushrooms from pan; add wine to skillet and reduce to a glaze. Add cream and reduce slightly over high heat; toss in cilantro and lime juice. Turn heat to medium and cook through, 3-4 minutes. Return shrimp and mushrooms to pan; add butter, one tablespoon at a time, swirling after each addition. Place six toasts on two warm plates; top with shrimp. Intersperse shrimp with mushrooms on plates; spoon sauce over all. Serve hot along with a chilled white Graves.

- Makes 2 servings.

1992 Merv Griffin's Paradise Island's National Sexy Seafood Recipe Contest

Chefs on Merv Griffin's Paradise Island selected the winning recipe from hundreds of entries. From Northfield, Minnesota, Joan W. Churchill's Grand Prize win included a week of luxurious accommodations and entertainment for two at the Ocean Club Golf & Tennis Resort on Paradise Island.

Recipe courtesy of Merv Griffin's Paradise Island and Joan Churchill

$10,000

SWEETBREADS EN BROCHETTE

*Although Webster defines **sweetbreads** in a succinct 9 words, unless you know what a "thymus" is, further explanation is required. It takes him 42 words to define **thymus** which, in a word, translates into "glands." Oh goody, gored glands for dinner... But, you be the judge.*

1 pound veal sweetbreads
24 mushrooms
⅓ cup lemon juice
1 teaspoon Worcestershire sauce
1 teaspoon salt
⅛ teaspoon pepper
⅛ teaspoon dry mustard

KAISER ALUMINUM FOIL for
  broiling
4 10-inch skewers
12 bacon slices, halved
½ cup melted butter or margarine
Chopped parsley

• Simmer the sweeetbreads in boiling salted water, covered, for 25 minutes. Drain and place in cold water; remove the membranes and veins. Cut them into 24 pieces, cover and refrigerate for several hours or overnight.

• Remove stems from the mushrooms. Place the mushroom caps in a mixing bowl; combine the lemon juice, Worcestershire sauce, salt, pepper and mustard. Pour over the mushroom caps and refrigerate several hours or overnight, tossing occasionally.

• Line the firebox with foil; let the coals burn down until they are covered with gray ash.

• Roll up the bacon pieces and string on the skewers, alternating them with the sweetbread pieces and mushroom caps. Brush with melted butter; grill 15 to 20 minutes, turning often and brushing with butter. When the sweetbreads are golden and the mushrooms are done, place on a warm platter, pour the remaining butter over all and sprinkle with parsley.

• Makes 4 servings.

1962 Kaiser's Great National Cookout Championship for Men

In this unmistakably all-male contest, "Sweetbreads En Brochette" was the unanimous choice for First Place, the entry of food salesman George Gail Stout of Arvada, Colorado — Clearly, this guy could sell anything remotely edible... Even so, some said he had nerve to enter sweetbreads in a barbecue contest ("guts" would be a more accurate term).

Sports Illustrated *covered the sporting event, reporting that from more than 2,000 recipes submitted, 25 finalists participated in the cook-off held in the Ale Ale Kai Garden of the Hawaiian Village in Waikiki. Finalists clad in white caps and aprons literally marched to the competition area to the tune of "The Road to Mandalay."*

Other winners were "Baker's Dozen Decker," a grilled, multilayered sandwich baked in biscuit dough which was entered by a surgeon pediatrician; a mortician's entry was "Barbecued Lamb Shanks Armenian;" "Porcupineapple" was an elaborate arrangement of a whole pineapple sliced in one-inch sections which was skewered together with pork chops in between and held together with toothpicks, then basted with a ginger-honey sauce.

Joan Crawford was on hand throughout the cook-off and presented the awards, including Jeep station wagons to four runners-up. Summarizing the tone of the contest, one judge was heard to comment, "You can't serve ladylike dishes at a barbecue." And so our hero and Grand Prize winner, George Gail Stout, returned to Colorado in a blaze of glory to roast on his laurels.

Recipe courtesy of the Ekco Company and Packaging Corporation of America

$50,000 FOR THE ASSISTANCE LEAGUE OF ESCONDIDO VALLEY

LASAGNA PRIMAVERA

Pray for leftovers. This light, colorful lasagna features fresh vegetables and introduces a new and unusual method of blanching the vegetables with the pasta to make preparation a snap.

1 (8-ounce) package lasagna noodles
3 carrots, cut into ¼-inch thick slices
1 cup broccoli flowerettes
1 cup zucchini, cut into ¼-inch thick slices
1 cup crookneck squash, cut into ¼-inch thick slices

2 (10-ounce) packages frozen chopped spinach, thawed
8 ounces ricotta cheese
26-ounce jar NEWMAN'S OWN® Marinara Sauce with Mushrooms
12 ounces mozzarella cheese, shredded
½ cup grated Parmesan cheese

- Preheat oven to 400°. Bring 3 quarts water to a boil in a 6-quart pan over high heat. Add lasagna noodles and cook 5 minutes. Add carrots; cook 2 more minutes. Add broccoli, zucchini and crookneck squash and cook the final 2 minutes or until pasta is tender. Drain well.

- Squeeze liquid out of spinach. Combine spinach with ricotta cheese. In a 3-quart rectangular baking pan, spread ⅓ of the Newman's Own Marinara Sauce with Mushrooms. Line pan with lasagna noodles. Put half of each of the vegetables, spinach mixture and mozzarella cheese on the noodles. Pour half of the remaining Newman's Own Marinara Sauce with Mushrooms over these layers. Repeat layers and top with remaining sauce. Sprinkle with Parmesan cheese.

- Place on a 10 x 15-inch baking sheet which has been lined with foil. Bake, uncovered, in a 400° oven about 30 minutes or until hot in the center. Let stand 10 minutes before serving. (Casserole may be prepared up to 2 days before baking and refrigerated, covered, until one hour before baking. If cold, bake for one hour at 350°.)

- Serve with Italian bread or rolls, a green salad with Newman's Own® Light Italian Dressing and a bottle of full-bodied red wine.

- Makes 8 servings.

1992 Newman's Own® & GOOD HOUSEKEEPING's Second Annual Recipe Contest

Competitors entered main dish recipes in six categories of Newman's Own products. GOOD HOUSEKEEPING selected one finalist from each product category plus one finalist from a special category for a school class. Each won trips to New York City with a guest of choice, plus $1,000 for incidental expenses.

While in New York, finalists joined Paul Newman at the Rainbow Room for lunch. Andrew Wilkinson, the Rainbow Room's Executive Chef, prepared and served finalists' dishes to Mr. Newman who sampled and judged the seven top recipes himself. His favorite, a recipe developed by Janet Sutherland of Escondido, California, was awarded the $50,000 Grand Prize.

The six runners-up each won $10,000 for his or her favorite charity. Even the stores where finalists purchased their Newman's Own products selected charities to which $5,000 was donated. Here are the categories, runners-up, and charities that benefitted:

NEWMAN'S OWN® Ranch Salad Dressing "Newman's Own Lamburgini"

Karen Durrett, Portland, Oregon: $10,000 — March of Dimes

NEWMAN'S OWN® Olive Oil & Vinegar Salad Dressing "Whitecap Pizza"

Linda Mangen, Valrico, Florida: $10,000 — University of Tampa Scholarship Fund

NEWMAN'S OWN® Light Italian Salad Dressing "Spinach, Turkey, and Apple Salad"

Marie Sheppard, Chicago, Illinois" $10,000 — The Howard Brown Memorial Clinic for AIDS Patients

SCHOOL GROUP — NEWMAN'S OWN® Sockarooni Pasta Sauce "Bagelroonies"

Ms.Dana Reed's CDC — Special Education Class, Westview Middle School, Morristown, Tennessee: $10,000 — Special Olympics

NEWMAN'S OWN® Diavolo Sauce "Kaleidoscope Chowder"

Larry Elder, Charlotte, North Carolina: $10,000 — Lions Club and Habitat for Humanity

NEWMAN'S OWN® All-Natural Bandito Salsa "Sundance's Salsa Steak in a Sack"

Julie DeMatteo, Clementon, New Jersey: $10,000 — Catholic Charities of Trenton and the Respiratory Distress Syndrome Foundation

Given all the fun and the philanthropy, it's no wonder that thousands of recipe contesters have strived to be a part of an effort whose company motto is "Shameless exploitation in pursuit of the public good."

Recipe courtesy of Newman's Own, Inc.

$4,000

SAUCY LINGUINE SCRAMBLE

This vegetarian main course, rich in Italian flavor, teams up with good nutrition for a winning combination.

6 EGGS
¼ cup milk
¼ cup taco sauce
¼ cup grated Parmesan cheese
1 tablespoon chopped sun-dried
  tomatoes, optional
1 teaspoon basil leaves, crushed
  or 1 tablespoon chopped fresh
  basil leaves
½ teaspoon salt

⅛ teaspoon pepper
3 cups hot cooked linguine,
  drained
2 small plum tomatoes, quartered
  and sliced
1 small zucchini, quartered and
  sliced
¼ cup sliced drained pitted ripe
  olives
Fresh basil leaves, optional

- In medium bowl, beat together eggs, milk, taco sauce, cheese, sun-dried tomatoes, if desired, and seasonings until well blended.

- In 10- to 12-inch omelet pan or skillet, stir together egg mixture and linguine. Cook over medium heat, tossing gently until eggs begin to thicken, about 10 minutes. Add tomatoes, zucchini and olives. Toss gently until eggs are thickened but still moist, about 3 minutes. Garnish with basil leaves, if desired.

- Makes 4 servings.

1988 National Egg Cooking Contest

For many years the American Egg Board has sponsored annual contests which are entered first through state competitions held in most of the continental 48 states. Gloria Piantek of Skillman, New Jersey hatched a Grand Prize winner with her quick and easy pasta scramble.

Recipe courtesy of the American Egg Board

STELLAR STARTERS

$1,000

CRANBERRY APPLE COLADA

Cheers... Here's to the cranberry, jewel of the bog, true native American, established here long before the arrival of the <u>Mayflower</u> .

6 ounces OCEAN SPRAY
  CRANAPPLE® Cranberry
  Apple Drink, chilled
1½ ounces gold rum
½ ounce white rum

2 ounces cream of coconut
2 ounces OCEAN SPRAY®
  Jellied Cranberry Sauce, cut up
1 slice sweet, red-skinned apple,
  garnish

- Put all ingredients, except apple, in a blender. Blend on high for a few seconds or until ingredients are thoroughly combined.
- Pour into a chilled hurricane glass filled with crushed ice. Garnish with apple slice.
- Makes 1 drink.

1991 Ocean Spray® Distinctive Taste Recipe Contest

Before sailing across Cape Cod Bay to establish Plymouth Colony, the pilgrims first spent some time in Truro, Massachusetts near the tip of the Cape. Appropriately, Ellen Burr of Truro captured top prize in the Cocktails/Mocktails category of this contest with her pretty 'n' pink drink that makes for spirited competition among the colada family of flavors.

Recipe courtesy of Ocean Spray Cranberries, Inc.

$1,000

LUSCIOUS STRAWBERRY PARTY PUNCH

Who could argue with this smoothie of a party potion?

6 cups OCEAN SPRAY
CRAN•STRAWBERRY™
Cranberry Strawberry Drink,
chilled

2 quarts strawberry ice milk or ice
cream, softened

2 cups frozen strawberries,
thawed

2 (12-ounce) cans lemon-lime
soda, chilled

- Combine cranberry strawberry drink, ice milk and strawberries in a large punch bowl. Use a rotary beater or wire whisk to thoroughly combine ingredients until creamy. Gently stir in soda just before serving.

- Makes about 50 ⅓-cup servings.

1991 Ocean Spray® Distinctive Taste Recipe Contest

Elsie Wigdahl of Ruthven, Iowa delivered a double one-two punch that won her the victory in the Punch category of this contest which featured Ocean Spray's blended juice drinks. Four category winners each won $1,000 for the best in Cocktails/Mocktails, Desserts, Entrees, and Punches. Twelve finalists, three from each category, received $250.

Recipe Courtesy of Ocean Spray Cranberries, Inc.

TRIP FOR TWO TO ENGLAND

RUSSIAN BLINI

Finger food fit for a king, or czar, when filled and rolled with sour cream, caviar, or smoked salmon.

2 cups milk
1 package yeast
½ cup lukewarm water
2 cups KING ARTHUR®
   Unbleached All-Purpose Flour
½ cup KING ARTHUR® Stone
   Ground Whole Wheat Flour

3 eggs, separated
2 teaspoons sugar
½ teaspoon salt
¼ cup sour cream
4 tablespoons melted butter, to
   grease griddle

- Scald 1 cup of milk and cool to lukewarm. Dissolve yeast in water; add to lukewarm milk. Stir in 1½ cups flour and ½ cup whole wheat flour. Cover with towel and let stand in warm spot for two hours.

- Scald remaining milk and let cool to lukewarm. Stir down dough. Add milk, lightly beaten egg yolks, sugar, salt, sour cream and remaining flour. Mix until smooth. Beat egg whites until stiff. Fold into batter. Cover and let stand ½ hour. Bake on griddle, pouring so that each blini is about 3 inches across. Turn as usual for pancakes.

- Makes about 55 blini.

1991 King Arthur® Flour WinterBake

In this baking competition for adults and children, finalists in the Adult and Junior Divisions were guests of King Arthur Flour at The Inn at Essex in Essex, Vermont, a luxury hotel reminiscent of a country inn. Their recipes were baked by the New England Culinary Institute and judged by an independent panel of food experts. In the Adult Division, Gretchen Cominetto of Midland Park, New Jersey won the one week trip for two to England in a history-making year marked by Russian liberation from communism.

Recipe courtesy of the King Arthur Flour Co.

$3,000

HERBED BACON, RED PEPPER, & GOAT CHEESE TART

Quiche-like appetizer tart redolent with fresh basil and parsley. Bacon, Chèvre, garlic, and roasted red peppers combine to produce a feast for sophisticated palates, and real men too.

1 refrigerated unbaked folded pie crust
1 pound BACON, cut crosswise into 1-inch slices
1 medium onion, chopped (about 1 cup)
2 cloves garlic, peeled and crushed
1 cup whipping cream

3 eggs
4 ounces goat cheese
¼ cup minced fresh basil
¼ cup minced fresh parsley
Salt and pepper to taste
1 jar (7-ounces) roasted red peppers, drained and cut into ½-inch pieces

• Preheat oven to bake pie crust (see package). Arrange pie crust in 10-inch tart pan with a removable bottom; press against side and trim excess dough. Place on a cookie sheet and bake according to package directions for unbaked pie crust. Set aside. Reset oven to 375°.

• Cook bacon, either in microwave or on stove top until crisp. Drain well on paper towels; crumble. Reserve 1 tablespoon bacon drippings; sauté onion and garlic in the drippings in a small skillet just until tender, about 3 or 4 minutes.

• In a blender or food processor, blend sautéed mixture with cream, eggs and goat cheese until smooth. Add basil, parsley, reserved crumbled bacon, salt and pepper; blend just to mix well. Pour half of bacon mixture into prepared tart crust. Top with red pepper pieces, then with remaining bacon mixture. Bake for 30 to 35 minutes or until puffed and browned. Cool slightly (about 10 minutes) before slicing.

• Makes 12 wedges; serves 6.

1991 Second Annual "Makin' Bacon" Recipe Contest

Calling this Grand Prize recipe in the Appetizer category her "uptown" appetizer, Janice Elder from Charlotte, North Carolina, caught a late 1980's up-trend in the popularity of goat cheese.

Recipe courtesy of the National Live Stock and Meat Board

TRIP FOR TWO TO SAN FRANCISCO & $500
SOUTHWEST APPETIZER CHEESECAKE

Crust:

⅔ cup finely crushed tortilla chips

2 tablespoons PARKAY®
Margarine, melted

Filling:

1 cup BREAKSTONE'S®
Cottage Cheese

3 packages (8 ounces each)
PHILADELPHIA® BRAND
Cream Cheese, softened

4 eggs

1 package (10 ounces)
CRACKER BARREL® Sharp
Natural Cheddar Cheese,
shredded

1 can (4 ounces) chopped green
chilies

Topping:

1 container (8 ounces)
BREAKSTONE'S® Sour
Cream

1 container (8 ounces)
BREAKSTONE'S® Gourmet
Jalapeño Cheddar Dip

1 cup chopped tomato

½ cup chopped green onions

¼ cup sliced pitted ripe olives

Crust:

- Preheat oven to 325°

- Mix crushed chips and margarine; press onto bottom of 9-inch spring-form pan. Bake 15 minutes.

Filling:

- Place cottage cheese in blender container; cover. Blend on high speed until smooth. Mix cottage cheese and cream cheese at medium speed with electric mixer until well blended. Add eggs, one at a time, mixing well after each addition. Blend in cheddar cheese and chilies; pour over crust. Bake 1 hour.

Topping:

- Mix sour cream and dip; spread over cheesecake. Bake 10 minutes. Loosen cake from rim of pan; cool before removing rim of pan. Refrigerate. Top with remaining ingredients and additional sour cream, if desired.

- Makes 16 to 20 servings.

Recipe developed by Debbie Vanni from Libertyville, Illinois for the 1987 "Philly" Hall of Fame Recipe contest. Recipe courtesy of Kraft General Foods, Inc.

$5,000

CHEESE & SPINACH TORTILLA PIZZA

From south of the border and east of the Atlantic comes this intercontinental appetizer pizza with three cheeses.

2 large flour tortillas (10-inch)
2 teaspoons vegetable oil
¼ cup sour cream
1 package (10 ounces) frozen chopped spinach, thawed and squeezed dry
1 large tomato, seeded and chopped (1½ cups)
½ cup sliced ripe olives

1 cup (4 ounces) SARGENTO® Fancy Shredded Mild Cheddar Cheese
1 cup (4 ounces) SARGENTO® Shredded Monterey Jack *or* Low Moisture Part-Skim Mozzarella Cheese
½ cup (2 ounces) SARGENTO® Fancy Shredded Parmesan Cheese
½ cup thinly sliced green onions

- Preheat oven to 450°. Place tortillas on foil-lined baking sheet. Brush oil evenly over tortillas. Bake 3 to 4 minutes or until golden brown.

- Reduce oven temperature to 350°. Spread sour cream evenly over tortillas; top with spinach, tomato and olives. Sprinkle Cheddar, Monterey Jack and Parmesan cheeses evenly over tortillas. Bake 8 minutes more or until cheese is melted. Sprinkle with green onions. Cut into wedges with pizza cutter or scissors.

- Makes 12 appetizers.

1991 Sargento® "Cheese Makes the Recipe" Contest

The big cheese in this contest was Eileen M. Watson from Oviedo, Florida with her creation using three cheeses in a pizza with a great Mexitalian accent. Other prizes were three $1,000 First Prizes in three categories and eleven microwave ovens were awarded to 11 semi-finalists.

Recipe courtesy of the Sargento Cheese Company, Inc.

$5,000

BRUSCHETTA MOZZARELLA

Delicioso... captures the flavors of one of America's favorite melting-pot cuisines.

1 loaf (1 pound) Italian bread
⅓ cup olive oil
1 clove garlic, minced
½ teaspoon salt (optional)
¼ teaspoon coarse grind black
   pepper
½ cup thinly sliced green onions
   (2 large)

¾ cup chopped tomato (1 small)
1½ cups (6 ounces)
   SARGENTO® Shredded Low
   Moisture Part-Skim Mozzarella
   Cheese
Fresh parsley sprigs (optional)

• Preheat oven to 500°. Cut bread in half lengthwise. Place cut side up on foil-lined baking sheet. Combine oil, garlic, salt and pepper; drizzle over bread. Sprinkle with green onions and tomato; top with Mozzarella cheese. Bake in upper half of oven for 5 to 7 minutes or until cheese is melted and edges of bread are browned.

• Cut into 1-inch pieces. Place on serving platter; garnish with parsley, if desired.

• Makes about 28 appetizers.

1990 Sargento® "Cheese Makes the Recipe" Contest

Grand Prize winner Bonnie W. Walkes of Roswell, Georgia achieved the **vera cucina Italiana** — *true cooking of Italy — with her appetizer in a savor-the-flavor Italian tempo.*

Recipe courtesy of the Sargento Cheese Company, Inc.

115

$1,125

OYSTERS BROILED IN CHAMPAGNE WITH STURGEON CAVIAR BEURRE BLANC

Exquisite delicacies.

6 MARYLAND OYSTERS
3 ounces Champagne

6 turns of the mill black pepper

Caviar Beurre Blanc:
¼ teaspoon shallot, chopped
2 ounces white wine
2 ounces heavy cream
2 ounces butter

Pepper to taste
½ teaspoon lemon juice
1 tablespoon caviar

- Preheat oven to Broil. Shuck oysters, reserving the juice, and loosen from the shell. Pour the reserved juice over the oysters and splash each with one-half ounce of champagne. Give each oyster one turn of the pepper mill. Broil for 60 seconds on a rack 6 to 8 inches from the heat.

Caviar Beurre Blanc:

- Place shallots and wine in a small sauté pan and heat over medium flame; reduce wine to almost dry. Add heavy cream and reduce by one-half. Remove from flame and slowly stir in butter. Season with pepper and lemon. Add caviar to sauce. Spoon over warm oysters and serve immediately.

- Makes 6 oysters on the half shell.

NOTE: Oysters may be garnished with Tomato Concasse and fresh herbs.

1990 — 11th Annual National Oyster Cook-Off

For many a Marylander living in the heart of Chesapeake Bay country, the oyster is his world, as illustrated in this competition — all four category winners were men, two of them from Maryland. The judges' unanimous choice for Grand Prize, however, was this recipe from Robert Fedorko, who hailed from Hilton Head Island, South Carolina.

Recipe courtesy of the National Oyster Cook-Off, the Maryland Department of Agriculture, Office of Seafood Marketing, and St. Mary's County Department of Economic and Community Development

TRIP FOR TWO TO LONDON, PARIS, ROME

GOLDEN GREEKS

Elegant triangular-shaped phyllo dough puffs filled with an exotic, savory chicken filling.

¼ cup light soy sauce
¼ cup dry sherry
1 tablespoon honey
2 tablespoons Chinese oyster
   sauce
3 cloves star anise

3 thin slices fresh ginger root
2 scallions, cut in 1-inch sections
4 boned chicken breasts
¼ pound melted butter
½ pound phyllo dough or strudel
   leaves

- Combine soy, sherry, honey, oyster sauce, spices and scallions in a saucepan, simmer 5 minutes. Add chicken breasts, bring liquid to a boil. Cover the pan, reduce the heat, and simmer chicken gently for 20 minutes. Remove cover, cook 15 minutes longer, turning chicken often to color evenly. Cut into thin crosswise slices.

- Preheat oven to 425°. Melt butter. Cut phyllo into strips 2 inches wide by 10 to 12 inches long. For each serving, brush two strips lightly with melted butter. Lay 2 or 3 slices of chicken in a corner of one strip. Fold the corner over the chicken to form a triangle. Continue to fold in uniform triangles until the chicken is completely wrapped with the first strip of phyllo. Lay the wrapped chicken in the corner of the second strip of phyllo and repeat the process. Arrange the triangles well apart on an ungreased baking sheet. Bake 12 to 15 minutes, until golden brown. Serve warm.

- Makes 30 to 36 triangles.

1973 Seagram's V.O.® & GOURMET MAGAZINE®'s
International Hors d'Oeuvre Recipe Contest

From more than 10,000 entries, 5 finalists were selected by a panel of experts from GOURMET MAGAZINE and were flown with their guests to San Francisco for a round of festivities. "Golden Greeks" was pronounced the Grand Prize winner at an Academy Awards-style ceremony at Ernie's, the famous French restaurant, where chefs prepared and served finalists' recipes.

Recipe courtesy of Joseph E. Seagram & Sons, Inc./Seagram's V.O.

$3,000

CONFETTI STUFFED PEPPERS

The eyes have it — these are as bright and beautiful as can be and nothing could be easier or faster to prepare; serve them as a side dish too.

5 small sweet peppers, red, green and/or yellow
SARAN WRAP® for the Microwave
½ cup chopped onion (1 medium-size)

2 ounces chopped mushrooms (about ½ cup)
1 cup shredded Cheddar cheese
Crumbled bacon, sliced green onion and sliced pimiento for garnish (optional)

- Cut peppers into quarters; core and seed. Place on 11-inch microwave-safe quiche pan or platter. Cover with microwave-safe Saran Wrap. Microwave at full power 3 minutes, rotating dish one-quarter turn after 2 minutes. Cool slightly.

- Combine onion and mushrooms in 9-inch microwave-safe pie plate. Cover with microwave-safe Saran Wrap. Microwave at full power 2 minutes.

- Spoon onion-mushroom mixture onto pepper quarters. Sprinkle with cheese. Microwave, uncovered, at full power 2 to 3 minutes until cheese melts. Garnish with crumbled bacon, green onion and pimiento, if you wish.

- Makes 20 appetizers.

1986 FAMILY CIRCLE and Saran Wrap®'s Microwave Cooking Recipe Contest

At the beginning of the decade less than 10% of the homes in America had one, by 1985 everybody wanted one, and by 1989 75% of the homes in America had a microwave oven. At the height of the "want" period, this contest featured microwave cooking in three categories — Main Dishes, Appetizers, and Side Dishes. Today, microwave ovens are practically standard equipment and finding an American kitchen without one is rare. This Grand Prize recipe from Jackie Roberts of Mississippi is a great example of the magic of microwave cooking in minutes.

---

*Recipe courtesy of Dow Brands L.P.
and FAMILY CIRCLE/The New York Times Company*

$1,000

VIBRANT RICE & CHICKEN SOUP

"Coriander, tomato, lime juice and cayenne give Melani's soup its distinctively Mexican flavor. Add avocado and low-fat cheese and you have a fiesta of flavors and textures in every spoonful"—PREVENTION.

3 skinless chicken-breast halves
4 cups water
1 can (14 ounces) low-sodium
  chicken stock
1 onion, chopped
3 carrots, sliced
2½ cups cooked Uncle Ben's
  Converted Rice
3 tablespoons lime juice

⅛ teaspoon ground cayenne
  pepper
1 small avocado, cubed
2 tomatoes, cubed
3 tablespoons minced fresh
  coriander
4 ounces (1 cup) queso fresco or
  farmer cheese, cubed

- In a 4-quart pot over medium heat, bring the chicken, water, stock and onion to a boil. Reduce the heat and simmer for 25 minutes. Add the carrots and simmer for 20 minutes.
- Remove the chicken from the pot and set aside until cool enough to handle. Remove the bones and cut the chicken into bite-sized pieces. Return chicken to pot. Stir in the rice, lime juice and pepper. Heat for 3 to 5 minutes, but don't boil. Stir in the avocado, tomatoes and coriander. Heat through.
- Divide the cheese among 4 soup bowls. Add the soup.
- Makes 4 servings.

1991 PREVENTION's Cooking for Health Recipe Contest

Meeting PREVENTION's strict standards for fat, cholesterol, and sodium content was the challenge of this contest. Rising to meet that challenge was Melani Juhl-Chandler of Palo Alto, California. Of her Grand Prize soup, one judge commented, "It tastes great, it looks great and it's great for you. This dish is what our contest is all about."

$3,000

PICANTE ONION SOUP

Pedro introduces Pierre to the joys of picante in this cross-cultural version of French onion soup.

3 cups thinly sliced onions
1 garlic clove, minced
¼ cup butter or margarine
2 cups tomato juice
1 can (10½ ounces) condensed
   beef broth and 1 can water (or
   2⅔ cups single-strength beef
   broth may be substituted for
   condensed beef broth and
   water)

½ cup PACE® Picante Sauce
1 cup unflavored croutons
1 cup (4 ounces) shredded
   Monterey Jack cheese

- In a 3-quart saucepan over medium-low heat, cook onions and garlic in butter until tender and golden brown, about 20 minutes, stirring frequently. Stir in tomato juice, broth, water and picante sauce. Bring to a boil; reduce heat and simmer uncovered 20 minutes.

- Ladle into soup bowls; sprinkle with croutons and cheese. Serve with additional picante sauce.

- Makes 4 servings, about 5 cups soup.

1988 "Pick Up The Pace" Recipe Contest

Joyce Sproul of Pembroke Pines, Florida won the top cash prize and a case of picante sauce for her spicy twist on an all-time favorite soup. Other awards were two category First Prizes of $1,000 each, three Second Prizes of $500, and 100 runners-up received Pace's 40th Anniversary Collection Cookbook.

Recipe courtesy of Pace® Picante Sauce and Pace Foods, Inc.

$5,000

PEPPERONI PIZZA SOUP

This could be the "starter" of something big in cafés across America and in trattorias from Milan to Palermo.

8 slices French baguette bread (½-inch)
1 tablespoon olive oil
2 tablespoons (½ ounce) SARGENTO® Fancy Supreme Shredded Parmesan Cheese
1 can (14½ ounces) chunky pasta-style stewed tomatoes
1 can (about 14 ounces) chicken broth

2 cups sliced zucchini (¼-inch)
1 large red bell pepper, cut into ¾-inch pieces
1 can (2¼ ounces) sliced ripe olives, drained
2 ounces thinly sliced pepperoni
1½ cups (6 ounces) SARGENTO® Fancy Supreme Shredded Pizza Double Cheese
Fresh basil sprigs, optional

• Preheat oven to 400°. Brush bread slices with oil; sprinkle with Parmesan cheese. Place on baking sheet; bake 6 minutes or until golden brown.

• In large saucepan, combine tomatoes, chicken broth, zucchini and bell pepper. Heat to a boil, reduce heat. Simmer uncovered about 5 minutes or until vegetables are crisp-tender. Stir in olives and pepperoni; simmer 1 minute.

• Ladle soup into four soup bowls; sprinkle evenly with Pizza Double cheese. Top each serving with 2 bread slices. Garnish with basil sprigs, if desired.

• Makes 4 servings, about 5 cups soup.

1992 Sargento® "Cheese Makes the Recipe" Contest

Besides the Grand Prize, other prizes in this contest included 3 First Prizes of $1,000 each and 11 Semi-Finalist Prizes of microwave ovens. "Pepperoni Pizza Soup" is to pepperoni pizza what French onion pizza is to "French Onion Soup," one of the most popular bistro menu items in France. There's a good chance that this creation of Priscilla Yee's from Concord, California would play in Palermo, and Peoria too.

Recipe courtesy of the Sargento Cheese Company, Inc.

$1,000 & MICROWAVE OVEN FOR HOME EC DEPARTMENT

WEST TEXAS TORTILLA SOUP

Outpacing the competition, this quick and easy variation of classic Mexican tortilla soup is ladled over diced cheese and topped with noodle-like strips of corn tortillas.

2 cloves garlic, minced
2 tablespoons butter or margarine
2 teaspoons ground cumin
2 cans (about 14 ounces each) chicken broth
2 cans (14½ ounces each) stewed tomatoes, undrained, coarsely chopped

1 cup PACE® Picante Sauce
½ cup coarsely chopped cilantro
8 ounces provolone or Monterey Jack cheese, cut into ¼-inch cubes
4 corn tortillas, cut into 2 x ¼-inch strips

• Cook garlic in butter in large saucepan or Dutch oven 2 minutes. Add cumin; cook and stir 1 minute. Add broth, tomatoes and Pace Picante Sauce; bring to a boil. Reduce heat; cover and simmer 30 minutes. Remove from heat; stir in cilantro.

• Place ¼ cup of the cheese in the bottom of each of 8 soup bowls. Ladle 1 cup soup over cheese; top with tortilla strips.

• Makes 8 servings, about 8 cups soup.

1992 — 4th Annual Pace® Picante Sauce Young Cooks Recipe Contest

For ages 12 to 18 only, these competitions reward young cooks for their creativity with Pace Picante Sauce. From the hacienda of 17-year-old high school junior D'Lynn Masur of West, Texas comes this Grand Prize recipe that reveals once again how fond Americans are of Mexican foods.

Recipe courtesy of Pace® Picante Sauce and Pace Foods, Inc.

$5,000

CAJUN SALAD WITH SIX SEASONINGS DRESSING

As colorful as Cajun culture itself, this lively blend of flavors in a main dish shrimp salad is guaranteed to pep up the taste buds. For a knock-out appetizer, marinate 1½ to 2 pounds of shrimp in the dressing and mound on a beautifully garnished serving platter.

1 pound medium or large shrimp, peeled, deveined and cooked
1 can (15-ounces) pinto beans, drained
1 can (11-ounces) whole kernel corn, drained

1 can (2.2-ounces) sliced ripe olives, drained
1 green bell pepper, seeded and chopped
12 cherry tomatoes, halved

Six Seasonings Dressing:

½ cup olive oil
½ cup catsup
1 tablespoon cider vinegar
2 tablespoons McCORMICK/ SCHILLING® Parsley Flakes
1½ teaspoons McCORMICK/ SCHILLING® Creole Seasoning

½ teaspoon McCORMICK/ SCHILLING® Garlic Powder
½ teaspoon McCORMICK/ SCHILLING® Cumin
½ teaspoon McCORMICK/ SCHILLING® Lemon Peel
¼ teaspoon McCORMICK/ SCHILLING® Ground Red Pepper

Optional:

Salad Greens

- In a large bowl combine shrimp, beans, corn, olives and bell pepper.
- In a small bowl combine dressing ingredients; blend well. Pour over shrimp mixture and toss to coat. Fold in cherry tomatoes. Cover and chill. Toss and serve on a bed of lettuce, if desired.
- Makes 6 servings.

1992 McCormick/Schilling® "Festival of Flavor" Recipe Contest

In 1992 McCormick/Schilling sponsored two almost simultaneous contests — this one, a regional contest open only in the four western states of Idaho, Nevada, Utah, and Wyoming, and a nationwide "Spice Up Your Life" contest. In both contests Louisiana Creole-style recipes were the top prizewinners.

Recipe developed by Connie Emerson, Reno, Nevada.
Courtesy of McCormick & Co., Inc.

$2,500

ONE POTATO, TWO POTATO BACON SALAD WITH LEMON-MAYONNAISE DRESSING

Potato salad with a twist — Bacon and sweet potatoes double up with the expected spuds in a creamy lemon-mustard mayonnaise dressing.

1½ pounds sliced BACON, cut in 1-inch pieces
1½ pounds *each* boiling potatoes and sweet potatoes, peeled and cut into 1-inch pieces
1 egg
2 tablespoons fresh lemon juice
1 teaspoon Dijon-style mustard

½ teaspoon grated lemon rind
¼ teaspoon *each* salt and white pepper
⅔ cup olive oil
2 teaspoons white vinegar
1 teaspoon honey
1 cup thinly sliced celery

- Cook bacon in a large frying pan over medium heat until crisp; drain on paper towel. Reserve 2 tablespoons bacon drippings. Finely crumble enough bacon to measure ¼ cup; reserve. Place boiling potatoes in a large saucepan, cover with water. Bring to a boil; add sweet potatoes and cook 10 to 12 minutes or until potatoes are tender. Drain well.

- Meanwhile, place egg, lemon juice, mustard, lemon rind, salt, and pepper in a food processor or blender container. Cover and blend until thoroughly combined. Remove cover and with motor running, add reserved bacon drippings and oil in a slow, steady stream. Blend until thoroughly combined. Remove dressing to a small bowl; stir in vinegar, honey and reserved bacon. Place potatoes, celery, bacon pieces and dressing in a large bowl, tossing lightly to coat. Serve warm.

- Makes 8 servings.

1990 "Makin' Bacon" Recipe Contest

As one of four category winners, Sandra Rygle of Carmichaels, Pennsylvania sliced and diced her way to a big win. There were more than 800 entries in this competition which offered four $2,500 prizes to winners in Salads, Appetizers, Main Dishes, and for ages 10 to 17 only, in Microwave Bacon Recipes.

Recipe courtesy of the National Live Stock and Meat Board

$5,000

MEDITERRANEAN POTATO SALAD

Feta cheese accentuates a Greek goddess dressing of yogurt, mayonnaise, olive oil, fresh herbs, and capers. In an unusual cooking method, the potatoes are first boiled in chicken broth and garlic, then drained and sprinkled with white wine vinegar. Served on a bed of red leaf lettuce, garnishes of pine nuts and Kalamata olives provide classical finishing touches for this Greek-style potato salad.

6 medium red potatoes, skins on, cubed
2 cups chicken broth
1 clove garlic, minced
2 tablespoons white wine vinegar
½ cup yogurt
¼ cup mayonnaise
¼ cup olive oil
1 teaspoon salt, or to taste
1 tablespoon minced fresh dill *or* 1 teaspoon dried

1 tablespoon minced fresh oregano *or* 1 teaspoon dried
2 tablespoons tiny capers (non-pareilles), with juice
8 ounces CHURNY® ATHENOS® Feta Cheese, coarsely crumbled
Red lettuce leaves
¼ cup pine nuts, lightly toasted
2 dozen black olives, preferably imported, such as Kalamata

- Cook potatoes in chicken broth with garlic until just tender. Drain and reserve broth for other use. Sprinkle vinegar on potatoes and cool.

- Blend yogurt, mayonnaise, olive oil, salt, herbs, and capers. Add feta cheese. Gently fold into potatoes. Chill overnight, if possible, to blend flavors. Remove from refrigerator 1 hour before serving. Line platter with lettuce leaves. Mound potatoes in center. Sprinkle with pine nuts and arrange olives around edge.

- Makes 8 servings.

1992 Churny® Athenos® Feta Cheese Recipe Contest

As the most popular of the Greek cheeses, feta cheese has its origin in the hills above Athens. Helen Conwell of Fairhope, Alabama was the gold medalist of this culinary olympics with her potato salad à la Grecque.

Recipe courtesy of Churny® Athenos® Feta Cheese

$4,000

PEARLS O' BARLEY SALAD

With lots o' Swiss cheese, cucumber, parsley, olives, and...

3 cups water
½ cup QUAKER® Scotch Brand
　Pearled Barley (see Note)
½ teaspoon salt (optional)
½ cup (2 ounces) cubed Swiss
　cheese
½ medium cucumber, cut into
　matchstick pieces
⅓ cup sliced celery
⅓ cup sliced green onions
¼ cup finely chopped parsley

¼ cup sliced pimiento-stuffed
　green olives
¼ cup Italian salad dressing
¼ teaspoon dried oregano leaves,
　crushed
⅛ to ¼ teaspoon ground red
　pepper
Fresh spinach leaves, rinsed and
　trimmed
2 to 3 tablespoons dry-roasted
　sunflower kernels
Tomato wedges (optional)

- Bring water to a boil; stir in barley; cover, and simmer 50 to 60 minutes, or until tender, stirring occasionally. Drain.

- In large bowl, combine barley with remaining ingredients, except spinach leaves, sunflower kernels and tomato wedges. Marinate several hours or overnight. Serve in large bowl or platter lined with spinach leaves. Sprinkle with sunflower kernels. Garnish with tomato wedges.

- Makes 8 servings.

NOTE: If substituting ⅔ cup Quaker Scotch Brand Quick Pearled Barley, decrease water to 2 cups and simmer time to 10 to 12 minutes. Proceed as recipe directs.

1985 Quaker® Oats "$tretching Food Dollars" Recipe Contest

Barley is as ancient as history itself. From 4000 to 2000 B.C. it was a basic weight unit—a shekel contained 180 grains of barley; in 1700 B.C. in Old Babylon a wagon could be rented at a per day cost of 40 "qu" (about 1½ quarts) of barley. And when the children of Israel came out of the wilderness into the land of plenty it was described in Deuteronomy 8:8 as, "A land of wheat, and barley, and..." With this recipe from Elaine Schultz of Miami, Florida there are not only pearls o' barley, but pearls o' history too.

Recipe courtesy of the Quaker Oats Company

$5,000

FIESTA RICE & BLACK BEAN SALAD

Colorful and lively, with a guacamole-style dressing.

1 cup UNCLE BEN'S®
AROMATICA® or
CONVERTED® Brand Rice
1 can (15 ounces) black beans,
rinsed and drained
1 cup thawed frozen corn kernels
1 small red bell pepper, chopped
¾ cup sliced green onions
¼ cup plus 2 tablespoons chopped
cilantro
2 to 3 jalapeño peppers, seeded
and minced

1 large clove garlic
2 ripe avocados
¼ cup plain yogurt
1 tablespoon lemon juice
¾ teaspoon ground cumin
¾ teaspoon salt
¼ teaspoon freshly ground black
pepper
Red leaf lettuce leaves
Tortilla chips

- Cook rice according to package directions; cool to room temperature. Toss rice with beans, corn, red pepper, ½ cup of the onions, ¼ cup of the cilantro and jalapeño peppers in a large bowl.

- Mince garlic in blender or food processor. Peel, seed and cut one of the avocados into chunks; add to blender with yogurt, remaining onions, remaining cilantro, lemon juice, cumin, salt and pepper. Blend until smooth, scraping down sides once. Toss with rice mixture; chill.

- Just before serving, peel, seed and cut remaining avocado into ¾-inch pieces. Gently toss with salad. Serve on lettuce leaves with tortilla chips.

- Makes 6 servings, about 8 cups salad.

1991 Uncle Ben's® "Cook & Tell" Cook-Off

A contest within six contests. During 1990 and 1991 Uncle Ben's sponsored six contests; the best of the entries culminated in a cook-off in Aspen, Colorado. Once again, the ever-popular flavors of the southwest were judged the best in this recipe submitted by Virginia C. Anthony of Jacksonville, Florida.

Recipe courtesy of Uncle Ben's, Inc.

$5,000

CRAB LOUIS EN BLOX

Inspired by the classic luncheon salad created in San Francisco at the turn-of-the-century. Serve à la Louis on a bed of Bibb lettuce and garnish with wedges of tomato and hard-cooked eggs. Or, serve the 1-inch cubes on party picks as appetizers.

6 envelopes KNOX® Unflavored
  Gelatine
¼ cup sugar
2½ cups boiling water
1 cup mayonnaise
½ cup Wish-Bone® Deluxe
  French or Thousand Island
  Dressing

½ cup chili sauce
2 cups flaked cooked crabmeat
½ cup chopped celery
1 hard-cooked egg, chopped
  (optional)

- In large bowl, mix Knox Unflavored Gelatine and sugar. Add boiling water and stir until gelatine is completely dissolved. With wire whip or rotary beater, blend in mayonnaise, Wish-Bone Dressing, chili sauce, crabmeat, celery, and egg.

- Pour into 9 x 13-inch shallow baking pan and chill until firm. Cut into squares to serve.

- Makes about 10 dozen (1-inch) squares.

1975 "Knox® Blox" Recipe Contest

Peggy Creed of Florissant, Missouri was the creative cook whose rendition of "Crab Louis" stood out in the crowd of entries. Although the real "Louis's" identity remains a mystery, he, too, created a winning crab salad.

KNOX® is a registered trademark of the Thomas J. Lipton Company.
Reprinted by permission.

$10,000

HAM & POTATO CRUNCH SALAD

It's the crispy, crunchy topping of buttery browned Betty Crocker Potato Buds and shredded cheese that make this homespun main dish salad unique.

⅓ cup butter or margarine
2 cups BETTY CROCKER®
  Potato Buds mashed potatoes
  (dry)
¼ teaspoon onion salt
1 jar (6 ounces) marinated
  artichoke hearts, drained
  (reserve liquid)
1 cup chopped celery
½ cup salad oil

¼ cup tarragon vinegar
1 teaspoon salt
1 jar (2 ounces) diced pimientos,
  drained
2 cups cut-up fully cooked
  smoked ham
6 cups coarsely shredded iceberg
  lettuce
½ cup shredded Jarlsberg or Swiss
  cheese

- Heat butter in 10-inch skillet over medium-low heat until melted. Stir in Potato Buds and ¼ teaspoon onion salt. Cook, stirring constantly, until the potatoes are dark brown, 5 to 8 minutes; reserve.

- Chop artichoke hearts; place in 2-quart saucepan. Stir in reserved artichoke liquid, the celery, oil, tarragon vinegar, salt and pimientos; heat until hot. Mix ham, lettuce and artichoke heart mixture in large bowl. Sprinkle with browned potatoes and the cheese. Serve immediately.

- Makes 6 servings.

1983 Betty Crocker® Potato Buds Recipe Contest

Of all the cooks in America, none is better known — or more in the mainstream — than Betty Crocker. Here, Betty Crocker was looking for inventive main dishes using at least ½ cup of Potato Buds and the recipes had to be submitted on 3x5 cards. With 40% of the judges' vote rating "originality," the highest marks went to Gloria Ward of Yuma, Arizona whose imagination went way beyond mashed potatoes.

Recipe courtesy of General Mills, Inc.

$3,000

THAI CHICKEN FETTUCINE SALAD

An adventure into the tantalizing flavors, colors, and textures of Thai cuisine. With no last-minute preparation required, this spicy salad is an ideal main course for casual entertaining.

1 cup PACE® Picante Sauce
¼ cup chunk-style peanut butter
2 tablespoons honey
2 tablespoons orange juice
1 teaspoon soy sauce
½ teaspoon ground ginger
6 ounces dry fettucine, cooked according to directions, well drained

3 chicken breast halves, boned, skinned and cut into 1-inch pieces (about 12 ounces)
2 tablespoons vegetable oil
Lettuce or savoy cabbage leaves (optional)
¼ cup coarsely chopped cilantro
¼ cup peanut halves
¼ cup very thin, short red bell pepper strips

• Combine picante sauce, peanut butter, honey, orange juice, soy sauce and ginger in a small saucepan. Cook and stir over low heat until blended and smooth. Reserve ¼ cup picante sauce mixture; toss remaining picante sauce mixture with hot cooked fettucine.

• Cook chicken in oil in large skillet until browned and cooked through, about 5 minutes. Add reserved picante sauce mixture; mix well. Line large platter with lettuce leaves, if desired. Arrange fettucine mixture over lettuce; top with chicken mixture. Sprinkle with cilantro, peanut halves and pepper strips. Cool to room temperature before serving. Serve with additional picante sauce.

• Makes 4 servings.

1990 "Pick Up The Pace" Recipe Contest

The supermarkets of Jackie Stevens' Nashville, Tennessee homeland are worlds apart from Thailand, yet her winning recipe conjures up images of a country of canals, where sampans loaded with fresh produce offer a picturesque floating marketplace.

Recipe courtesy of Pace® Picante Sauce and Pace Foods, Inc.

$5,000

TURKEY BERRY SALAD WITH LEMON DRESSING

A low-fat feast — and berry pretty too.

1 (8-ounce) carton lemon lowfat yogurt
1 tablespoon honey
½ teaspoon grated ginger root
¼ teaspoon shredded lemon zest (peel)
½ pound fresh spinach leaves

½ pound BUTTERBALL® Slice 'N Serve Honey Roasted Breast of Turkey, cut into ¾-inch cubes
1 cup sliced fresh strawberries
1 medium banana, sliced
½ cup coarsely chopped pistachio nuts

- To make dressing, stir together yogurt, honey, ginger root and lemon zest in small bowl. Place spinach leaves on 4 serving plates. Divide and arrange turkey, strawberries and banana on each plate. Spoon dressing over salad and sprinkle with nuts. Pass remaining dressing.

- Makes 4 servings.

1991 Butterball® Slice 'N Serve "Meal Makers" Recipe Contest

Thanks to Butterball, turkey isn't just for Thanksgiving feasts. Recipes in the Entrée, Soup, Salad, and Casserole categories were required to use Butterball Slice 'N Serve Breast of Turkey; one First Prize of $2,000 and a Second Prize of $1,000 were awarded in addition to the Grand Prize, which went to Beverly Ann Crummey from Brooksville, Florida for her winning combination salad.

Recipe courtesy of Armour Swift-Eckrich

$2,500

CURRIED TURKEY TWIST

1 pound TURKEY BREAST CUTLETS or TENDERLOINS, cut into ½ x 2-inch strips
2 teaspoons peanut oil
¼ teaspoon garlic powder
¼ teaspoon curry powder
⅛ teaspoon ground ginger
Non-stick vegetable cooking spray

2 ounces fresh snow peas, blanched
½ cup fresh mushrooms, sliced
8 cherry tomatoes, halved
¼ cup red bell pepper, seeded and cut into ¼ x 2-inch strips
¼ cup green bell pepper, seeded and cut into ¼ x 2-inch strips
2 cups rotini pasta, cooked according to package directions and drained

Chutney Dressing:
⅓ cup peanut oil
⅓ cup mango chutney
2 tablespoons fresh lemon juice
1½ teaspoons curry powder

½ teaspoon salt
½ teaspoon bottled hot pepper sauce

- In small bowl combine turkey, oil, garlic powder, curry powder and ginger. Cover and refrigerate 30 minutes. Coat large non-stick skillet with vegetable cooking spray. Over medium-high heat, sauté turkey mixture 4 to 5 minutes or until turkey is no longer pink in center. In large bowl combine turkey, snow peas, mushrooms, tomatoes, red pepper, green pepper, pasta and dressing. Cover and refrigerate 20 minutes to allow flavors to blend.

Chutney Dressing:

- In blender combine oil, chutney, juice, curry powder, salt and hot pepper sauce. Blend until mixture is smooth.
- Makes 6 servings.

1991 National Turkey Lovers' Recipe Contest for Teens

In addition to submitting a recipe, entries required two accompanying essays. From more than 500 entries, sixteen-year-old Julie Bowman from Raleigh, North Carolina won the Grand Prize for some "pretty" terrific teen cuisine.

Recipe courtesy of the National Turkey Federation

$25,000

HONEY CREAM DRESSING

Melliferously smooth and creamy — quick and easy too.

1 can (11 ounces)
  CAMPBELL'S® Condensed
  Cheddar Cheese Soup
½ cup milk

½ cup sour cream
½ cup honey
3 cups thawed frozen whipped
  topping

- In bowl blend soup, milk, sour cream, and honey until smooth; chill 4 hours or more. Fold in whipped topping. Serve on fruit salads.
- Makes about 5½ cups.

1979 Campbell's® Creative Cooking Contest

A blockbuster of a contest. Five finalists were chosen in each of the seven categories — 35 big prizewinners in all. Recipes required the use of one or more varieties of Campbell's Soups or Franco-American, Swanson, or V8 products.

First prize winners in each category chose between free groceries for one year or $5,000; the other 28 finalists received free groceries for a month or $400. As if that weren't enough, 50 third-prize winners crammed grocery carts to overflowing and, finally, 10,000 fourth-prize winners received a Campbell's cookbook of 250 recipes designed to help them "enjoy the art of creative cooking." Grand Prize winner Charlie Poulos of Knoxville, Tennessee, a food service manager, was given the choice of free groceries for five years or $25,000. Summing up his winning recipe, he commented to one food editor, "It's not much work, it looks pretty and it tastes good." Within the framework of the 1970's "granola decade," honey was considered a wonder food and was recommended for everything from a sore throat to cancer. Culinarily speaking, it sweetened everything from herbal tea to, well, salad dressing and many contest-winning recipes reflected the switch to a taste of honey. At a time when there were more women working outside the home than stayed home, this Grand Prize recipe also met the quick and easy standard.

"CAMPBELL'S," "FRANCO-AMERICAN" and "V8" are registered trademarks of Campbell Soup Company. Recipe provided courtesy of Campbell Soup Company.

$1,000

CRANBERRY CHERRY RELISH

Bright ruby-red relish made from bog-in-a-bag cranberries and cherries. If serving with chicken or poultry, add more cranberries; add more raisins if serving with ham.

1½ cups fresh OCEAN SPRAY®
  Cranberries *or* Fresh Frozen
  Cranberries
1 orange
1 lemon
2 cups dark brown sugar, packed
1½ cups seedless raisins

1 cup fresh *or* canned cherries,
  pitted
½ cup vinegar
½ teaspoon cinnamon
½ teaspoon ground cloves
½ teaspoon nutmeg
½ cinnamon stick

- Rinse cranberries; sort out soft berries and stems. Quarter orange and lemon; remove seeds. Cut into small pieces.

- In a large saucepan combine and thoroughly mix all ingredients. Bring to a boil, reduce heat, and simmer about 15 minutes. Remove cinnamon stick. Cool. Keeps for 2 to 3 weeks in refrigerator, or relish can be frozen in plastic containers.

- Makes 6 cups.

1980 Ocean Spray® National Cranberry Cook-Off

Ocean Spray discovered how cranberries were being used in American homes when it celebrated its 50th anniversary by announcing this recipe contest. From 6,000 entries, fifteen finalists were selected from the General Federation of Women's Clubs, the Grange, and Extension Service Homemaker Clubs throughout the country. Finalists competed in a cook-off held in the ballroom kitchens of the Beverly Wilshire Hotel in Los Angeles. Helen Lacine of Grinell, Iowa garnered the Grand Prize and a silver tray with her very-cherry cranberry recipe.

Recipe courtesy of Ocean Spray Cranberries, Inc.

$12,000

CRANBERRY SAUSAGE STUFFING

Jellied cranberry sauce and apple juice add zing to traditional sausage stuffing.

1 (15-ounce) package ARNOLD®
  Stuffing
1 pound pork sausage, panfried
  and drained
4 medium onions, finely chopped
  (1½ cups)

6 stalks celery, finely chopped
  (2½ cups)
2 eggs, slightly beaten
1 can (8-ounces) jellied cranberry
  sauce, beaten until thin
1 to 2 cups apple juice

- Mix the stuffing mix, cooked sausage, chopped onion and celery, eggs and cranberry sauce. Add apple juice, a little at a time, until entire mixture is dampened but not mushy. (For less moist stuffing, use less apple juice.)
- Stuff 18 to 20 pound turkey and cook as directed for weight of turkey.

NOTE: To stuff 8 to 10 pound bird, cut recipe in half. Any remaining stuffing can be baked separately in covered casserole for 30 minutes at 350°.

1982 "Strut Your Stuffin'" Recipe Contest

Only seven ingredients are required to make this Grand Prize recipe, an old European recipe brought to America and made a tradition by the Gunther-Mohr-Fitting Family.

Recipe courtesy of Best Foods Baking Group/CPC International Inc.

$1,000

GARLIC & CHILE RELLENO SOUFFLÉ

Softened butter and dry
  breadcrumbs for mold
5 tablespoons butter, softened
3 tablespoons all-purpose flour
1 cup hot milk
¼ teaspoon plus 1 pinch salt
⅛ teaspoon white pepper
4 large egg yolks, well beaten

1 can (17-ounces) peeled green
  chiles, drained and patted dry,
  cut in 1-inch pieces
8 cloves FRESH GARLIC,
  minced
5 large egg whites
½ cup grated Monterey Jack
  cheese

- Preheat oven to 375°. Grease a 1½-quart soufflé mold or Pyrex baking dish generously with butter, and dust well with breadcrumbs; set aside. Heat 3 tablespoons of the butter until it foams; add flour, cook over medium heat until it starts to brown, stirring constantly. Add hot milk and cook for 4 minutes, stirring constantly, until thickened. Season with ¼ teaspoon of the salt and white pepper. Let cool slightly and add the beaten egg yolks, then the chiles, and mix well.

- Sauté garlic in remaining 2 tablespoons butter until golden brown. Add to the above mixture.

- Beat egg whites with a pinch of salt until stiff. Fold beaten egg whites into first mixture; then fold in the grated cheese. Pour into prepared mold and bake for 35 to 40 minutes, until puffed and brown.

- Makes 4 to 6 servings.

1991 Gilroy Great Garlic Recipe Contest and Cook-Off

These annual festival/cook-offs held in Gilroy, California began in the late 1970's to challenge the claim by Arleux, France as the garlic capital of the world. By 1981 attendance surpassed that of the Super Bowl — 110,000 followed their noses to Gilroy to mingle among 105 garlic concessions and 6½ tons of minced garlic. The publicity from the event translated into garlic consumption going up 1,000 percent! The 1991 Grand Prize winner was Maria Sandoval from Alameda, California who also received a crown of garlic.

Recipe courtesy of the Gilroy Garlic Festival Association, Inc.

$3,000

BULGUR, GAZPACHO STYLE

Here, crushed wheat — a Middle Eastern staple — is tricked up with the popular Spanish ingredients for gazpacho. Serve warm as a side dish or cold as a salad.

3 tablespoons olive oil
¼ cup sliced green onions, both white and green parts
¼ cup diced sweet green pepper
1 cup bulgur
SARAN WRAP® for the Microwave
1 can (6 ounces) spicy-hot tomato-vegetable juice

1 can (10½ ounces) condensed beef broth
Juice of 1 lime
1 teaspoon leaf thyme, crumbled
¼ teaspoon garlic powder
1 large tomato, chopped
1 medium-size cucumber, pared and chopped
¼ cup chopped fresh parsley

- Place oil in shallow, round microwave-safe casserole, about 9 inches in diameter. Stir in green onion, green pepper and bulgur. Cover with microwave-safe Saran Wrap. Microwave at full power 3 minutes.

- Add vegetable juice, beef broth, lime juice, thyme and garlic powder. Cover with microwave-safe Saran Wrap, pleated slightly at one side to vent. Microwave at full power 6 minutes. Then microwave at half power (50%) for 7 to 8 minutes until bulgur is tender. Mix in tomato, cucumber and parsley. Let stand, covered, on solid surface 5 minutes. Garnish with cucumber slices, lime slices and parsley, if you wish.

- Makes 6 servings.

1986 FAMILY CIRCLE and Saran Wrap®'s
Microwave Cooking Recipe Contest

During the 1980's Americans were quick to adopt the microwave oven as their latest "electric servant." As the new industry burgeoned, creating demand for microwavable foods, equipment, and microwave-safe plastic wrap, recipe contests like this one helped us consider the possibilities. In a cross-cultural coup, Elaine Schultz from Miami, Florida won the Grand Prize in the Side Dish category with her tabbouleh-gazpacho crossover.

---

*Recipe courtesy of Dow Brands L. P. and
FAMILY CIRCLE/The New York Times Company*

$3,000 IN CASH & PRIZES

MEL'S SWEET RED PEPPER RELISH

Move over, Peter Piper... make room for Mel's pickled peppers.

8 cups chopped LE ROUGE
  ROYALE® Sweet Red Peppers
  (12 to 15 whole peppers)
3 cups chopped onions (4 to 5
  large onions)

2 tablespoons salt
4 tablespoons mustard seed
2¼ cups sugar
5 cups vinegar

NOTE: Canning instructions are given due to the large quantity of sweet red peppers. For institutional purposes, relish can be put into containers and refrigerated until used.

- Chop vegetables by putting into food processor or meat grinder.
- Put all ingredients into large pot. Cook over high heat about 45 minutes, stirring often to prevent sticking. Mixture should cook down by one-third.
- Ladle mixture into hot sterilized jars, adjusting lids. Process in a water bath canner for 10 minutes.
- Makes 6 to 8 pints.

1992 Sun World "Royale" Recipe Contest

From the heart of California's produce capital, Sun World introduced this contest seeking dishes "fit for royalty" and featuring Le Rouge Royale sweet red peppers. First Place prize, $2,000, a $500 Sun World product voucher, and a trip for two to Southern California was awarded to Lindsay "Mel" Mattison of Cherry Valley, California for her zesty relish. "Sweet Red Peppers and Corn Fritters" won the $1,000 Second Place prize plus a $250 product voucher; "Savory Southwest Flan" won Third Place prize of $500 and a $100 voucher. In a departure from typical contest rules, entrants were encouraged to send photos with their recipes.

Recipe courtesy of Sun World International

$7,500

BROCCOLI LEMON SAUCE OVER STEAMED VEGETABLES

Although his well-known distaste for broccoli may not have altered the course of history while George Bush was in the White House, it may fairly be said that this contest — and this recipe — altered the history of broccoli.

3 pounds small red potatoes, quartered
1 large sweet red pepper, cut into ½-inch-thick strips
2 cups broccoli flowerets
1 can (10¾ ounces) CAMPBELL'S® Condensed Cream of Broccoli Soup

½ cup mayonnaise
¼ cup minced green onions
1 tablespoon lemon juice
¼ teaspoon dried thyme leaves, crushed

- In 6-quart Dutch oven over high heat, in 1 inch boiling water, in steamer basket, steam potatoes 10 minutes. Add pepper and broccoli; steam vegetables 5 minutes more or until tender.
- Meanwhile, in 2-quart saucepan over medium heat, combine soup, mayonnaise, onions, lemon juice and thyme. Heat through, stirring occasionally. Pour over vegetables.
- Makes 8 servings.

1991 Campbell's Soup/WOMAN'S DAY "How To Get George Bush To Eat Broccoli" Recipe Contest

No question about it, broccoli suffered a serious image problem when George Bush was President. Together, Campbell's Soup and WOMAN'S DAY magazine devised a plan to polish its tarnished reputation via a contest featuring Campbell's Condensed Cream of Broccoli Soup. As a result, broccoli received the ultimate invitation — dinner at the White House — through the efforts of Grand Prize winner Priscilla Yee of Concord, California.

Final judging was done by editors from WOMAN'S DAY in three categories — (1) Meat, Poultry and Seafood, (2) One-Pot Main Courses/ Casseroles, and (3) Sauces and Side Dishes. In addition to the $5,000 Grand Prize, there were 3 First Prizes of $2,500 (one awarded to one First Prize winner in addition to Grand Prize), 3 Second Prizes of $1,500 each, and 3 $500 Third Prizes.

"CAMPBELL'S" is a registered trademark of Campbell Soup Company. Recipe provided courtesy of Campbell Soup Company.

$4,000

PEPPY CORN TIMBALES

Impressive accompaniment to any meal.

2 tablespoons butter
½ cup chopped green onions with tops
½ cup chopped red pepper
½ cup chopped green pepper
4 cups thinly sliced bok choy*
6 EGGS
1 can (8.5 ounces) cream-style corn

1 cup (4 ounces) shredded mozzarella cheese
1 cup low-fat cottage cheese
½ cup grated Parmesan cheese
¼ cup flour
¼ teaspoon salt
¼ teaspoon ground red pepper

Bok choy is a cabbage which resembles Swiss chard, with long, thick-stemmed, light green to pearly white stalks. The flavor is similar to cabbage.

- Preheat oven to 350°. In large skillet over medium heat, cook onions, peppers and bok choy in butter until tender but not brown. Remove from heat and set aside.

- Place remaining ingredients in blender container. Cover and blend at medium speed until smooth. Occasionally, turn off blender and scrape down sides of container with rubber spatula. Carefully add reserved vegetable mixture to blender container. Using a large spoon, carefully stir until ingredients are evenly combined. Pour mixture into 10 (6-ounce) or 6 (10-ounce) greased custard cups. Bake until puffy and golden brown, about 35 minutes. Let stand 5 minutes before serving timbales from cups or inverting timbales onto serving plate.

- Makes 5 to 6 servings.

1990 National Egg Cooking Contest

At the American Egg Board there has never been a doubt about which came first, the chicken or the egg. This year there wasn't a doubt as to which recipe should win the blue ribbon and Grand Prize in the Adult Division — this one, the entry of Latrelle Pevey of Springfield, Georgia.

Recipe courtesy of the American Egg Board

BLUE RIBBON BONUSES

BLUE RIBBON

$10,000

GINGERBREAD SCONES WITH LEMON BREAKFAST CREAM

We have the Scots to thank for these teacakes (pronounced "skonns") that are often served with thick cream or butter and jam.

Scones:

¼ cup sugar
1¾ cups all-purpose flour
¾ cup QUAKER® OATS (Quick or Old Fashioned, uncooked)
4 teaspoons baking powder
1 teaspoon ground ginger
½ teaspoon cinnamon

¼ teaspoon ground nutmeg
⅛ teaspoon ground cloves
⅓ cup (5⅓ tablespoons) margarine
⅓ cup skim milk
⅓ cup dried currants or raisins
2 egg whites, slightly beaten
2 tablespoons molasses

Lemon Breakfast Cream:

¾ cup part-skim ricotta cheese

2 tablespoons frozen lemonade concentrate, thawed

Scones:

- Heat oven to 425°. Reserve 1 teaspoon of sugar; combine remaining sugar with next 7 ingredients, mixing well. Cut in margarine until crumbly. Add combined milk, currants, egg whites and molasses, mixing just until moistened. Turn out onto lightly floured surface; knead gently 5 to 10 times. Pat dough to ¾-inch thickness. Cut with 2½-inch heart-shaped or round biscuit cutter. Place on ungreased cookie sheet. Sprinkle tops with reserved 1 teaspoon sugar. Bake 9 to 11 minutes or until golden brown.

Lemon Breakfast Cream:

- Place ricotta cheese and lemonade concentrate in blender or food processor; cover. Blend on high or process until smooth. Serve with warm scones. (For thinner Lemon Breakfast Cream consistency, add ½ cup low-fat lemon yogurt.)

- Makes 10 scones.

Recipe developed by Julia E. Winter of Grosse Pointe Park, Michigan for the 1990 First Annual Quaker® Oats "It's the Right Thing To Do" Recipe Contest. Recipe courtesy of the Quaker Oats Company.

$20,000

MUSTARD-ONION HAMBURGER BUNS

4 cups unsifted unbleached flour
2½ cups whole wheat flour
⅓ cup instant nonfat dry milk
  powder
⅓ cup instant chopped onion
2 teaspoons salt
2 envelopes Fast-Rising Dry
  FLEISCHMANN'S® YEAST
1¼ cups water

⅔ cup Dijon-style or whole-grain
  mustard
⅓ cup butter or margarine
¼ cup honey
1 tablespoon butter or margarine,
  melted
Instant chopped onion, sesame
  seeds and poppy seeds for
  topping

- Set aside 1 cup of the unbleached flour. Mix together the remaining 3 cups unbleached flour, whole wheat flour, milk powder, instant onion, salt and yeast in a large bowl.

- Combine water, mustard, butter and honey in medium-size saucepan. Heat to 130° (mixture should feel comfortably hot to the touch). Mix into dry ingredients. Stir in enough of the reserved 1 cup flour to make a fairly stiff dough. Turn dough out onto lightly floured surface. Knead until smooth and elastic, 8 to 10 minutes. Cover; let rise 10 minutes. Divide dough into 12 equal pieces. Form each into a smooth ball. Place about 2 inches apart on greased cookie sheets; press to flatten slightly. Cover; let rise in warm place, away from drafts, until doubled in volume, 35 to 45 minutes. Brush tops of rolls with melted butter. Sprinkle with instant chopped onions. Sprinkle half the buns with sesame seeds and half with poppy seeds. Bake in a preheated 350° oven 20 to 25 minutes or until buns are browned and they sound hollow when tapped with fingers. Remove to wire racks to cool.

- Makes 12 buns.

1984 Fleischmann's® "Healthy Bakers' Dozen" Recipe Contest

Triumphing over more than 7,000 entries entered in the healthful bread categories of Nuts, Grains, Fruits, and Vegetables was Grand Prize winner Charlotte Gevurtz from Beaverton, Oregon.

---

*Recipe courtesy of Fleischmann's, Specialty Brands,
A Division of Burns Philp Food, Inc.*

$10,000 & G.E. APPLIANCES
LERICI ONION FLAT BREAD

4½ to 5 cups unsifted bread flour
2 tablespoons plus 1 teaspoon
  sugar
1 teaspoon salt
¼ cup lukewarm water (105° to
  115°)
1 package active dry yeast
1 large egg, slightly beaten
1 cup lukewarm milk

½ cup HELLMANN'S® (BEST
  FOODS) Real Mayonnaise
3 tablespoons margarine
1¼ cups coarsely shredded
  onions, drained
Garlic powder
2 tablespoons sesame seeds
Paprika

- In small bowl, stir together 2 cups flour, 2 tablespoons sugar and the salt. In large bowl, stir together water and 1 teaspoon sugar. Sprinkle yeast over water; stir until dissolved. Let stand 5 minutes. In small bowl, stir together egg, milk, and mayonnaise; stir into yeast mixture. Beat in flour mixture. Stir in enough remaining flour to form a soft, not sticky, dough. On floured surface, knead 2 minutes, or until dough is smooth and satiny. Place in oiled bowl; turn dough over so that top is greased. Cover with towel. Let rise in warm place, free from drafts, until double in bulk, 45 to 60 minutes.

- In medium skillet, melt 2 tablespoons margarine over medium-low heat. Add onions. Stirring occasionally, cook 5 minutes, or until onions are translucent. Cool.

- Punch down dough. Knead in ½ cup onions. Form into ball on floured surface. Using rolling pin and hands, roll and stretch dough to 15 x 10-inch rectangle. Place in oiled 15½ x 10½ x 1-inch jelly roll pan. Melt remaining margarine; brush over dough. Sprinkle with garlic powder to taste and 2 tablespoons sesame seeds. Spread the remaining onions over top; sprinkle with paprika. Let rise in warm place, free from drafts, about 15 minutes, or until slightly puffy. Bake in a preheated 375° oven for 35 minutes, or until well browned. Cut lengthwise down middle of bread, then crosswise into 1-inch slices. Serve warm or cool.

- Makes about 2½ dozen slices.

Recipe developed by Anna Lea Steenburgen of Virginia Beach, Virginia for the 1983 Hellmann's® $100,000 Baking Contest. Recipe courtesy of Best Foods/ CPC International Inc.

5 KitchenAid APPLIANCES

SUNSHINE CARROT BREAD

½ cup warm water (105° to 115°)
2 envelopes active dry yeast
⅓ cup sugar
1 tablespoon grated orange rind
½ cup orange juice, at room
 temperature
1 cup shredded carrots

½ cup raisins
2 teaspoons ground cinnamon
1 teaspoon salt
2 eggs
4½ cups unsifted all-purpose flour
1 egg yolk
1 tablespoon water

Orange Glaze:

½ cup confectioners' sugar

2 to 3 teaspoons orange juice

• Pour warm water into large bowl. Sprinkle yeast and 1 tablespoon of the sugar over water; stir to dissolve. Let stand 5 minutes. Add the remaining sugar, orange rind, orange juice, carrots, raisins, cinnamon, salt, eggs and 2 cups of the flour. Mix at low speed until thoroughly blended; beat at medium speed 2 minutes. Mix in 2 cups more flour, ½ cup at a time.

• Turn dough out onto lightly floured surface. Knead about 5 minutes, adding up to ½ cup of the remaining flour, until smooth and elastic. Place in oiled large bowl; turn to coat. Cover; let rise in warm place until doubled in bulk, about 1 hour. Punch dough down; knead briefly. Divide dough into 6 equal portions. Shape each into a ball. Place 3 balls side by side in each of 2 greased 8½ x 4½-inch loaf pans. Covers let rise in warm place, away from drafts, until doubled in bulk, about 45 minutes.

• Combine egg yolk and water in small cup. Brush over tops of loaves. Bake at 350° for 35 to 45 minutes or until golden brown. Cool breads on racks. Drizzle with Orange Glaze (mix confectioners' sugar with orange juice to glazing consistency).

• Makes 2 loaves, 10 slices each.

Recipe developed by Toby Ann Apgar from Bridgewater, New Jersey for the 1986 KitchenAid® Holiday Yeast Bread Contest. Recipe courtesy of KitchenAid, Inc.

$35,000 SCHOLARSHIP

APRICOT CARROT DELIGHT BREAD

Naturally sweet carrots team up with apricots and raisins in this wholesome, flavorful quick bread.

1½ cups shredded carrots
¾ cup sugar
¼ cup vegetable oil
3 egg whites
1½ cups all-purpose flour
2 teaspoons vanilla
2 teaspoons almond extract
¾ teaspoon baking soda
½ teaspoon salt
¼ teaspoon baking powder
¼ teaspoon ground cloves
½ cup finely chopped dried
   apricots
½ cup white raisins
Apricot rosettes for garnishing

- Preheat oven to 350°. Spray 9 x 5-inch loaf pan with non-stick cooking spray. In large bowl, combine carrots, sugar, oil and egg whites. Stir in remaining ingredients. Pour mixture into pan. Bake for 60 to 70 minutes or until wooden toothpick inserted in center comes out clean. Cool 10 minutes. Loosen sides from loaf pan and remove from pan. Cool completely before slicing.

- To make rosettes, flatten 20 dried apricots on waxed paper with a rolling pin. Roll one into a cone, press additional apricots to form petals. Secure with toothpick.

- Makes 1 loaf, 12 servings.

1992 Johnson & Wales University's Third Annual High School Recipe Contest

In cooperation with the American Cancer Society, Johnson & Wales University in Providence, Rhode Island conducts these competitions for high school and secondary school vocational facility seniors only. Twenty student chefs competed for a range of scholarships to the University and judging was done on taste, cost effectiveness and utilization, nutritional value, originality and creativity, presentation and appearance. Showing promise as a pastry chef was Grand Prize winner Pamela A. Cavanaugh from Oceanside, New York.

Recipe courtesy of Johnson & Wales University

TRIP FOR TWO TO NEW YORK & JAMES BEARD COOKING COURSE

RAISED MEXICAN CORN BREAD

2 packages FLEISCHMANN'S®
Active Dry Yeast
1 cup cornmeal plus some for
pans
½ teaspoon baking soda
1 cup buttermilk
1 medium onion, chopped fine
½ cup oil
1 tablespoon salt

1 tablespoon sugar
2 eggs
1½ cups sharp Cheddar cheese,
grated
1 cup cream-style corn
3 hot chili peppers, chopped fine
6½ to 7 cups flour
¼ cup margarine, melted

- In large bowl mix well yeast, 1 cup cornmeal and the soda; set aside. In saucepan heat buttermilk, onion, oil, salt and sugar until very warm (120° to 130°). Stir into cornmeal mixture. Beat in eggs, then cheese, corn and peppers. Stir in 5 cups flour 1 cup at a time until well mixed. Turn out on lightly floured surface; knead in enough remaining flour until dough is not sticky and is smooth and elastic. Place in greased bowl; turn to grease top. Cover and let rise in warm, draft-free place until double, about 1½ hours.

- Grease two 9 x 5 x 3-inch or 10 x 4 x 3-inch loaf pans; dust lightly with cornmeal. Divide dough in half. On lightly floured surface roll out each to 18 x 8-inch rectangle; roll up into loaf. Place seam side down in pan. Brush with some margarine. Cover; let rise in warm, draft-free place until double, 30 to 45 minutes. Bake in preheated 400° oven 25 to 30 minutes. Remove from pans to rack. Brush with remaining margarine. Cool completely. May be tightly wrapped and frozen.

- Makes 2 loaves.

1977 WOMAN'S DAY/James Beard
Creative Cookery Recipe Contest

James Beard was the Chief Judge of this contest. Entries were requested using any one or more of 12 different products and more than 1,500 prizes were awarded. Fleischmann's yeast provided the inspiration for Grand Prize winner Helen Bemis Black of Arlington Heights, Illinois.

Recipe courtesy of WOMAN'S DAY Magazine/Hachette Magazines, Inc.

$4,000

EGGSCITING HAM & CHEESE BRAID

An eggstraordinary breakfast in bread.

2 tablespoons butter
½ cup chopped green onions with tops
½ cup chopped red pepper
6 EGGS
¼ cup low-fat milk
½ teaspoon salt
½ teaspoon basil leaves, crushed
1 cup (4 ounces) diced ham or turkey ham

1 package (10 ounces) frozen chopped broccoli, thawed and well drained
1 cup (4 ounces) shredded Swiss or Cheddar cheese
2 teaspoons lemon juice
1 can (10 ounces) refrigerated pizza crust
1 EGG
1 tablespoon water
Poppy seeds

- In large skillet over medium heat, cook onion and red pepper in butter until tender but not brown. Beat together eggs, milk, salt and basil until blended. Stir in ham. Pour over vegetables in pan. Gently scramble until eggs are thickened but still moist. Remove from heat and set aside. In medium bowl, toss together broccoli, cheese and lemon juice. Set aside.

- Unroll dough onto greased baking sheet and pat to form a 14 x 9-inch rectangle. Spread reserved egg mixture in a 3-inch wide strip length-wise down center of dough. Top with reserved broccoli mixture. Make cuts in dough at 1-inch intervals on both sides of rectangle just to edge of filling. Fold dough strips diagonally over filling, overlapping strips and alternating from side to side to give a braided appearance.

- In small bowl, beat together 1 egg and water. Brush top of dough with egg mixture. Sprinkle with poppy seeds. Bake in a preheated 375° oven until golden brown, about 25 minutes. Cut into slices to serve.

- Makes 6 servings.

Recipe developed by Laurin Lentz of Nicholasville, Kentucky for the Junior Division (Grades 6 through 12) of the 1990 National Egg Cooking Contest. Recipe courtesy of the American Egg Board.

TRIP FOR TWO TO ENGLAND

APPLE-NUT COFFEE CAKE

Sour cream coffee cake with bits of apple throughout and a nutty-rich streusel topping.

1 cup KING ARTHUR®
   Unbleached All-Purpose Flour
½ teaspoon baking powder
½ teaspoon baking soda
⅛ teaspoon salt
½ cup sugar
¼ cup shortening
1 egg

½ teaspoon vanilla
1 apple, cored and chopped
½ cup sour cream
¼ cup walnuts, crushed
¼ cup brown sugar
1 tablespoon butter
½ teaspoon cinnamon

- Preheat oven to 350°. Grease and flour an 8-inch round cake pan.

- In a medium bowl stir together flour, baking powder, soda, and salt. In a large bowl beat together sugar and shortening until fluffy. Beat in egg and vanilla. Stir about half the flour mixture into the sugar mixture. Stir in sour cream. Stir in the rest of the flour mixture. Stir in apple and spread evenly in prepared pan.

- Put nuts, brown sugar, butter and cinnamon in a small bowl and mix until crumbly. Sprinkle over coffee cake. Bake for 25 to 30 minutes or until done. Serve warm.

- Makes one 8-inch coffee cake.

1992 King Arthur® Flour WinterBake

After enjoying WinterBake festivities at The Inn at Essex in Essex, Vermont, Meghan Barron of Arnold, Maryland won the Grand Prize — a one-week trip for two to England — in the Junior Division for ages 7 to 18. "Reuben Pizza" was the Grand Prize recipe in the Adult Division and the winner also won a one-week trip for two to England. Second and third place winners received solid pewter medals.

Recipe courtesy of the King Arthur Flour Co.

$18,000

TORTILLA SUNRISE

Good morning, Latin America... Sandwiched between two tortillas, the "sun" rises from its bed of peppy ground beef.

½ pound ground beef
¼ cup finely chopped onions
2 tablespoons minced fresh parsley
2 tablespoons minced fresh cilantro (optional)
2 tablespoons minced fresh mushrooms
½ teaspoon jalapeño salsa (or ⅛ teaspoon hot pepper sauce)
½ teaspoon salt

¼ teaspoon fresh ground black pepper
6 tablespoons PLANTERS® Peanut Oil
2 tablespoons grated Parmesan cheese
8 (8-inch) flour tortillas
5 small eggs
1 tablespoon milk
1 lemon or lime, quartered
Parsley sprigs

- In a small bowl combine ground beef, onions, parsley, cilantro, mushrooms, salsa, salt and pepper. Blend well. Heat 2 tablespoons Planters Peanut Oil in a large skillet over medium heat. Add meat mixture; break up as it cooks until no longer pink and mixture is a fine even texture. Drain well. Cool slightly. Stir in Parmesan cheese.
- Spoon ¼ meat mixture in the center of one flour tortilla. Form a depression in the middle of meat. Carefully break and slip 1 egg into depression. Brush the edges of filled tortilla and another unfilled tortilla with a mixture of 1 egg beaten with 1 tablespoon milk, rubbing the outside edges of tortillas until they become very sticky. Invert unfilled tortilla over filled one and firmly press edges together, crimping with a fork to seal. Repeat with remaining tortillas and filling.
- Heat ¼ cup Planters Peanut Oil in a large skillet over medium heat. Fry, one at a time, 7 to 8 minutes, turning once. Drain. Keep warm while cooking remaining tortillas. Garnish with lemon and parsley sprigs to serve.
- Makes 4 servings.

Recipe developed by Harry A. Peterson from Temple City, California for the 1981 Planters® Oil "Great Cuisines of the World" Recipe Contest. Recipe courtesy of the Planters LifeSavers Company

$1,000

GRAPE-NUTS OMELET CALIFORNIA

As early as 1928 Californians were garnering their share of Grand Prizes as revealed by this recipe from days gone by.

2 tablespoons onion, chopped
2 tablespoons green pepper, chopped
2 tablespoons parsley, chopped
2 tablespoons butter
½ teaspoon salt
1½ cups canned tomatoes

3 eggs
3 tablespoons water
½ teaspoon salt
¼ teaspoon pepper
5 tablespoons grated cheese
½ cup GRAPE-NUTS® Cereal

- Cook onion, pepper, and parsley in fat until tender. Add salt and tomatoes and simmer 15 minutes. (This sauce may be made beforehand, and reheated.)
- Beat the eggs until mixed, but not foamy; add water, salt, and pepper and mix well. Pour gently into hot buttered omelet pan. Cook over low fire. As omelet becomes firm on bottom, lift edges a little with fork and shake pan occasionally. When egg is nearly set, sprinkle grated cheese and Grape-Nuts over it. Spread lightly with part of tomato mixture. Cut across omelet, being careful not to cut all the way through. Fold over carefully and place on hot platter. Pour rest of tomato mixture over omelet and serve.
- Makes 4 servings.

1928 The Postum Company's Grape-Nuts® Recipe Contest

In 1928 the $1,000 Grand Prize won by Frances Lewis Trussel of San Marcos, California was a <u>very</u> big deal considering that the average annual income was $2,470, the price of a new car was $525, and the average house had a price tag of $7,782. In those days, a loaf of bread cost 9¢, a gallon of milk 57¢, gold was valued at $20.67 an ounce, and Grape-Nuts were touted as contributing to good health — that's about the only thing that hasn't changed.

$4,000

BRUNCH-TIME ROLLED OMELET

The ultimate omelet — beaten eggs are baked in a jelly roll pan and sprinkled with sliced green onions, pieces of ham, shredded carrots, cheese, and green chilies, then rolled and sliced.

Non-stick cooking spray
4 EGGS
1 cup low-fat milk
½ cup flour
2 tablespoons butter, melted
½ teaspoon salt
½ cup sliced green onions with
  tops

2 ounces prosciutto or ham, thinly
  sliced and cut into strips
½ cup shredded carrots
¼ cup chopped pine nuts,
  optional
1 cup (4 ounces) shredded
  Monterey Jack cheese
2 tablespoons diced green chilies

- Preheat oven to 350°. Line bottom and sides of a 15½ x 10½ x 1 inch jelly roll pan with aluminum foil. Generously spray bottom and sides of foil with cooking spray. Set aside.

- Beat together eggs, milk, flour, butter and salt until well blended. Pour into prepared pan. Sprinkle with onions and prosciutto. Bake until eggs are set and lightly browned, about 18 minutes. Immediately sprinkle with carrots, nuts, if desired, cheese and chilies. Starting from short edge, roll up, using foil to lift and roll omelet. To serve, cut omelet into 1¼-inch slices.

- Makes 4 servings.

1989 National Egg Cooking Contest

*"The omelette is to **haute cuisine** what the sonnet is to poetry," said Alexander Dumas, the French gastronome of renown and writer of the **Dictionary of Cuisine**. Compliments go to Grand Prize winner Frances Kovar from Staten Island, New York for an unusual and most elegant "omelette."*

Recipe courtesy of the American Egg Board

$2,500

SPINACH BACON BUNDLE

Beyond breakfast... a well-seasoned mixture of bacon, spinach, artichoke hearts, provolone cheese, and black olives rolled up in pizza crust.

1 pound SLICED BACON, cut into 1-inch pieces

1 package (10-ounces) frozen, chopped spinach, defrosted and well drained

1 jar (6-ounces) marinated artichoke hearts, drained and chopped

6 ounces provolone cheese, cut into ½-inch pieces

1 can (2¼-ounces) sliced black olives, drained

1 egg, beaten

2 cloves garlic, minced

¼ teaspoon *each* dried basil leaves and instant minced onion

⅛ teaspoon ground red pepper, optional

1 package (10-ounces) refrigerated pizza crust

1 egg white, beaten

1 teaspoon sesame seeds

- Preheat oven to 350°. Cook bacon in large frying pan over medium heat until crisp; drain on paper towel. Combine bacon, spinach, artichokes, cheese, olives, egg, garlic, basil, minced onion and red pepper; reserve.

- Place pizza crust on lightly greased baking sheet; press out dough starting at center to form a 14 x 10-inch rectangle. Spread bacon mixture to within one inch of edges. Starting from long side, roll up jelly roll fashion, sealing ends and seam. Place seam side down; brush with egg white and sprinkle with sesame seeds. Bake 25 minutes or until golden brown. Let stand 5 minutes; cut into slices with serrated knife.

- Makes 6 servings.

1990 "Makin' Bacon" Recipe Contest

One of four Grand Prize winners, Karen Durrett of Portland, Oregon, proved that bacon isn't just for breakfast any more with her winning recipe in the Main Dish category. Three other $2,500 Grand Prizes were awarded in the Appetizer, Salad, and Microwave Bacon (for ages 10 to 17 only) categories.

Recipe courtesy of the National Live Stock and Meat Board

TRIP FOR TWO TO FRANCE

BAYS GRILLED SHRIMP WITH PAPAYA SALSA

2 tablespoons *each*: oil, lime juice, soy sauce
1 to 2 teaspoons red pepper sauce
½ teaspoon freshly ground coriander seeds

1½ pounds large shrimp, shelled and deveined
1 *each*: sweet red pepper and yellow pepper, cut into 1-inch cubes, seeded, blanched

Papaya Salsa:
1 peeled and seeded papaya, cut into ½-inch cubes
1 fresh jalapeño pepper, seeded, minced

1 green onion, minced
1 tablespoon *each* : sugar, chopped cilantro, finely chopped sweet red pepper

6 BAYS® English Muffins, split, lightly toasted and buttered

12 thin slices papaya
Cilantro sprigs

- In a large resealable plastic bag, combine oil, lime juice, soy sauce, red pepper sauce and ground coriander. Add shrimp and pepper squares, tossing to coat well. Close bag; marinate 30 minutes at room temperature.
- For Papaya Salsa, combine salsa ingredients, cover and set aside.
- Drain shrimp and pepper and thread on skewers, reserving marinade. Broil over hot coals until shrimp turn pink, 7 to 10 minutes, basting often with marinade. Fan 2 papaya slices on two muffin halves on each plate. Remove shrimp and peppers from skewers and arrange on muffin halves with salsa. Garnish with cilantro.
- Makes 6 servings.

1990 Bays® English Muffins National Recipe Contest

Here's a taste of the Grand Prize won by Jim Pleasants, a retired Army colonel from Williamsburg, Virginia: "A trip for two to France with a week of cooking lessons at the famous La Varenne cooking school in Burgundy. The school, located in the gracious 17th century Chateau du Fey, provides the perfect romantic and historical setting with over 100 acres of beautiful woodlands featuring an ancient walled garden..."

Recipe courtesy of Bays English Muffins

TRIP FOR TWO TO TUSCANY, ITALY

SMOKED SALMON WITH GINGER-LIME BUTTER

Put the champagne on ice — These are a must for meandering mornings with the brunch bunch or as an appetizer for the gourmet group.

1 tablespoon minced fresh ginger root
1 teaspoon lime zest
1 teaspoon fresh lime juice
½ cup unsalted butter at room temperature (1 stick)

6 BAYS® ENGLISH MUFFINS, split
9 ounces thinly sliced good quality smoked salmon
Fresh dill

- Combine ginger, lime zest, lime juice and butter. Set aside or store in covered jar in refrigerator up to 5 days.
- Lightly toast muffins in toaster or bake at 400° for 6 to 7 minutes. Spread each half with ginger-lime butter. Arrange 2 or 3 slices smoked salmon on top. Garnish with fresh dill sprigs.
- Makes 12 servings.

NOTE: To serve as an hors d'oeuvre, cut the muffin halves into 4 triangular pieces, then bake on cookie sheets and toast. Proceed as above, using only one slice salmon on each.

1991 Bays English Muffins National Recipe Contest

First-time contest entrant and Grand Prize winner Margaret McDaniel from Sun Valley, Idaho won... "A trip for two to Italy, including a week of classes at Lorenza Dé Medici's famous Villa Table cooking school. Nestled in the hills of Tuscany, the school is located in Dé Medici's landmark 11th century abbey home, which is opened in the fall and spring to small groups of students. At the school, mornings are filled with classes and demonstrations, followed by luncheons featuring the morning's preparations. Trips to the surrounding countryside occupy the afternoons. Throughout the stay, the winner can enjoy exquisite wine from the abbey's own winery, observe the making of local cheese, meats and breads, and explore the wooded countryside dotted with olive groves..."

Recipe courtesy of Bays English Muffins

TRIP FOR TWO TO BANGKOK, THAILAND

GLAZED SALMON MEDALLIONS

These have a definite British accent — In the old days, English muffins were sold in the streets of England by the "muffin man" whose trademarks were his tray of muffins and a bell; in 1729 a lady from Durham, England invented dry mustard by grinding mustard seeds in a mill, becoming famous for "Durham mustard."

1 pound skinless salmon fillets
1 package (10-ounces) frozen
   chopped spinach, cooked, well
   drained
1 tablespoon butter or margarine
Pinch nutmeg

Salt and freshly ground pepper to
   taste
4 BAYS® English Muffins, split
   and lightly toasted
8 slices tomato

English Mustard Sauce:
1 tablespoon dry mustard
½ cup mayonnaise
2 teaspoons bottled steak sauce

2 teaspoons Worcestershire sauce
3 to 4 tablespoons cream

- Preheat oven to Broil. Broil salmon on greased broiler pan until barely cooked in center, 5 to 7 minutes. Combine cooked spinach with butter, nutmeg, salt and pepper.

English Mustard Sauce:

- Combine dry mustard, mayonnaise, steak sauce and Worcestershire; gradually mix in cream to desired consistency (makes about ¾ cup). Brush Bays English Muffin halves with English Mustard Sauce. Top each half with spinach, a tomato slice and portion of salmon. Top generously with sauce; broil 2 minutes until glazed.

- Makes 4 servings.

**1992 Bays® English Muffins "Entrée to Thailand"
Recipe Contest**

First-time contest entrant Gail Gettleson of Bloomfield Hills, Michigan won the Grand Prize from among more than 1,500 entries. Her prize — one week of instruction for two at The Oriental Hotel's cooking school in Bangkok, Thailand and a choice of four days in the mountains of Chiang Mai or the beach resort of Phuket.

Recipe courtesy of Bays English Muffins

$10,000

SWISS BREAKFAST PARFAIT

Guaranteed to get kids, and adults, to eat breakfast. With only 4 ingredients, this appealing "pudding" can be made the night before, then layered with sliced strawberries in parfait glasses the next morning.

1 cup QUAKER® OATS (Quick or Old Fashioned), uncooked

2 (8-ounce) cartons nonfat or low-fat vanilla yogurt

1 (8-ounce) can crushed pineapple in juice, undrained

2 tablespoons sliced almonds (optional)

2 cups sliced fresh strawberries (or substitute 2 cups frozen strawberries, thawed, sliced)

- In medium bowl, combine oats, yogurt, pineapple and almonds; mix well. Cover; refrigerate overnight or up to 1 week.

- To serve, layer oat mixture and strawberries in 4 parfait glasses. Garnish with additional sliced strawberries, if desired. Serve chilled.

- Makes 4 servings.

1992 Second Annual Quaker® Oats "It's the Right Thing To Do" Recipe Contest

Recipe makeovers — favorite recipes that have been changed to make them more healthful — are what Quaker was seeking in this contest of four categories. Anne Dwyer, an elementary school teacher from Ft. Collins, Colorado whipped up a winner that demonstrates how eating a delicious, nutritious breakfast is not only the right, but the bright, thing to do.

Recipe courtesy of the Quaker Oats Company

FUN FOOD FINALS

THE STORY OF THE INTERNATIONAL CHILI SOCIETY'S WORLD CHAMPIONSHIP CHILI COOKOFFS

PART I

Lawlessness On The Old Chili Trail

...or...

How The Best Was Won (Or Was It?)

Some said that laws governing the making of the best Bowl O' Red were very precise indeed. Other folks simply declared that the only law of chili making was not having any law at all.

In 1967, to bean or not to bean, that was the question (except in Boston). It all started when...

Carroll Shelby — champion race car driver and designer of the Mustang Shelby Cobra, respected chili devotee, and a Texan to boot — saw red after reading an article that boasted "Nobody Knows More About Chili Than I Do." Them's fightin' words thought he. The author, humorist H. Allen Smith of New York, by making outrageous claims and boldly insisting that any decent bowl of chili *must* contain beans, was promptly challenged to a chili showdown.

And so it was that on October 21, 1967 Mr. Smith faced his opponent — Wick Fowler, the official chef of The Chili Appreciation Society, International — on the sagging front porch of the Chisos Oasis Saloon in Terlingua, Texas. Battling it out in front of 500 "chiliheads" (a term of endearment for chili-loving lawless varmints), a tie was declared by blindfolded judges at the "First Original World's Championship Chili Cookoff."

To his dying day, however, H. Allen Smith insisted that he had soundly whupped his challenger's "sissy Texas a—" (his words). Besides the beans and other ingredients, said he, the secret to superior chili is in the "genius of the cook" — one should never measure anything.

And so a new frontier opened up and the annual chili wars began in earnest.

Although it's difficult to argue with a guy whose name begins with an initial, Mr. Smith did not have the last word as Part II reveals.

$15,000

"NEVADA ANNIE" HARRIS'S 1978 WORLD CHAMPIONSHIP CHILI

A more genteel (read somewhat less hot) chili calling for a 12-ounce can of beer and a 12-ounce bottle of (?) mineral water. Note that only half the can of beer goes in the chili — the remainder is consumed.

3 medium-sized onions
2 medium-sized green peppers
2 large stalks celery
2 small cloves garlic
½, or more, small fresh jalapeño pepper
8 pounds lean chuck, coarsely ground
1 can (7 ounces) diced green chiles
2 cans (14½ ounces each) stewed tomatoes

1 can (15-ounces) tomato sauce
1 can (6 ounces) tomato paste
2 bottles (3 ounces each) chili powder
2 tablespoons cumin powder
Tabasco sauce to taste
1 can (12 ounces) beer
1 bottle (12 ounces) mineral water
2 to 3 bay leaves
Garlic salt
Salt and pepper to taste

- Dice and sauté first five ingredients. Add meat and brown. Add remaining ingredients, including ½ can beer (drink the remainder, says Annie). Add water just to cover top. Cook about 3 hours on low heat. Stir often. Freezes well.

- Serves 12 to 16.

1978 International Chili Society's
World Championship Chili Cookoff

As the first of the red hot chili-mommas to win the competition (it took just a little over a decade to do it), Laverne "Nevada Annie" Harris of Las Vegas brought a touch of feisty femininity to the male-dominated raging and rowdy world of chili warriors. The alfresco cookoff was held at the dusty, turn-of-the-century Tropico Gold Mine in the Mojave Desert where Annie struck the Mother Lode with her champion chili. Besides winning the $15,000 Grand Prize, Annie toted home a silver-plated chili bowl trophy.

Recipe courtesy of the International Chili Society

PART II
THE POT THICKENS

No bull about it, Mr. H. Allen Smith's article raised a ruckus. Short of a shoot-out, year after year there's a whole lot of fightin' and feudin' and clashin' and bashin' going on over who makes, and what constitutes, the best bowl of chili.

Somewhere along the line someone, a Texan no doubt, developed some "laws" for these megaton chili cookoff blow-outs. For example, in Rule No. 1:

"True chili is defined by the International Chili Society as any kind of meat, or combination of meats, cooked with chili peppers, various other spices, and other ingredients with the exception of items such as beans or spaghetti which are strictly forbidden."

However, in Rule No. 10:

"Each contestant must cook a minimum of two quarts of chili. Contestants are permitted to prepare only 1 pot of competition chili which may be submitted for judging. If they desire to prepare additional pots, for public tasting, such pots must contain beans or spaghetti."

More unusual rules regarding a contestant's special arrangements for participating in the cookoff are Rule Nos. 14 and 16:

"Official support team members may not exceed 25 people (of which a maximum of 10 can be included in the individual contestant's musical group). More than 25 must be approved by cookoff Chairman."

"All contestants who have special requirements or who plan to arrive by special vehicle (i.e. decorated cars or trucks, hot air balloons, or parachutes) are asked to notify the sponsors at least three days in advance..."

Tempted to make a foray into the fray? Be forewarned, just about the only thing that isn't disputed about chili is its popularity.

*Although the late **great northern** Mr. H. Allen Smith did not win the war of the beans, think of the fuse he could have lit had he written a follow-up article titled "Nobody Knows More About Having Fun Than I Do."*

$20,000

FRED DREXEL'S 1981 WORLD CHAMPIONSHIP BUTTERFIELD STAGELINE CHILI

Manly and meaty for the rough 'n' tough. This version contains a massive amount of beef brisket and ground pork with a shot of tequila and a can of beer thrown in for good measure.

4 white onions
1½ whole garlic bulbs, peeled
3 whole canned green chiles
10 pounds lean beef brisket, chopped fine
¼ cup cooking oil
3 tablespoons cumin
Salt to taste
Pinch of oregano
¼ teaspoon hot dry mustard

1½ cups tomato sauce
1½ cups whole tomatoes
½ ounce tequila
1 can (12 ounces) beer
2 pounds fresh ground pork
2 bottles (1.7 ounces each) Gebhardt chili powder
2 beef bouillon cubes
½ teaspoon brown sugar

- Chop onion, garlic and chiles fine. Brown brisket and onions in oil. Add all remaining ingredients. Heat to boiling, reduce heat, cover and simmer 2 to 3 hours, stirring occasionally, except last 30 minutes.
- Makes 15 or more hearty servings.

1981 International Chili Society's World Championship Chili Cookoff

Fred Drexel of Van Nuys, California led the six members of his Butterfield Stageline Chili Team to victory over 62 other entries. Mr. Drexel, the president of Automated Phone Corp., also received a three-foot-high chili pot trophy as the year's chili champeen.

Recipe courtesy of the International Chili Society

PART III

FUN RAISING & FUND RAISING

Nobody knows more about having fun than the International Chili Society folks. During the three-day extravaganzas millions of dollars have been raised, many of which benefit a wide variety of charities and non-profit organizations.

In the tongue-in-cheek spirit of Mr. Smith's 1967 article that sparked one of the fiercest wars in history, the World Championship Chili Cookoffs have been among the Nation's hottest spectator sports. Their popularity is evidenced not only by coverage on the ESPN Cable Network and local radio stations, but by much media hype.

Attracting more than 30,000 attendees annually, on-lookers get in on all the action and sample chili kickshaws with names like "Buzzard's Breath Chili," "Danté's Inferno Armadillo Chili," and "50,000-Watt Chili." There has even been chocolate chili, featuring Mexican chocolate with a pinch of cinnamon and ginger.

Besides the cookoff itself, highlights of the 1992 three-day event held at "Rawhide," an 1880's western town in Scottsdale, Arizona, included:

- First Annual World Championship Chili Cookoff Men's and Women's Celebrity Golf Tournament
- Miss Chili Pepper and Mr. Hot Sauce
- Skydivers
- Chris Mitchum's Celebrity Rodeo
- Board of Governors Hayride and Steak Fry
- KMLE Country 108 Radio Dance and Show

On the competitive circuit, chili aficionados have tried just about everything short of whipping up their killer concoctions in a kerosene can and flambéeing the contents. And they've thrown in everything from filet mignon to filé powder, and critters such as kangaroo and rattlesnake, plus an assortment of booze — bourbon, tequila, beer from north and south of the border, and moonshine from the hills of Virginia.

Standing in the wings to support the cookoffs are sponsors such as Hunt-Wesson, Inc., Budweiser, Tabasco Sauce, Pepsico, and many others. And, yep, Pepto Bismol is among 'em too.

$25,000

CAROL HANCOCK'S 1985 WORLD CHAMPIONSHIP SHOTGUN WILLIE CHILI

RED ALERT. Watch out for the pepper paste and proceed with caution. After negotiating that dangerous curve and heeding the STOP signs at 14 garlic cloves and 16 tablespoons of chili powder, you're back on the road again with this chili named for singer Willie Nelson.

Pepper Paste:
½ pound dried red chili peppers

4 cups beef broth	6 pounds beef bottom round
½ teaspoon sugar	roast, cubed or coarsely ground
14 cloves garlic, crushed	Salad oil
2 tablespoons red wine vinegar	4 medium onions, finely diced
1 teaspoon Tabasco pepper sauce	16 tablespoons chili powder
1½ tablespoons dried oregano	2 tablespoons ground cumin
leaves	1 can (15 ounces) tomato sauce
1 cup water	1 tablespoon monosodium
1 teaspoon ground red pepper	glutamate (optional)
Salt to taste	1½ cups pepper paste, recipe
	below

Pepper Paste:

- Boil dried red chili peppers in water to cover for approximately 1 hour, or until pulp separates from skin. Discard seeds; scrape pulp from skin; mash into a paste. Makes 1½ cups.

- In large heavy skillet brown beef, one fourth at a time, in hot oil. Remove meat to chili pot as it browns. In same skillet, sauté onions until tender. Add onions and remaining ingredients to meat, blending well. Cover and simmer 2 hours, stirring occasionally.

- Makes 3 quarts, or 12 (1-cup) servings.

1985 International Chili Society's
World Championship Chili Cookoff

Definitely something to get fired up about, it was the rootin' tootin' secret blend of seasonings she rustled up and named for her friend Willie Nelson that clinched the Grand Prize win for Carol Hancock of Los Altos, California.

Recipe courtesy of the International Chili Society

CHILI STARS

History records that Jesse James consumed a few bowls of "red" before pulling many of his bank heists. It is also said that Will Rogers judged a town by its chili and that Billy the Kid even allowed as how anyone who likes chili ain't all bad.

Perhaps the notorious behavior of the two more shady characters can be blamed on the effect of the little red-hot pods of the *Capsicum* (chile pepper) family of which there are 5 species and some 300 varieties. If it's true that "you are what you eat," then at least a partial explanation is provided for the reputation of the wild west and the explosive personalities that dominated it.

In any case, over the years many celebrities have added to the chili controversy with their own specialties and blends of TNT. Among them, listed with their secret ingredients, are:

- Craig Claiborne (heavy on the garlic and beef broth)
- Perry Como (corn)
- "Festus" Ken Curtis (venison)
- Pete Fountain (onion soup)
- A. J. Foyt (Spanish chorizo sausage and Mexican beer)
- James Garner (honey and brown sugar)
- Janet Guthrie (3 cans of refried beans and grated lemon rind)
- Tom T. Hall (jalapeño bean dip)
- Parnelli Jones (sugar)
- Les McCann (bacon)
- Minnie Pearl (only 10 ingredients, 3 of 'em heat)
- Carroll Shelby (goat cheese)

These wild, racy recipes, and many others, can be found in the International Chili Society's **Official Chili Cookbook**.

THE LAST WORD... MAYBE

That recognized authority, the august Mr. Webster, obviously did not consult with a Texan before constructing his definition of "chili con carne" (literally, chile peppers with meat):

> **chili con carne**: a spiced stew of ground beef and minced chilies or chili powder usu. with beans.

To bean, or not to bean that is still the question. The conclusion can be drawn that, except in Texas, the question can never be definitively resolved — not even in a *chiliad*, defined by Mr. Webster in precisely the same language as *millenium*, "a period of 1000 years."

And so the chili war happily simmers on.

Want to enter the fracas? To become a card carrying member and Charter Chilihead of the International Chili Society, or to order the **Official Chili Cookbook** *containing anecdotes and history, plus Mr. Allen's humorous 1967 article in its entirety and many recipes, contact:*

International Chili Society
P.O. Box 2966
Newport Beach, California 92663

BEST GUBERNATORIAL CHILI

FIRE BRIGADE CHILI

This one should carry a HAZ-MAT warning label.

3 pounds beef chuck, diced
3 cups water
1 cup beef broth
1 can (8 ounces) tomato sauce
6 tablespoons garlic powder
¼ cup hot chili powder
¼ cup mild chili powder
3 tablespoons cumin

3 tablespoons minced onion
2 tablespoons paprika
1 tablespoon ground red pepper
1 tablespoon sugar
2 teaspoons salt
Chopped tomato and green onion,
　shredded Cheddar cheese and
　sour cream, for garnish

- In large skillet brown meat over high heat in 3 batches, transferring to a Dutch oven with a slotted spoon. Add remaining ingredients. Bring to a boil; reduce heat and simmer, uncovered, stirring occasionally, 1½ to 2 hours. Garnish as desired.
- Makes 6 cups.

1987 LADIES' HOME JOURNAL Great Chili Cook-Off

LADIES' HOME JOURNAL invited the Governors of all fifty states to submit their favorite, but not necessarily original, chili recipes for judging in a blind taste test. Among the judges were food columnists William Rice of the **Chicago Tribune** *and Pierre Franey of* **The New York Times**, *the JOURNAL's own food editors, and Dotty Griffith, food editor of* **The Dallas Morning News** *and author of "Wild About Chili."*

This winning recipe, submitted by Oregon's Governor Neil Goldschmidt, had been an earlier prizewinner from the Great Northwest Chili Cook-Off. Second Place went to the State of Washington and third place to Virginia — Texas wasn't even among the Honorable Mentions! A consolation, at least, was that there was not a bean to be found in the winning recipe, but LADIES' HOME JOURNAL did not guarantee Ms. Griffith's safe return to Dallas.

$1,000

MY "OUT-OF-THIS-WORLD" FIERY FRUITED CHILI

¼ cup vegetable oil
2 pound mixture of lean cubed beef, pork and lamb
1 (16-ounce) package frozen chopped onions
2 (16-ounce) cans tomatoes, drained
2 (6-ounce) cans tomato paste
¼ cup chili powder
1 envelope Italian salad dressing mix
1 (4-ounce) can hot chiles, chopped

2 (16-ounce) cans red kidney beans, drained
2 teaspoons cumin powder
1 (32-ounce) bottle OCEAN SPRAY CRANAPPLE® Cranberry Apple Drink, reserving 3 tablespoons
11 ounces cream cheese, softened
1 cup halved green grapes
2 tablespoons chopped maraschino cherries
Toasted rye bread triangles
1 (20-ounce) can pineapple chunks

- Heat oil in a Dutch oven or large pot. Add meat and brown on all sides. Remove from pan and set aside. Add onion to pot. Cook until the onions become translucent, about 5 minutes. Return meat to pot. Add tomatoes, tomato paste, chili powder, salad dressing mix, chiles, kidney beans, cumin and cranberry apple drink; stir. Cover and cook 1½ hours over medium-low heat, stirring occasionally.

- Meanwhile, combine cream cheese with enough of the reserved cranberry apple drink to make spreading consistency. Add grapes and cherries, mix well. Spread on rye triangles. Set aside until serving time.

- Add pineapple chunks and juice to chili. Break up tomatoes with a fork. Bring to a boil. Serve with rye triangles.

- Makes 8 servings.

1991 Ocean Spray® Distinctive Taste Recipe Contest

Angelina Martis of Merrillville, Indiana took top prize in the Entrées category for her chili recipe that "bog"gles the imagination. A dish of contrasts, it stands alone in showcasing the versatility of cranberries.

Recipe courtesy of Ocean Spray Cranberries, Inc.

TRIP TO NEW YORK
AMERICAN PIECE-A-PIE

As the first prizewinning dish I (the author) ever tasted, this was my introduction to the world of contest cooking and the recipe that launched this cookbook...

It was 1954 and our family had been invited to spend the day and have dinner with friends. When my friend, Evelyn, asked her Mother, "Mom, what's for dinner?" I realize now that I was intrigued with the answer: "It's something called 'American Piece-A-Pie.' I just cut the recipe out of the paper because it was a winner at the Pillsbury Bake-Off and sounded good. Since you kids like pizza so much, I thought we'd give it a try."

At a time when Americans seemed to believe that pizza was their own invention, what could be more American than chili-cheeseburger pizza...

1½ to 2 cups PILLSBURY BEST® All Purpose or Unbleached Flour
1 tablespoon sugar
½ teaspoon salt
½ teaspoon chili powder
1 package active dry yeast
¼ cup water

3 tablespoons shortening
¼ cup tomato sauce (from 8-ounce can, reserving remaining for topping)
1 egg
2 tablespoons margarine or butter, melted, if desired

Hamburger Topping:
½ pound ground beef
¼ cup chopped onion
¾ cup reserved tomato sauce
½ teaspoon chili powder

⅛ teaspoon pepper
8 ounces (2 cups) shredded American cheese

- Lightly spoon flour into measuring cup; level off. In large bowl, combine 1 cup flour, sugar, salt, ½ teaspoon chili powder and yeast; blend well. In small saucepan, heat water, shortening and ¼ cup tomato sauce until very warm (120° to 130°). Add warm liquid and egg to flour mixture. Blend at low speed until moistened; beat 2 minutes at medium speed. By hand, stir in an additional ¼ to ½ cup flour until dough pulls cleanly away from sides of bowl.

- On floured surface, knead in ¼ to ½ cup flour until dough is smooth and elastic, about 3 minutes. Place dough in greased bowl; cover loosely with plastic wrap and cloth towel. Let rise in a warm place (80° to 85°) until light and doubled in size, 30 to 45 minutes.

Hamburger Topping:

- Meanwhile, prepare Hamburger Topping. In medium skillet brown ground beef and onion; drain. Stir in ¾ cup tomato sauce, ½ teaspoon chili powder, and pepper.

- Heat oven to 425°. Grease 15 x 10 x 1-inch baking pan. Punch down dough several times to remove all air bubbles. Press dough into greased baking pan; brush with melted margarine. Top with hamburger mixture and sprinkle evenly with cheese. Bake at 425° for 15 to 20 minutes or until crust is golden brown and cheese is melted. Serve hot.

- Makes 6 servings.

1954 — Pillsbury Bake-Off® 6

The Grand Prize this year was won by "Open Sesame Pie" which made history of its own — the recipe and the story are included in the "Pillsbury Bake-Off® Grand Prize Hall of Fame" section. As the creator of "American Piece-A-Pie," Jamie Marie Chisam of Oak Park, Illinois was one of the Junior Winners who won a trip to New York, including a stay at the Waldorf-Astoria Hotel, and a pocketful of spending money.

Reprinted by permission of The Pillsbury Company

$1,000 SAVINGS BOND

PEPPERONI "PIZZA" CASSEROLE

A pizzazzy new way to paraphrase "pizza."

2 bags UNCLE BEN'S® Rice
Boil-in-Bag Family Servings (or
4 cups cooked UNCLE
BEN'S® CONVERTED®
Brand Rice or UNCLE BEN'S®
RICE IN AN INSTANT® may
be substituted)
2 eggs
¼ cup (1 ounce) grated Parmesan
cheese
1 teaspoon oregano leaves,
crushed

½ teaspoon garlic powder
1 jar (14 to 16 ounces) spaghetti
sauce
3 to 5 ounces sliced pepperoni
1 can (4 ounces) sliced
mushrooms, drained
1 green bell pepper, thinly sliced
into rings
1 package (8 ounces) shredded
mozzarella cheese

- Preheat oven to 350°. Cook rice according to package directions.
  Combine rice, eggs, Parmesan cheese, oregano and garlic powder; mix
  well. Spread into greased 13 x 9-inch baking pan. Bake 10 minutes or
  until firm.

- Spread spaghetti sauce over rice; top evenly with pepperoni, mushrooms, pepper rings and mozzarella cheese. Continue baking 15
  minutes or until hot and bubbly.

- Makes 8 servings.

1990 Uncle Ben's® Teen Cuisine Recipe Contest

*Matt Itallie, an eighth grader from Poughkeepsie, New York showed Uncle
Ben how to make a champion "pizza" in this contest for high school and
junior high school students only.*

Recipe courtesy of Uncle Ben's, Inc.

TRIP FOR TWO TO ENGLAND
REUBEN PIZZA

Crust:
1 tablespoon or packet active dry
　yeast
1 cup warm water (110°)
1 teaspoon sugar
1½ tablespoons oil
1 clove garlic, pressed

1½ tablespoons caraway seeds
½ teaspoon salt
3 cups KING ARTHUR®
　Unbleached All-Purpose Flour
Olive oil to brush on crust

Topping:
½ pound grated Swiss cheese
2 cups well-drained sauerkraut
1 pound sliced corned beef

1 pound grated mozzarella cheese
Freshly ground pepper

• In a large bowl, dissolve yeast in warm water, add sugar, and allow to stand for 5 minutes, until foamy. Add oil, garlic, caraway seeds and salt. Add flour one half cup at a time, stirring until dough begins to pull away from sides of bowl. Knead dough on a floured board for 5-10 minutes, adding more flour as needed. Place dough in greased bowl, turning once to coat top. Cover with plastic wrap and allow dough to rise in a warm place for about 15 minutes. Do not allow dough to become overlight. When dough has risen, divide into two pieces and roll each piece to fit a 12-inch round pizza pan, or a 13 x 9-inch rectangular pan. Form a small rim around the edge of the pizza. Place in greased pan, prick dough all over with a fork and allow to rise for another 15 minutes. Brush crust lightly with olive oil and bake in the middle of a preheated 400° oven for about 10 minutes, or until lightly browned.

• Divide topping ingredients evenly between the two pizzas and place on top of crust in the following order: Swiss cheese, sauerkraut, corned beef, mozzarella and pepper. Bake for 10-20 minutes more, until cheese is bubbling. Serve immediately.

• Makes two 12-inch round or two rectangular pizzas.

Recipe developed by Emily Koch of Schenectady, New York for the 1992 King Arthur® Flour WinterBake. Recipe courtesy of the King Arthur Flour Co.

$32,000

ROUND REUBEN PIZZA

Reuben offers a new perspective on pizza, with secret ingredients from "crust" to crest.

Crust:

5 cups cooked rice

1 cup (4 ounces) shredded KRAFT® Natural Swiss Cheese

¼ cup (1 ounce) KRAFT® 100% Grated Parmesan Cheese

2 eggs, beaten

2 teaspoons caraway seed

Filling:

2 packages (8 ounces each) PHILADELPHIA® BRAND Cream Cheese, softened

2 tablespoons KRAFT® Horseradish Mustard

1 can (16 ounces) sauerkraut, drained, rinsed

½ pound sliced corned beef, cut into strips

2 cups (8 ounces) shredded KRAFT® Natural Swiss Cheese

¼ cup (1 ounce) KRAFT® 100% Grated Parmesan Cheese

⅓ cup sliced pitted ripe olives

¼ cup chopped pimiento, drained

¼ cup chopped fresh parsley

Crust:

• Preheat oven to 450°. Mix rice, Swiss and Parmesan cheese, eggs and caraway seed; press onto bottom and sides of greased 12-inch pizza pan. Bake 15 to 18 minutes or until lightly browned.

Filling:

• Mix cream cheese and mustard until well blended. Spread over crust. Layer sauerkraut, meat, Swiss and Parmesan cheese over cream cheese mixture. Bake 10 minutes or until Swiss cheese is melted. Top with olives, pimiento and parsley.

• Makes 8 servings.

1984 Kraft® Cheesefest Lifestyle Recipe Contest

In this "cheesefest lifestyle" contest, six categories— (1) For Singles, (2) For Couples, (3) For Men Only, (4) For Working Women, (5) For Young Marrieds and (6) For Family Fare—required using at least one of ten varieties of Kraft cheese products. This Grand Prize recipe proves once again that Reuben's always a winner.

Recipe courtesy of Kraft General Foods, Inc.

$10,000 & 7 KitchenAid APPLIANCES

BRANIZZA

Pizza-style meatloaf with the works, but not the guilt.

1½ cups KELLOGG'S® ALL-
  BRAN® Cereal
1½ pounds lean ground round
  beef
2 egg whites, slightly beaten
¼ cup skim milk
1 cup chopped onions
2 teaspoons Italian seasoning

1 can (8 ounces) tomato sauce
  with Italian seasoning
1 can (8 ounces) pizza sauce
2 cups (8 ounces) shredded part-
  skim mozzarella cheese
1 large green bell pepper, thinly
  sliced
½ cup grated Parmesan cheese

- Preheat oven to 400°. In a large mixing bowl, combine Kellogg's All-Bran Cereal, beef, egg whites, milk, onions and seasoning. Let stand 5 minutes or until cereal is softened.

- Evenly press meat mixture into an 11 x 15 x 2-inch baking pan. Stir together tomato and pizza sauces; spread over meat mixture. Sprinkle sauce with mozzarella cheese, pepper slices and Parmesan cheese.

- Bake about 30 minutes or until cheese is bubbly and edges begin to brown. Cut into 18 slices. Serve hot.

- Makes 18 slices.

1991 Kellogg's® All-Bran® "Healthy Life" Recipe Contest

Grace Crispo of Norwell, Massachusetts developed this winning recipe while trying to increase her family's dietary fiber. Selected as the best from more than 4,000 entries, Grace's version of pizza offers a healthy alternative to enjoying two American favorites — meat loaf and pizza.

Recipe courtesy of the Kellogg Company

$1,000

BEEF 'N' BREW

*These picnic-going slices of twice-marinated roast beef **must** be prepared in advance.*

5-pound sirloin-tip roast of beef
1 bottle (16-ounces) beer
¼ cup flour
¼ teaspoon salt

½ teaspoon garlic salt
½ teaspoon onion salt
⅛ teaspoon pepper
¼ cup vegetable oil

Marinade:

½ cup vegetable oil
¼ cup red wine vinegar
½ cup tomato purée
½ cup prepared marinara sauce
¼ cup Burgundy wine

½ cup dry sherry
½ teaspoon salt
¼ teaspoon onion salt
¼ teaspoon garlic salt
⅛ teaspoon pepper

- Place roast in plastic bag. Add beer, close tightly, place in bowl. Refrigerate overnight (at least 12 hours), turning roast once or twice. Preheat oven to 325°. Remove roast from bag, reserving beer. Combine flour, salt, garlic and onion salts, and pepper. Rub mixture into roast. Insert meat thermometer in center of thickest part of roast. Place on rack in roasting pan. Roast, uncovered, 1 hour and 50 minutes to 2 hours, basting roast every 10 to 15 minutes with ¼ vegetable oil mixed with ½ cup of the reserved beer. Meat thermometer should register 140° for rare. Meat should be rare to medium rare for more complete absorption of marinade. Let roast cool completely.

Marinade:

- Combine marinade ingredients, mixing well, and place in a large casserole. Slice roast for sandwiches (not too thick) and place in marinade. Refrigerate, covered, overnight — at least 12 hours. Or serve warm with marinade heated thoroughly and poured over meat. Next day, take beef to picnic in casserole. Serve on pumpernickel along with beer or red wine.

- Makes 12 servings.

Recipe developed by Carole Gilbert of Parsippany, New York for the 1971 McCALL'S Fourth-of-July Picnic Cooking Contest. Recipe courtesy of McCALL'S/The New York Times Company Women's Magazines.

$5,000 & TRIP TO NEW YORK

CHICKEN AVOCADO STUFFED SOURDOUGH SANDWICHES

Grilled chicken and avocado sandwiches with Avocado Hollandaise.

4 (1-inch-thick) slices sourdough bread
Butter or margarine
2 cups diced or cubed cooked chicken

1 cup (4 ounces) shredded Swiss cheese
1 teaspoon lemon pepper (or to taste)
2 small AVOCADOS, cubed

Avocado Hollandaise Dressing:

2 large eggs
¼ cup lemon juice
½ cup hot, melted butter or margarine

1 AVOCADO, chopped
1 teaspoon salt
Dash ground red pepper
Onion powder to taste

- With a sharp knife, cut open one end of each slice of bread to form a pocket. Butter the bread slices on both sides.

- In a bowl, combine the chicken, cheese, pepper and avocado, and mix until blended; spoon the mixture into the bread pockets and secure with wooden picks if necessary. In a hot skillet over medium heat, grill the sandwiches until browned on both sides. Serve with Avocado Hollandaise Dressing.

Avocado Hollandaise Dressing:

- In a food processor or blender, blend the eggs with the lemon juice until lemon-colored. At low speed, slowly add the hot butter and blend until smooth. Add the avocado; blend until smooth. Mix in the salt, red pepper and onion powder.

- Makes 4 servings.

1991 McCALL'S California Avocado Recipe Contest

Leave it to a Californian to come up with the top prizewinning recipe in this contest co-sponsored by McCALL'S and the California Avocado Commission. Linda Towson of Rancho Cucamonga, California flew across the country to participate in the Great Avocado Cook-Off held in New York.

Recipe courtesy of McCALL'S/The New York Times Company Women's Magazines and the California Avocado Commission

$5,000

GOLDEN GATE GRILL

As one of the world's greatest convenience foods, this sandwich is dressed up San Francisco deli-style.

12 ounces BUTTERBALL® Deli Turkey Breast, thinly sliced
1 egg, beaten
¼ cup milk or half and half
8 slices large oval sourdough French bread
Grated Parmesan or Romano cheese
1 small avocado, seeded, peeled and sliced

1 tomato, thinly sliced
2 tablespoons chopped fresh cilantro
4 slices red onion, separated into rings
4 slices Monterey Jack cheese
2 tablespoons butter or margarine, softened
1 clove garlic, minced
⅛ teaspoon crushed red pepper

- Combine egg and milk. Dip one side of bread in egg mixture, then in Parmesan cheese. Arrange turkey on undipped side of 4 slices of bread. Place avocado, tomato, cilantro and red onion on turkey. Top with Monterey Jack cheese and remaining bread, dipped side up.

- Combine butter, garlic and red pepper. Preheat a large skillet over medium heat. Melt 1 tablespoon butter mixture in skillet. Brown both sides of two sandwiches until crisp. Repeat with remaining butter and sandwiches. Serve immediately.

- Makes 4 sandwiches.

1987 Swift-Eckrich "Taste America" Deli Recipe Contest

Let's talk turkey... and salami, pepperoni, ham, corned beef, pastrami, and bologna too. For this contest Swift-Eckrich asked for entries for Appetizers, Entrées and Sandwiches using any of its wide variety of deli meat products. In addition to the Grand Prize, there were 15 First Prizes of $750 each and 50 $250 Second Prizes. Since he is credited with inventing the sandwich, the Earl of Sandwich should have been a judge — he would have loved this contest.

Recipe courtesy of Armour Swift-Eckrich

$5,000

LAWRY'S LUSCIOUS LUAU BURGER

Here's the real cheeseburger in paradise — the cheese and a pineapple slice are tucked inside each well-seasoned and sauced burger.

2 pounds lean ground beef
¼ cup water
1 teaspoon LAWRY'S® Seasoned Salt
1 teaspoon onion salt
½ teaspoon LAWRY'S® Lemon Pepper

1 tablespoon Worcestershire sauce
¼ cup minced or finely grated green pepper
1 (20-ounce) can sliced pineapple (10 slices), drained and juice reserved
8 tablespoons cheese spread

Mustard Sauce:
1 cup mayonnaise
¼ cup Dijon-style mustard
¼ cup reserved pineapple juice

½ teaspoon LAWRY'S® Lemon Pepper
4 English muffins, split

- Preheat oven to Broil. Combine ground beef, water, Seasoned Salt, onion salt, Lemon Pepper, Worcestershire sauce and green pepper; mix well. Shape into 16 equal sized balls and flatten into patties ½ inch larger than pineapple slice. Place a pineapple slice on 8 patties and place 1 tablespoon cheese spread on top of pineapple slice. Cover with remaining patties, sealing securely by pressing edges of patties together. Set aside.

Mustard Sauce:

- Blend together mayonnaise, mustard, reserved pineapple juice and Lemon Pepper. Brush a little on each muffin half and brown under broiler. Keep warm.

- Broil hamburger patties 8 inches from heat, 10 to 12 minutes or until done, turning once. Place hamburgers on prepared muffin halves and top with remaining Mustard Sauce. Garnish with broiled pineapple slices quartered.

- Makes 8 servings.

Recipe developed by Catherine Bugnitz of Florissant, Missouri for the 1977 Lawry's® "World's Greatest Hamburger" Recipe Contest. Recipe courtesy of Lawry's® Foods, Inc.

$10,000

NAPA VALLEY BASIL-SMOKED BURGERS

2 pounds ground sirloin
¼ cup SUTTER HOME
ZINFANDEL
¼ cup lightly packed minced
fresh basil
¼ cup minced red onion
¼ cup fine fresh Italian bread
crumbs
8 sun-dried tomatoes packed in
oil, drained and finely chopped
1 to 2 teaspoons garlic salt
Vegetable oil for brushing on grill
rack

8 fresh basil sprigs moistened
with water for tossing onto the
fire
6 large seeded sandwich rolls,
split
6 slices Monterey Jack cheese
⅔ cup light mayonnaise
2 tablespoons prepared basil pesto
Red leaf lettuce leaves
6 large tomato slices, about ¼-
inch thick
Paper-thin red onion rings
Fresh basil sprigs (optional)

- In a grill with a cover, prepare a medium-hot fire for direct-heat cooking.

- In a medium-sized bowl, lightly combine the sirloin, Zinfandel, minced basil, minced onion, bread crumbs, sun-dried tomatoes, and garlic salt to taste. Divide the meat mixture into 6 equal portions and shape into round patties.

- Brush the grill rack with vegetable oil. Toss the basil sprigs directly onto the coals, then place the patties on the grill and cook, turning once, until done to your preference (5 to 8 minutes on each side). During the last few minutes of cooking, place the rolls, cut side down, on the outer edges of the grill to toast lightly. During the last minute or so of cooking, top each patty with a cheese slice.

- Meanwhile, in a small bowl, combine the mayonnaise and pesto. Spread the mixture on the cut side of the toasted rolls. On the bottom half of each roll, layer the lettuce, burger, tomato slice and onion ring. Add basil sprigs, if desired, and roll tops.

- Makes 6 burgers.

Recipe developed by Jim Pleasants of Williamsburg, Virginia for the 1990 Sutter Home Winery "Build A Better Burger" Recipe Contest. Recipe courtesy of Sutter Home Winery.

$10,000

LAMBURGERS À LA GREQUE WITH CILANTRO-MINT CHUTNEY

Cilantro Mint Chutney:

⅔ cup plain yogurt
4 tablespoons yellow onion, chopped
3 medium jalapeño peppers, seeded and chopped
3 tablespoons fresh ginger root, chopped

1½ cups fresh cilantro leaves
⅔ cup fresh mint leaves
2 large garlic cloves, chopped
1 teaspoon kosher salt
1 pinch sugar

Burger:

2 pounds lean ground sirloin
2 pounds lean ground lamb
2 cloves garlic, minced
1 cup Feta cheese, crumbled
⅔ cup Kalamata olives, minced
2 teaspoons kosher salt
½ cup fruity extra-virgin olive oil

2 teaspoons *each* ground cumin and ground coriander, mixed
12 medium pita pockets (thicker variety)
Slices of tomato, thinly sliced red onion, red lettuce leaves, for garnish

Cilantro Mint Chutney:

- Combine all ingredients in a blender or processor and blend thoroughly. Chill to incorporate the flavors (may be prepared a day ahead).

- In a grill with a cover, prepare a medium-hot fire with natural hardwood charcoal for direct-heat cooking.

- To make the burgers, combine sirloin, lamb, garlic, Feta cheese, olives, and salt in a large bowl. Carefully divide the mixture into 12 patties. Brush the meat with olive oil (this will aid in the searing of the meat), then sprinkle with the spice mixture. Brush the grill with olive oil. Place the patties on the grill, turning once, until cooked to your preference (5-8 minutes per side). Place the burgers in lightly toasted pita pockets. Serve with a dash of the chutney and the garnish for the guest to assemble as desired.

- Makes 12 burgers.

Recipe developed by Robert Chirico of Greenfield, Massachusetts for the 1991 Sutter Home Winery "Build A Better Burger" Recipe Contest. Recipe courtesy of Sutter Home Winery.

LINCOLN CONTINENTAL

CURRIED ORIENTAL TIDBITS

Will satisfy any snack attack or a case of the midnight munchies.

2 (3-ounce) cans LaCHOY® Chow
  Mein Noodles
1 (8-ounce) can LaCHOY® Water
  Chestnuts, drained, sliced
1 cup whole, unblanched almonds
¼ cup grated Parmesan cheese

¼ cup butter, melted
1 tablespoon LaCHOY® Soy
  Sauce
1 teaspoon curry powder
¼ teaspoon seasoned salt

- Preheat oven to 325°.
- In a large bowl combine noodles with water chestnuts and almonds. Mix remaining ingredients; add to noodle mixture, tossing lightly until well blended. Spread mixture evenly on ungreased 15 x 10 x 1-inch baking pan.
- Bake for 15 minutes, stirring occasionally. Serve warm.
- Makes about 6 cups.

1978 LaChoy® "Swing American" Recipe Contest

Besides a Lincoln Continental, Grand Prize winner Maurine Vaughan from Richmond, Virginia was awarded a 6-piece set of His-and-Hers Samsonite luggage. A total of 1,531 prizes were awarded, including five First Prizes of $1,000 plus 6-piece sets of His-and-Hers luggage, 10 microwave ovens, 15 diamond cocktail rings, 500 Lady Manhattan signature blouses, and 1,000 Vera designer scarves.

Recipe courtesy of Hunt-Wesson, Inc.

$2,500

HOG WILD PARTY MIX

Guaranteed for success at your next pigskin party or Super Bowl bash.

1 pound sliced BACON, cut into
  1-inch pieces
3 quarts freshly popped popcorn,
  unsalted
1 can (5 ounces) chow mein
  noodles

1 can unsalted cashews or walnuts
⅓ cup butter or margarine, melted
¼ to ½ teaspoon seasoned salt
½ cup grated Parmesan cheese

• Preheat oven to 350°.

• Cook bacon in a large frying pan over medium heat until crisp; drain
on paper towel.

• Combine popcorn, noodles and cashews. Combine butter and seasoned salt; drizzle over popcorn mixture, tossing lightly to coat. Stir in
bacon. Spoon popcorn mixture into two 13 x 9 x 2-inch baking pans.
Bake 5 to 8 minutes or until heated through. Sprinkle with cheese,
tossing lightly.

• Makes about 4½ quarts.

1990 "Makin' Bacon" Recipe Contest

*Retiree John Winch of South Euclid, Ohio must have enjoyed developing
this Grand Prize recipe in the Appetizer category. Hope he went hog wild
with that extra $2,500 in his pocket too; three other category Grand Prize
winners also won $2,500 each.*

Recipe courtesy of the National Live Stock and Meat Board

JUST FOR FUN

RECIPE CONTEST LORE AND MORE

Mid-1800's

The origins of competition cooking are pure Americana. Their roots can be traced directly to family farms of the mid-nineteenth century. It was then that state and county fairs began honoring creative homemakers with bright colored ribbons for their delicious homemade specialties.

These cooks were not professionals. They were our foremothers who not only loved to cook, but whose main ingredient *was* love. Whether it was a blue First Prize, a purple Grand Champion, or a gold Best of Show ribbon that was placed beside a treasured heirloom cake, bread, or preserve, these dedicated cooks experienced the incomparable thrill of winning.

Early 1900's

Despite the fact that most home cooking was done on mostly inaccurate, unmanageable stoves — at least by today's standards — commercial recipe contests began to appear about the turn of the century. In 1904 the Charles B. Knox Gelatin Company, Inc. announced what is possibly the earliest commercial recipe contest. Fannie Farmer, cooking school founder and cookbook author famous for establishing accurate, level measurements in cookery, was one of its judges.

KNOX'S GELATINE

What to Do with Your Empty Knox Gelatine Boxes :
Save them—send them to me any time before Jan. 1, 1905, in bundles of 13 only, and send a new recipe with each bundle of 13.
For the BEST Recipe Received **$1,000 Steinway Piano**
I AM GOING TO GIVE A
which the winner may personally select, and additional **VALUABLE GIFTS** for other good recipes. Commence saving the boxes now.
Write me a postal for particulars.
KNOX'S GELATINE — Recipe Dept. 3 Knox Ave., Johnstown, N. Y.
The only guaranteed Gelatine. Your money cheerfully returned if you are not more than pleased — CHAS. B. KNOX.

When writing to advertisers please mention LESLIE'S MAGAZINE.

"KNOX" is a registered trademark of the Thomas J. Lipton Company; reprinted by permission.

A Steinway piano was the Grand Prize offered in this contest but it was the Third Prize recipe that was bound for destiny as an American classic. Mrs. John E. Cooke of New Castle, Pennsylvania was awarded a sewing machine for her for "Perfection Salad" and the Knox company distributed the recipe far and wide. It has been reprinted in countless cookbooks and, as often happens with prizewinning recipes, has become so absorbed in American kitchen culture that its origin has been obscured with time and use.

When "Perfection Salad" won the Knox contest, gelatin was very much in vogue. Its popularity skyrocketed even farther after modern refrigeration debuted in the 1930's.

Knox's Gelatine

The only odorless—the absolutely pure—the one guaranteed Gelatine. It may not be in highest favor with poorly informed or indifferent housewives, but it certainly is pronounced the best by all the rest.

Third Prize Winner.

A $100 SEWING MACHINE.

PERFECTION SALAD.

½ package Knox's Gelatine,
½ cup cold water,
½ cup vinegar,
Juice of one lemon,
1 pt. boiling water,
½ cup sugar,
1 teaspoon salt,
2 cups celery cut in small pieces,
1 cup finely shredded cabbage,
¼ can sweet red peppers, finely cut.

Soak Gelatine in cold water two minutes, add vinegar, lemon juice, boiling water, sugar and salt. Strain, and when beginning to set add remaining ingredients. Turn into a mold and chill. Serve on lettuce leaves with mayonnaise dressing, or cut in dice and serve in cases made of red or green peppers.

A delicious accompaniment to cold sliced chicken or veal.

MR. CHARLES B. KNOX,
DEAR SIR:

Enclosed please find receipt for salad. It is one of the finest salads I have ever had, was made with Knox's Gelatine and can be served in so many different ways. I am going to have this salad served at our next church supper if I can, where we always feed from two hundred to two hundred and fifty people. This salad is especially fine with fried oysters. I never use anything except Knox's Gelatine because it "jells" so quickly. Trusting this will meet with your approval, I remain,

Yours,
MRS. JOHN E. COOKE,
174 Boyles Ave., New Castle, Pa.

BIRTH OF A CLASSIC RECIPE ... In 1905, Charles Knox ran a cookery contest, and Fannie Farmer was one of the judges. The third prize, a sewing machine, was awarded to Mrs. John E. Cooke of New Castle, Pa., who submitted a recipe she called Perfection Salad. The recipe was widely distributed and was greeted with such enthusiasm it is now considered an American classic. Just about every newspaper and magazine in the country has run the recipe for Perfection Salad since that time.

The leaflet that announced the contest winners read sternly, "Knox's Gelatine—the only odorless—the absolutely pure—the one guaranteed Gelatine. It may not be in highest favor with poorly informed or indifferent housewives, but it certainly is pronounced the best by all the rest."

"KNOX" is a registered trademark of the Thomas J. Lipton Company;
reprinted by permission.

1920's

In 1925 the Hawaiian Pineapple Company (Dole) sponsored a recipe contest won by Mrs. Robert Davis of Norfolk, Virginia. Another favorite American dessert was born when her "Pineapple Upside-Down Cake" took top honors.

The Borden Company conducted contests in the 1920's seeking recipes using its condensed milk. In 1927 the Associated Salmon Packers of Seattle, Washington awarded cash prizes for recipes using canned salmon and in 1931 the Association of Pacific Fisheries sought canned salmon recipes as well.

The Postum Company, Incorporated awarded thousands of dollars for Grape-Nuts recipes in 1924 and again in 1928. In 1928 the $1,000 Grand Prize was awarded to "Grape-Nuts Omelet California" and the recipe is included in this collection in the "Brunch Bonanza" section. Today, GRAPE NUTS is a registered trademark of Kraft General Foods, Inc.

1930's

The advent of temperature controlled ovens and refrigerators and freezers emphatically changed not only how we cooked, but how we lived. These "electric servants" made easier preparation a reality, preparation in advance a possibility, and frozen desserts the height of fashionable entertaining. About the same time, convenience foods in canned and packaged form promoted creativity in the kitchen.

When BETTER HOMES AND GARDENS began offering monthly contests in September, 1937, the country was still suffering from the Depression and the $5 prize was considered large at the time. By 1967 the top prize had increased to $50 each for two Cooks-of-the-Month; today the two top winners are awarded $200 each and BETTER HOMES AND GARDENS has the distinction of sponsoring the oldest continuous recipe contests in the world.

1940's

Once restrictions on sugar and other rationed comestibles were lifted following World War II — coupled with increasing use and variety of canned and packaged goods — food manufacturers began to see the potential for promoting their products via recipe contests. As "super" markets offering thousands of items sprang up across the country following years of deprivation during the war, recipe contests were employed more and more as a promotional vehicle.

PINEAPPLE UPSIDE-DOWN CAKE

One of the first classic recipes to come from a contest... a genuine masterpiece of cake featuring canned pineapple slices.

1½ cups all-purpose flour
2 teaspoons baking powder
½ teaspoon salt
½ cup plus 2 tablespoons butter
  or margarine
1 cup granulated sugar
2 eggs, separated

½ cup milk
1 teaspoon vanilla extract
1 cup firmly packed light brown
  sugar
1 can (20 ounces) DOLE® Sliced
  Pineapple, drained
Maraschino cherries, for garnish

- Preheat oven to 350°.

- In medium bowl combine flour, baking powder and salt.

- In large mixer bowl cream ½ cup butter or margarine with sugar until light and fluffy. Add egg yolks one at a time, beating well after each addition. Stir in flour alternately with milk.

- In bowl beat egg whites until stiff peaks form; fold into batter. Stir in vanilla.

- In 8-inch cast-iron skillet melt remaining 2 tablespoons butter over medium heat. Top with brown sugar; add pineapple slices in a single layer. Pour batter over pineapple.

- Bake 40 to 45 minutes, until toothpick inserted in center comes out clean. Invert onto plate and garnish with cherries.

- Makes 8 servings.

Recipe developed by Mrs. Robert Davis of Norfolk, Virginia for the 1925 Hawaiian Pineapple Company (Dole) Cooking Contest. Recipe courtesy of the Dole Food Company, Inc.

The New Forty-Niners

Exactly one century after the California Gold Rush began when gold was discovered at Sutter's Mill in California on January 24, 1848, a golden age of contest cooking was ushered in halfway across the country at yet another mill — the Pillsbury mill. In 1949 a new breed of forty-niners struck culinary gold when The Pillsbury Company of Minneapolis, Minnesota announced its first "Grand National Recipe and Baking Contest," offering an astounding $50,000 Grand Prize.

In 1949 the Delmarva Poultry Industry also announced its first Chicken Festival, eventually resulting in two sister contests—the National Chicken Cooking Contest sponsored by the National Broiler Council and the regional Delmarva Chicken Cooking Contest.

Together, these three organizations launched what have essentially become amateur culinary olympics, creating a new gold rush in the process — in the kitchens of America. These competitions were all held annually for many years and are extravaganzas by any definition. Today, they are held biennially and are the acknowledged institutions in the world of recipe contests. In contesters' lingo, just "going to Pillsbury" or "going to Chicken" is in itself a valued prize for aspiring finalists.

1950's

In the decades following the first Pillsbury Bake-Off® and the chicken cooking contests, thousands of Americans have experienced the joy of competitive creative cooking and its lucrative rewards. Countless organizations have sponsored contests realizing the mutual benefit when customers and companies are connected.

One of the most notable recipe contest winners of the 1950's is the original Reuben Sandwich, the creation of Fern Snider from Omaha, Nebraska. As winner of the 1956 National Sandwich Idea Contest, the Reuben would become the inspiration for many winning Reuben recipes to follow, including "Reuben Croquettes," the $5,000 winner in a 1976 Uncle Ben's contest, "Baked Chicken Reuben," the $10,000 Grand Prize winner at the 1982 National Chicken Cooking Contest, and "Round Reuben Pizza" which won a whopping $32,000 in a Kraft Cheese contest in 1984.

1960's and 1970's

Some of the recipe contest milestones during these two decades were:

- The 1966 Pillsbury Bake-Off® recipe for "Tunnel of Fudge Cake" that inspired a new line of cake mixes and created a demand for the Bundt pan that has since become standard equipment in most kitchens.

- The "First Original World's Championship Chili Cookoff" showdown in Terlingua, Texas in 1967.

- The advent of the microwave oven that revolutionized American cooking during the 1970's.

- The 1971 National Chicken Cooking Contest recipe for "Dipper's Nuggets Chicken with Three Dipping Sauces" that is credited with starting the "nuggets" fast food trend.

- The first National Beef Cook-Off in 1974.

- And then there was the woman who ended up on Johnny Carson's "Tonight Show" in the late '70's after winning the Third Annual Worm Cooking Contest with her masterpiece, a worm quiche — now there's a quiche for real men!

The Future

The popularity of recipe contests has burgeoned over the years and interest in them shows no signs of letting up. As one food editor commented: "Recipe contests have long been a reliable barometer of current cooking trends. Prizewinning recipes quickly go on the menu in American households. It's staggering, the effect of these recipes. People will use them for generations."

Without doubt, recipe contests will continue to play a role in America's future culinary culture. For sponsors, the commercial reality is that recipe contests sell large quantities of their products, both through the contest process itself and through promotion of the prizewinning recipes. Moreover, by virtue of the many thousands of entries in every contest, a sponsor has the unique opportunity of peering through the windows of America's kitchens to see what's cooking. It is here that times, trends, and ideas are revealed, allowing sponsors to target advertising dollars most effectively towards the ones who buy and use their products.

In turn, the everyday American cook has the opportunity to show her or his culinary stuff and to be handsomely rewarded for the effort. Those who have won testify to the fun, fame, and fortune they have enjoyed through competition cooking.

The fact is, recipe contesting is a happy two-way street for both the sponsors and the good cooks of America. In the end, many win, a lot of good will results, and lifetime friends are made.

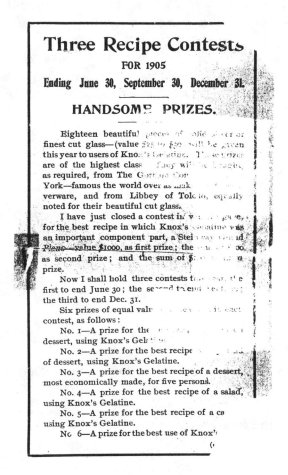

Three Recipe Contests

FOR 1905

Ending June 30, September 30, December 31.

HANDSOME PRIZES.

Eighteen beautiful pieces of solid silver or finest cut glass—(value $25 to $30 will be given this year to users of Knox's Gelatine. These prizes are of the highest class. They will be bought, as required, from The Gorham Co., New York—famous the world over as makers of silverware, and from Libbey of Toledo, equally noted for their beautiful cut glass.

I have just closed a contest in which I gave, for the best recipe in which Knox's Gelatine was an important component part, a Steinway Grand Piano—value $1000, as first prize; the sum of $500, as second prize; and the sum of $250 as third prize.

Now I shall hold three contests this year, the first to end June 30; the second to end Sept. 30; the third to end Dec. 31.

Six prizes of equal value in each contest, as follows:

No. 1—A prize for the best recipe of a dessert, using Knox's Gelatine.

No. 2—A prize for the best recipe of a dessert, using Knox's Gelatine.

No. 3—A prize for the best recipe of a dessert, most economically made, for five persons.

No. 4—A prize for the best recipe of a salad, using Knox's Gelatine.

No. 5—A prize for the best recipe of a ca using Knox's Gelatine.

No. 6—A prize for the best use of Knox's

1905 KNOX Recipe Contest Announcement

" KNOX " is a registered trademark of the Thomas J. Lipton Company; reprinted by permission.

FROM RECIPES TO RICHES — $ECRETS OF $UCCESS

Profile Of A Winning Recipe

In general, a winning recipe is one that has mouth-watering taste and a pleasant texture; one that can be prepared in 30 minutes or less not including cooking time; one that requires no more than 10 to 12 ingredients; one that utilizes a sponsor's product(s) appropriately; and one that the camera will love.

Before you grab that golden opportunity and enter a recipe contest, listen to what the pros have to say. The following are hints from contest judges and sponsors, food professionals, editors, and writers, and from recipe contest winners who have won repeatedly:

Follow Contest Rules Exactly

- If you think that judges will ignore the fact that you stretched the rules a little, you're wrong. (Food Editor)
- In some contests as many as 50% of the entries have to be eliminated because of not following the rules. (Contest Writer)

Taste Is Number One

- It's not the frills and garnishes that count, but just plain good eating. (Food Editor)
- Add seasonings in small quantities; be sure the main ingredient stands out and doesn't get lost. (Food Editor)
- Some beauties lose out because they don't taste as good as they look. (Judge)
- One otherwise good dish was a loser because the sauce was judged a poor match for the sponsor's product. (Judge)

Eye Appeal

- Remember that "eyes eat first;" consider flavor, texture, and color. (GOOD HOUSEKEEPING's Guidelines for Recipe Development)
- Some tasted great but lacked sufficient eye appeal and the garnish offered little contrast. (Judge)
- When adding color, use natural ingredients; avoid food coloring. (Pillsbury)

Ease of Preparation

- Short, simple good tasting dishes that can be prepared in an hour or less are generally the most favored. Intricate, time-consuming concoctions, delicious though they may be, usually don't make it to the finals. (Contest Writer)

Ingredients and Equipment

- Avoid a long list of ingredients.
- Lack of ready availability of ingredients keep some recipes from winning. Recipes have to be downgraded when special ingredients are required that are only available by mail order in small towns and rural areas. (Judge)
- Consider whether most home kitchens have the needed equipment and utensils. (Food Editor)

Notable Exceptions:

Because of unique creativity and marketability, there are exceptions to the above rules. These are the trend setters, the ground breakers, that rare stroke of genius:

Sesame Seeds — In 1954 the Pillsbury Bake-Off® Grand Prize winner, "Open Sesame Pie," featured sesame seeds in the crust. That ingredient alone caused a run on the exotic (at the time) little seed and grocery stores across the country ran out of stock after the recipe was published.

Bundt Pan — At the 17th Bake-Off® in 1966 "Tunnel of Fudge Cake" created a demand for the unfamiliar Bundt-shaped pan. Pillsbury was inundated with consumer requests — more than 200,000 of them — for help in locating the 12-cup fluted tube pan. Since then it has become standard equipment in most American kitchens and a new line of Pillsbury cake mixes was developed as a result.

Broad Appeal

- I believe judges look for a recipe that makes anyone reading it want to cook it. (Recipe Contest Winner)
- Pillsbury looks across mainstream America. (Recipe Contest Winner)
- The average American does not have the time, money, or know-how to be a gourmet cook; a winning recipe usually appeals to the average cook. (Contest Writer)

Consider the Cost

- Avoid expensive gourmet foods; judges express a dislike for expensive ingredients. (Contest Writer)
- Be practical; consider the cost of the dish and the skill involved in preparing it. (Contest Writer)

Tune in to Trends

- Judges look for recipes that fit current lifestyles. (Recipe Contest Winner)
- Many prizewinning recipes are light, nutritious, and healthful; keep fat, cholesterol, salt, and calories in mind. (Food Editor)
- Ethnic and regional dishes are popular as entrants are inspired by their heritage and demographics. (Pillsbury)

Be Creative

- Seek an ingenious use of an ingredient or a new method of shaping a familiar food. (Pillsbury)
- Many winners are simply a new twist on an old favorite. (Recipe Contest Winner)
- Elevate the mundane to the magnificent; come up with your own secret ingredient. I took a favorite recipe, added rum or rum flavoring and an exotic name and it won. (Recipe Contest Winners)
- There's a fine line between being way out in left field, yet being original. We want something unique, something there isn't fifty versions of already. (Pillsbury)

Clear Instructions

- Nothing is more discouraging to a cook or a judge than unclear rambling directions. (Food Editor)
- List ingredients in order of use — a must; don't abbreviate quantities; spell out "teaspoons," etc.
- Be precise with measurements. No "dash" of this or "pinch" of that, or "until it looks right." Include exact measurements and/or package sizes of all ingredients. (Pillsbury)
- Study recipe formats; submit recipes in the organization's preferred style if known; use all capital letters for the organization's product(s) in the ingredients list.

- Specify exact sizes of pots, pans, and casseroles. (Pillsbury)
- Include explicit cooking time, temperature, and a simple way to judge doneness — "cook five minutes until fork-tender." Include information that will avoid confusion — "mixture will be lumpy." (Food Editor)
- Include a tip on how to tell when a recipe is done — "until golden and bubbly." (Pillsbury)
- Include the number of servings a recipe makes.

Test Recipes

- Your recipe must work. A great recipe comes from a lot of near misses. (Recipe Contest Winner)
- Recruit family and friends for taste tests; welcome objective comments and keep refining. (GOOD HOUSEKEEPING's Guidelines for Recipe Development)
- If you are a contestant in a cook-off, prepare by making your dish at home until you can do it quickly and easily.

Create A Catchy Name

- Give your recipe a clever name with accurate descriptive words. (Pillsbury)
- Alliterative titles are popular and get the judges' attention. (Recipe Contest Winner)

Neatness Counts, But Don't Send in More Than Required

- I always send typewritten entries, trying not to make any errors or corrections. (Recipe Contest Winner)
- Unless contest rules specifically request or encourage them, do not submit your recipe with photographs, art work, drawings, or letters; these are nuisances that must be discarded. (Judge)

Enter Often

- If rules permit, I try to enter every category of a contest at least once; if time permits, I like to send a plain and a fancy recipe in each category. (Recipe Contest Winner)
- The more times you enter, the more likely you are to win.

Recipes MUST Be Original

- "Original" is defined as not previously published in the same or substantially the same form. Changing a minor ingredient in a recipe found in a cookbook, magazine, or on a package is not an original creation.

- Generally speaking, three *significant* changes (some contest sponsors require five) are accepted as constituting a new recipe.

- Not only is plagiarizing recipes unethical, but it is outright copyright infringement.

The Golden Rule — Don't Even Think About Cheating

Fortunately, it doesn't happen often, but the bad news is that recipes are occasionally stolen. The good news is that cheaters are ultimately caught:

- One contestant was sent home shamefacedly from a cook-off when it was discovered that her recipe was taken directly from another publication.

- In a major national contest everyone involved was acutely embarrassed upon discovering that the grand prize winner flouted recipe contest ethics and robbed the copyright holder by submitting a plagiarized recipe. When the fraud was discovered, a justifiably angry veteran recipe contest winner released the information to the press and cooking contest newsletter editors making it clear that:

> *"Reducing contest cooking to merely copying a recipe out of a book or magazine is nothing but pure plagiarism; it is an insult to the thousands of entrants who spent time, money and effort trying to create and develop a recipe."*

- Entering contests won't be fun for anyone if you win unfairly. (Contest Writer)

- And finally, before you are officially determined to be eligible to win any prize, in most contests you will be required to sign an Affidavit certifying that your recipe is your own creation. Typically, the wording is along these lines: "The recipe submitted is original and I own all rights to it. It is solely my own work and has never been entered in any contest and has not been previously published or offered for publication elsewhere..."

More Winning Wisdom

- The secret to winning is hard work, enthusiasm, and imaginative thinking. (Contest Writer)

- Start an idea notebook; ideas fade fast. (Contest Writer)

- Do what you do do well. Don't bake cookies if yours always burn; don't bake bread if yours never rises. (Contest Writer)

- Wear your judge's hat. Forget that the entries are yours and try to appraise them critically. (Contest Writer)

- Consider, is the time spent preparing the recipe worth the result? (Contest Writer)

- Sponsors prefer recipes that combine their product with familiar ingredients in an innovative way. (Contest Writer)

- Think like the sponsors and give them what they want; the focus shouldn't be on what the contestant prefers. (Recipe Contest Winner)

- Match your recipes to a sponsor's image and corporate posture. (Recipe Contest Winner)

- Use the product as stated in contest directions, but don't overdo it; some think that by using more of the sponsor's product their changes of winning will be greater, but that just isn't so. (Food Editor)

- Although most contests have their share of first-time winners, don't be discouraged if you don't make it on the first try. (Recipe Contest Newsletter)

- Study past winning recipes in an effort to understand what made them superior, objectively analyzing your recipes by comparison. (Contest Writer)

- Half-hearted efforts result in half-baked entries. (Recipe Contest Newsletter)

- Rule No. 1 — Have fun.

THE GOLD STANDARD OF RECIPE CONTESTS:

"The basis of all good cooking must be good taste and common sense, not mere fancy and make-believe."

LAROUSSE GASTRONOMIQUE
Encyclopedia of French Food, Wine, and Cookery,
Prosper Montagné (1865-1948)

PILLSBURY BAKE-OFF®
GRAND PRIZE HALL OF FAME

Eleanor Roosevelt was its first Guest of Honor, pronouncing it "an important part of the American scene"... the Waldorf Astoria Hotel in New York City hosted it... the Duke and Duchess of Windsor attended it... Art Linkletter M.C.'d it... everyday American cooks reveled in it... and a short time later it would become a registered trademark of The Pillsbury Company.

"It," of course, was the first "Grand National Recipe and Baking Contest," quickly dubbed the "Bake-Off" by the media in 1949 when The Pillsbury Company launched what would become an American institution. For close to half a century no other American food manufacturer has done more to recognize and reward the culinary achievements of the everyday American cook.

Fanfare and hoopla have always surrounded the Bake-Off® phenomenon. Although the cash prizes are tempting enough, America's creative cooks enter the competition for the drama, for the "chance to star in the show that's produced for them," said Ann Pillsbury, doyenne of the Pillsbury domain, in 1959.

And it's all First Class, all expenses paid; it's a glamorous media event where celebrities make cameo appearances. Over the years Pat Boone, Irene Dunne, Greer Garson, Helen Hayes, Abigail Van Buren, and Ronald Reagan have showed up, to name a few.

When Pillsbury offered a total of $100,000 in prizes to 100 of the best cooks in the country in 1949, it inaugurated what was to become one of the most competitive and looked-forward-to food events going. For the Pillsbury Bake-Off® contestant, there is no experience like it. Besides the competition itself, finalists are gloriously entertained wherever the Bake-Off® is held. When it was held in New Orleans in 1978, for example, they enjoyed the French Quarter, Antoine's, Pete Fountain, and cruising on the Mississippi.

As if all of this were not enough, many additional prizes are awarded besides cash — finalists have returned home with their ovens and mixers as souvenirs, and a $10,000 kitchen makeover is often an additional prize awarded to the Grand Prize winner. But as anyone who has ever been one of the 100 finalists will tell you, there are no losers at the Bake-Off®. Everyone's a winner and the best thing they take home are the memories.

The following are the Grand Prize winners — with some of the memories and a few of the recipes — from all of the Bake-Off®s held from 1949 to 1992:

1949 — Bake-Off® 1
NO-KNEAD WATER-RISING TWISTS
Theodora Smafield, Detroit, Michigan
$50,000

An orange, nut, and raisin sweet roll. The first eight Bake-Off®s were held at the Waldorf Astoria Hotel in New York; 97 women and 3 men were finalists in the first competition.

1950 — Bake-Off® 2
ORANGE KISS-ME CAKE
Lily Wuebel, Menlo Park, California
$25,000

Orange, raisin, walnut cake with a cinnamon walnut topping. A new class of competition was introduced this year; junior contestants aged 12 to 19 were eligible to enter and prizes were changed to accommodate the new division.

1951 — Bake-Off® 3
STARLIGHT DOUBLE DELIGHT CAKE
Mrs. Samuel P. Weston, La Jolla, California
$25,000

Moist chocolate cake and chocolate cream cheese frosting with a hint of mint. Arthur Godfrey and Art Linkletter were special guests.

1952 — Bake-Off® 4
SNAPPY TURTLE COOKIES
Beatrice Harlib, Chicago, Illinois
$25,000

Rich cookie resembling the familiar turtle candy. The first eighteen competitions were required to use Pillsbury's Best Flour.

1953 — Bake-Off® 5
"MY INSPIRATION" CAKE
Lois Kanago, Webster, South Dakota
$25,000

An elaborate two-layer cake that gives the appearance of four layers with its ribbon of chocolate running through the two layers; a toasted nut topping is baked in; the cake is assembled using chocolate and white frostings.

1954 — Bake-Off® 6
OPEN SESAME PIE
Mrs. Bernard A. Koteen, Washington, D.C.
$25,000

$25,000

OPEN SESAME PIE

Date chiffon pie with a novel sesame seed crust.

Pastry:

1 cup PILLSBURY All Purpose,
   Unbleached or Self Rising
   Flour *
2 tablespoons sesame seed,
   toasted **

½ teaspoon salt
⅓ cup shortening
3 to 4 tablespoons cold water

Filling:

1 envelope unflavored gelatin
¼ cup cold water
1 cup chopped dates
¼ cup sugar
¼ teaspoon salt
1 cup milk

2 eggs, separated
1 teaspoon vanilla
1 cup whipping cream, whipped
2 tablespoons sugar
Nutmeg

If using self rising flour, omit salt.
**To toast sesame seed, spread on cookie sheet; bake at 375° for 3 to 5 minutes
or until light golden brown, stirring occasionally. Or, spread in small skillet; stir
over medium heat for about 5 minutes or until light golden brown.*

• Heat oven to 450°. Lightly spoon flour into measuring cup; level off.
  In medium bowl, combine flour, sesame seed and ½ teaspoon salt.
  Using pastry blender or fork, cut shortening into flour mixture until
  mixture resembles coarse crumbs. Sprinkle flour mixture with water, 1
  tablespoon at a time, while tossing and mixing lightly with fork. Add
  water until dough is just moist enough to hold together. Shape dough
  into a ball. Flatten ball; smooth edges. On floured surface, roll lightly
  from center to edge into 10½-inch circle. Fold dough in half; fit evenly
  in 9-inch pie pan. Do not stretch. Turn edges under; flute. Prick
  bottom and sides of pastry generously with fork. Bake at 450° for 9 to
  15 minutes or until light golden brown. Cool completely.

• In small bowl, soften gelatin in ¼ cup water; set aside. In medium
  saucepan, combine dates, ¼ cup sugar, ¼ teaspoon salt, milk and egg
  yolks. Cook over medium heat 6 to 10 minutes or until mixture is
  slightly thickened, stirring constantly. Remove from heat. Add softened gelatin and vanilla; stir until gelatin is dissolved. Refrigerate
  until date mixture is thickened and partially set, stirring occasionally.
  Fold whipped cream into date mixture. In small bowl, beat egg whites
  until soft peaks form. Gradually add 2 tablespoons sugar, beating until

stiff peaks form. Fold into date mixture. Spoon filling into cooled baked pie shell; sprinkle with nutmeg. Refrigerate at least 2 hours before serving. Store in refrigerator.

• Makes 8 servings.

1954 — Pillsbury Bake-Off® 6

At a time when chiffon pies were the rage, Mrs. Bernard A. Koteen of Washington, D.C. caused quite a commotion in the supermarkets of America with her intriguing recipe. Just hours after it was announced the Grand Prize winner, many supermarkets ran out of sesame seed. Although it was considered somewhat exotic at the time, after 1954 it became a regularly stocked item on supermarket shelves.

Reprinted by permission of The Pillsbury Company

1955 — Bake-Off® 7
RING-A-LINGS
Bertha Jorgensen, Portland, Oregon
$25,000

No-knead sweet roll with a nut filling and orange glaze. During the 1950's homemakers took the time to be neighborly over a cup of coffee and a go-along. Not only was the first Bake-Off® Grand Prize winning recipe a sweet roll, but two others took top honors in the decade.

1956 — Bake-Off® 8
CALIFORNIA CASSEROLE
Mrs. Hildreth H. Hatheway, Santa Barbara, California
$25,000

Savory veal stew in a sour cream/chicken soup sauce with butter crumb poppy seed dumplings. A trend of the 1950's involved incorporating time-saving canned foods and soups with all manner of mysterious ingredients to produce the casserole, typically an economical and hearty one-dish meal.

1957 — Bake-Off® 9
ACCORDION TREATS
Mrs. Gerda Roderer, Berkeley, California
$25,000

Crisp, wedge-shaped butter cookies baked in an accordion-pleated foil pan. The Bake-Off® went on the road and was held at the Beverly Hilton Hotel in Los Angeles.

1958 — Bake-Off® 10
SPICY APPLE TWISTS
Dorothy DeVault, Delaware, Ohio
$25,000

Apple and spice pastry twists. The Bake-Off® returned to the Waldorf Astoria in New York.

1959 — Bake-Off® 11
MARDI GRAS PARTY CAKE
Eunice Surles, Lake Charles, Louisiana
$25,000

Butterscotch-buttermilk cake with coconut-butterscotch-nut filling and seafoam brown sugar frosting. Once again the Bake-Off® went west and was held in Los Angeles.

1960 — Bake-Off® 12
DILLY CASSEROLE BREAD
Leona P. Schnuelle, Beatrice, Nebraska
$25,000

$25,000

DILLY CASSEROLE BREAD

A real thoroughbread. Dill seed and cottage cheese are the secret ingredients in this favorite, moist, easy to make casserole bread.

2 to 2⅔ cups PILLSBURY'S
  BEST® All Purpose or
  Unbleached Flour
2 tablespoons sugar
2 to 3 teaspoons dried minced
  onion
2 teaspoons dill seed
1 teaspoon salt
¼ teaspoon baking soda

1 package active dry yeast
¼ cup water
1 tablespoon margarine or butter
1 cup creamed cottage cheese
1 egg
2 teaspoons margarine or butter,
  melted
¼ teaspoon coarse salt, if desired

- Lightly spoon flour into measuring cup; level off. In large bowl, combine 1 cup flour, sugar, onion, dill seed, 1 teaspoon salt, baking soda and yeast; blend well. In small saucepan, heat water, 1 tablespoon margarine and cottage cheese until very warm (120° to 130°). Add warm liquid and egg to flour mixture. Blend at low speed until moistened; beat 3 minutes at medium speed. By hand, stir in remaining 1 to 1⅔ cups flour to form a stiff batter. Cover loosely with plastic wrap and cloth towel. Let rise in warm place (80° to 85° F.) until light and doubled in size, 45 to 60 minutes.

- Generously grease 1½ or 2-quart casserole. Stir down dough to remove all air bubbles. Turn into greased casserole. Cover; let rise in warm place until light and doubled in size, 30 to 45 minutes.

- Heat oven to 350°. Uncover dough. Bake at 350° for 30 to 40 minutes or until deep golden brown and loaf sounds hollow when lightly tapped. Remove from casserole immediately; cool on wire rack. Brush warm loaf with melted margarine; sprinkle with coarse salt.

- Makes 1 (18-slice) loaf.

Food Processor Directions:

- In small bowl, soften yeast in ¼ cup warm water (105° to 115°). In food processor bowl with metal blade, combine 2 cups flour, sugar, onion, dill seed, 1 teaspoon salt, baking soda and 1 tablespoon margarine. Cover; process 5 seconds. Add cottage cheese and egg. Cover; process about 10 seconds or until blended. With machine running, pour yeast mixture through feed tube. Continue processing until blended, about 20 seconds or until mixture pulls away from sides of bowl and forms a ball, adding additional flour if necessary. Carefully scrape dough from blade and bowl; place in lightly greased bowl. Cover loosely with plastic wrap and cloth towel. Let rise in warm place (80° to 85°) until light and doubled in size, 45 to 60 minutes. Continue as directed.

1960 — Pillsbury Bake-Off® 12

The recipe for this dilly-icious cottage cheese bread has become so absorbed in American culinary culture that its roots are often forgotten. It's not uncommon to find it in many cookbooks despite it being one of Pillsbury's classic Grand Prize winners. Is it possible that all along you thought this was your Aunt Martha's Dill Bread? At the time Leona P. Schnuelle of Beatrice, Nebraska won the Grand Prize, one food editor commented, "Any dish with 'casserole' in the title these days is a shoo-in."

The only man in this competition was a U.S. Navy Chief Petty Officer who was chief steward aboard a submarine. He won a $1,000 First Prize for his orange cream pie topped with meringue which he dubbed "Sub-Meringue Pie."

Ivy Baker Priest, then Treasurer of the United States, was Guest of Honor at this Bake-Off® held at the Statler Hilton Hotel in Washington, D.C. As the only person authorized to do so, she obligingly autographed one dollar bills as souvenirs for finalists.

Reprinted by permission of The Pillsbury Company

1961 — Bake-Off® 13
CANDY BAR COOKIES
Alice Reese, Minneapolis, Minnesota
$25,000

Turtle-like bar cookie of caramel, pecan, and chocolate. Pillsbury noted a trend in the 1960's of one-step cakes, press-in-the-pan pie crusts, and bar cookies. Early in the decade this Grand Prize winner helped set the trend with its press-in-the-pan base. The Bake-Off® returned to Los Angeles for this year's competition.

1962 — Bake-Off® 14
APPLE PIE '63
Mrs. Erwin Smogor, South Bend, Indiana
$25,000

Rectangular shaped apple pie with a caramel and cream cheese topping. Art Linkletter M.C.'d and Mamie Eisenhower was Guest of Honor at this Bake-Off® held at the Waldorf Astoria in New York.

1963 — Bake-Off® 15
HUNGRY BOYS' CASSEROLE
Mira Walilko, Detroit, Michigan
$25,000

Beef and garbanzo bean casserole topped with almond and olive pinwheel biscuits. This year's competition was held in the International Ballroom of the Beverly Hills Hotel and James Beard was the only male judge.

1964 — Bake-Off® 16
PEACHEESY PIE
Janis Boykin, Melbourne, Florida
$25,000

Peach-flavored crust with peaches and cheesecake filling. As the youngest Bake-Off® Grand Prize winner, seventeen-year-old Janis created this recipe as a Home Economics class assignment and her teacher encouraged her to enter it in the Bake-Off®; her award was presented by Art Linkletter in Miami.

1966 — Bake-Off® 17
GOLDEN GATE SNACK BREAD
Mrs. John Petrelli, Las Vegas, Nevada
$25,000

No-knead, quick-rising cheese and onion bread. This was also the year of "Tunnel of Fudge Cake," which popularized the use of Bundt-shaped fluted tube pans and provided the inspiration for a new line of Pillsbury cake mixes. San Francisco was Bake-Off® headquarters for this appropriately named Grand Prize winner.

$5,000

TUNNEL OF FUDGE CAKE

Cake:

1¾ cups sugar
1¾ cups margarine or butter, softened
6 eggs
2 cups powdered sugar

2¼ cups PILLSBURY'S BEST®
  All Purpose Flour
¾ cup unsweetened cocoa
2 cups chopped walnuts *

Glaze:

¾ cup powdered sugar
¼ cup unsweetened cocoa

1½ to 2 tablespoons milk

Cake:

• Heat oven to 350°. Grease and flour 12-cup Bundt® or 10-inch tube pan. In large bowl, combine sugar and margarine; beat until light and fluffy. Add eggs, 1 at a time, beating well after each addition. Gradually add 2 cups powdered sugar; blend well. Lightly spoon flour into measuring cup; level off. By hand, stir in flour and remaining cake ingredients until well blended. Spoon batter into greased and floured pan; spread evenly. Bake at 350° for 58 to 62 minutes.** Cool upright in pan on wire rack 1 hour; invert onto serving plate. Cool completely.

Glaze:

• In small bowl, blend ¾ cup powdered sugar, ⅓ cup cocoa and enough milk for desired drizzling consistency. Spoon over top of cake, allowing some to run down sides. Store tightly covered.

• Makes 16 servings.

*Nuts are essential for the success of this recipe.
** Since this cake has a soft filling, an ordinary doneness test cannot be used. Accurate oven temperature and baking time are essential.

Recipe developed by Mrs. C. J. Helfrich of Houston, Texas for the 1966 Pillsbury Bake-Off® 17. Bundt® is a registered trademark of Northland Aluminum Company, Inc., Minneapolis, MN. Reprinted by permission of The Pillsbury Company.

1967 —Bake-Off® 18
MUFFIN MIX BUFFET BREAD
Mrs. Maxine Bullock, Topeka, Kansas
$25,000

Cream of vegetable soup and corn muffin mix in a yeast bread. "Convenience" became a byword of the 1960's as canned goods and packaged mixes combined to make cooking easier and quicker. Again the competition was held in California — Los Angeles this time.

1968 — Bake-Off® 19
BUTTERCREAM POUND CAKE
Mrs. Phyllis Lidert, Oak Lawn, Illinois
$25,000

Lemon-flavored cake with poppy seed filling. Dallas was the setting for the Bake-Off® this year.

1969 — Bake-Off® 20
MAGIC MARSHMALLOW CRESCENT PUFFS
Edna Holmgren Walker, Hopkins, Minnesota
$25,000

Hollow-centered sweet roll made with crescent rolls and cinnamon/sugar-coated marshmallows. This year's Bake-Off® marked Pillsbury's 100th anniversary and was held in Atlanta.

1970 — Bake-Off® 21
ONION LOVER'S TWIST
Nan Robb, Huachuca City, Arizona
$25,000

No-knead, yet from scratch, onion yeast bread. Although it took more than ten years for a bread to win the Grand Prize, breads of countless varieties have been popular entries since the first Bake-Off®. This one was held in San Diego.

1971 — Bake-Off® 22
PECAN PIE SURPRISE BARS
Pearl Hall, Snohomish, Washington
$25,000

Caramel pecan pie in bar cookie form. The ballroom of the Hilton Hawaiian Village in Honolulu was the scene of this Bake-Off®.

1972 — Bake-Off® 23 (Two Grand Prizes)
QUICK 'N CHEWY CRESCENT BARS
Mrs. Gerald Collins, Elk River, Minnesota
$25,000 — Refrigerated Foods Division
Only four ingredients with press-in-the-pan ease, using Pillsbury's Coconut Almond or Coconut Pecan Frosting Mix and Quick Crescent Dinner Rolls.

and

STREUSEL SPICE CAKE
Mrs. Carl DeDominicis, Verona, Pennsylvania
$25,000 — Grocery Products Division
A trend-setting pound cake baked in a tube or Bundt pan featuring a spiced streusel filling and topping. This year the Bake-Off® traveled to Houston.

1973 — Bake-Off® 24 (Two Grand Prizes)
QUICK CRESCENT PECAN PIE BARS
Mrs. Jerome Flieller, Jr., Floresville, Texas
$25,000 — Refrigerated Foods Division
and
BANANA CRUNCH CAKE
Bonnie Brooks, Salisbury, Maryland
$25,000 — Grocery Products Division
Sour cream banana cake with a coconut-pecan-oat crunch. It was back to California for this competition held in Beverly Hills. Among more than 100,000 entries there were two 12-year-old boys and one male graduate student who were finalists.

1974 — Bake-Off® 25 (Two Grand Prizes)
SAVORY CRESCENT CHICKEN SQUARES
Doris Castle, River Forest, Illinois
$25,000 — Refrigerated Foods Division
and
CHOCOLATE CHERRY BARS
Mrs. Emil Jerzak, Porter, Minnesota
$25,000 — Grocery Products Division
A combination of fudge cake mix and cherry fruit filling in bar form.

$25,000

SAVORY CRESCENT CHICKEN SQUARES

A unique sandwich using Pillsbury's Crescent Dinner Roll dough filled with a cream cheese and chicken mixture. After assembling, the tops are brushed with butter, then dipped in seasoned crouton crumbs before being baked a golden brown.

1 (3-ounce) package cream cheese, softened

2 tablespoons butter or margarine, melted

2 cups cooked, cubed chicken or two 5-ounce cans boned chicken

¼ teaspoon salt

⅛ teaspoon pepper

2 tablespoons milk

1 tablespoon chopped chives or onion

1 tablespoon chopped pimiento, if desired

1 (8-ounce) can PILLSBURY Refrigerated Quick Crescent or Italian Flavor Crescent Dinner Rolls

¾ cup seasoned croutons, crushed

- Preheat oven to 350°. In medium bowl, blend cream cheese and 2 tablespoons butter (reserve 1 tablespoon) until smooth. Add the next 6 ingredients; mix well. Separate crescent dough into 4 rectangles; firmly press perforations to seal. Spoon ½ cup meat mixture onto center of each rectangle. Pull 4 corners of dough to top center of chicken mixture, twist slightly and seal edges. Brush tops with reserved 1 tablespoon butter; dip in crouton crumbs. Bake on ungreased cookie sheet 20 to 25 minutes until golden brown. Refrigerate any leftovers.

- Makes 4 sandwiches.

1974 — Pillsbury Bake-Off® 25

There were two $25,000 Grand Prize winners in this Silver Anniversary competition held in Phoenix, Arizona. Mrs. Emil Jerzak of Porter, Minnesota won the Grand Prize in the Grocery Products Division with her recipe for "Chocolate Cherry Bars" and Doris Castle of River Forest, Illinois won the Grand Prize in the Refrigerated Foods Division by creating the only sandwich ever to win Grand Prize at the Bake-Off®.

Reprinted by permission of The Pillsbury Company

1975 — Bake-Off® 26 (Two Grand Prizes)
EASY CRESCENT DANISH ROLLS
Barbara Gibson, Fort Wayne, Indiana
$25,000 — Refrigerated Foods Division
and
SOUR CREAM APPLE SQUARES
Luella Maki, Ely, Minnesota
$25,000 — Grocery Products Division

Apple and cinnamon cake-like squares. This Bake-Off® was held at the Regency Hyatt Hotel in San Francisco.

1976 — Bake-Off® 27 (Two Grand Prizes)
CRESCENT CARAMEL SWIRL
Lois Ann Groves, San Antonio, Texas
$25,000 — Refrigerated Foods Division

Only five ingredients, one of them water — brown sugar, nuts, and butter swirl in, around, and through pinwheel slices of Crescent Roll dough arranged in a 12-cup fluted tube pan.

and
WHOLE WHEAT RAISIN LOAF
Lenora Smith, Harahan, Louisiana
$25,000 — Grocery Products Division

Healthy yeast bread fortified with whole wheat flour, rolled oats, and raisins and seasoned with cinnamon and nutmeg. This Grand Prize winner appeared smack in the middle of the "granola" decade, when the words "natural" and "healthful" were culinary watchwords. In this year of the U.S.A.'s Bicentennial, the Bake-Off® was held at the Statler Hilton Hotel in Boston, a significant city in early American history. This year also marked the change from annually held Bake-Off®s to biennial ones.

1978 — Bake-Off® 28 (Two Grand Prizes)
CHICK-N-BROCCOLI POT PIES
Linda L. Woods, Indianapolis, Indiana
$25,000 — Refrigerated Foods Division

Pillsbury biscuits form the "pie dough" for mini-pot pies baked in muffin tins. This was the first recipe contest Linda Woods had ever entered.

and
NUTTY GRAHAM PICNIC CAKE
Esther V.Tomich, San Pedro, California
$25,000 — Grocery Products Division

Brown sugar-glazed graham cracker crumb and nut cake. This year the Bake-Off® was held in the ballroom of the Hilton Hotel in New Orleans.

$40,000

ITALIAN ZUCCHINI CRESCENT PIE

4 cups thinly sliced zucchini
1 cup chopped onions
2 tablespoons margarine or butter
2 tablespoons parsley flakes
½ teaspoon salt
½ teaspoon pepper
¼ teaspoon garlic powder
¼ teaspoon basil leaves

¼ teaspoon oregano leaves
2 eggs, well beaten
8 ounces (2 cups) shredded
    Muenster or mozzarella cheese
1 (8-ounce) can PILLSBURY
    Refrigerated Quick Crescent
    Dinner Rolls
2 teaspoons prepared mustard

- Heat oven to 375°. In large skillet, cook zucchini and onions in margarine until tender, about 8 minutes. Stir in parsley flakes, salt, pepper, garlic powder, basil and oregano. In large bowl, combine eggs and cheese; mix well. Stir in cooked vegetable mixture.

- Separate dough into 8 triangles.* Place in ungreased 10-inch pie pan, 12 x 8-inch (2-quart) baking dish or 11-inch quiche pan; press over bottom and up sides to form crust. Firmly press perforations to seal. Spread crust with mustard. Pour egg-vegetable mixture evenly into prepared crust. Bake at 375° for 18 to 22 minutes or until knife inserted near center comes out clean.** Let stand 10 minutes before serving.

- Makes 6 servings.

*If using 12 x 8-inch (2-quart) baking dish, unroll dough into 2 long rectangles; press over bottom and 1 inch up sides to form crust. Firmly press perforations to seal. Continue as directed above.
**Cover edge of crust with strip of foil during last 10 minutes of baking if necessary to prevent excessive browning.

1980 — Pillsbury Bake-Off® 29

At a time when quiche was popular and zucchini was enjoying culinary popularity, this Grand Prize winning recipe was right on target. Millicent A. Caplan of Tamarac, Florida didn't have to travel far to claim her Grand Prize win at this Bake-Off® held at the Fountainbleau Hilton in Miami Beach, Florida.

Reprinted by permission of The Pillsbury Company

1980 — Bake-Off® 29
ITALIAN ZUCCHINI CRESCENT PIE
Millicent A.Caplan, Tamarac, Florida
$40,000

1982 — Bake-Off® 30
ALMOND FILLED COOKIE CAKE
Elizabeth Meijer, Danbury, Connecticut
$40,000

Rich ground almond-filled torte inspired by an old Dutch pastry recipe. San Antonio hosted this year's Bake-Off® and Bob Barker was there to present the awards. There were more than 30,000 entries in this year's Bake-Off®, distinguished by having the youngest finalist ever to compete — ten-year-old Janelle Smith.

1984 — Bake-Off® 31
COUNTRY APPLE COFFEE CAKE
Sue Porubcan, Whitewater, Wisconsin
$40,000

Pillsbury biscuits form the basis of this glazed apple coffee cake. The competition was held in San Diego in the Ballroom of the Sheraton Harbor Island Hotel and once again Bob Barker announced the winners and awarded the prizes.

1986 — Bake-Off® 32
APPLE NUT LATTICE TART
Mary Lou Warren, Colorado Springs, Colorado
$40,000

Apple-nut-raisin lattice tart with a hint of lemon in both filling and glaze. Disney World in Orlando hosted this year's event.

1988 — Bake-Off® 33
CHOCOLATE PRALINE LAYER CAKE
Julie Konecne, Minnesota
$40,000

Chocolate and praline cake topped with whipped cream and garnished with whole pecans and chocolate curls. This year's Bake-Off® venue was San Diego.

1990 — Bake-Off® 34
BLUEBERRY POPPY SEED BRUNCH CAKE
Linda Rahman, Petaluma, California
$50,000

Glazed sour cream and poppy seed cake with blueberry filling. The Bake-Off®— America's most prestigious cooking competition—was held in Phoenix this year.

1992 — Bake-Off® 35
PENNSYLVANIA DUTCH CAKE AND CUSTARD PIE
Gladys Fulton, Summerville, South Carolina
$50,000
Cake-pie combination featuring Pillsbury's Refrigerated Pie Crust with a filling of applesauce, sour cream, and molasses. There were nine men among the 100 finalists this year in Orlando and Willard Scott presented the awards.

"Going to Pillsbury" is an adventure in a food fantasyland, a place where finalists' dreams come true. But, instead of a fantasies, there are real stories of the sweet smells of success about America's most real people.

Over the decades, these adventures have been entertainingly and heartwarmingly recorded in the many Pillsbury publications — like the time one contestant whose luggage was lost was taken on a shopping trip by a member of the Pillsbury family... or the time that one woman whose husband's dying wish was for her to go to the Bake-Off® did so the day after his funeral. After she won a $2,000 prize, the applause was long and sincere from 99 fellow finalists and everyone in attendance.

"Going to Pillsbury" is the goal of all avid recipe contesters. Those who have been Pillsbury finalists declare that there is no experience like it. And that is why many, many thousands of American cooks reach for the Pillsbury gold star Bake-Off® after Bake-Off®... because just being a Pillsbury finalist and "Going to Pillsbury" is a great achievement indeed.

A WEEK IN THE LIFE OF A RECIPE CONTEST FINALIST

Notes From The Author's Diary

In 1977 I was one of 40 lucky finalists who won a trip to Hawaii to compete for a Grand Prize of $25,000 in the National Pineapple Cooking Classic. Although I didn't win the Grand Prize, or any of the other cash prizes, I felt that I was the big winner. Besides being a dream come true, the trip inspired the cover for AS GOOD AS GOLD. After checking in at the Royal Hawaiian Hotel in Honolulu, these were the highlights of a very special week in April, 1977:

SATURDAY

A get-acquainted cocktail reception and dinner on the hotel's Surf Room Terrace for travel-worn finalists from as far away as New Hampshire. Shaping the mood for the week ahead, the Hawaiian sun set as if on cue while finalists and their guests sipped mai tais from hollowed out pineapples garnished with tropical flowers.

SUNDAY

Following an orientation program of the week's events, finalists inspected the ingredients to be used in Tuesday's cook-off and acquainted themselves with the Hotpoint ranges. In the evening, Diamond Head provided the surreal backdrop for a festive luau on the Royal Hawaiian Hotel's ocean lawn and beachfront. Masses of fragrant jasmine and other jewel-like tropical flowers perfumed the air. Torches blazed as the most exotic of exotic dancers appeared... from Tahiti, Samoa, and other Polynesian island groups.

MONDAY

Not a typical Monday. The only work was an optional inspection of perishable ingredients to be used in the next day's cookoff. After a day of seeing the sights and compulsory shopping on Kalakaua Avenue, a highly ceremonial dinner was a sit-down affair (on floor mats) at the Natsunoya Tea House. By now, we were a big family wondering if we'd been whisked off to Japan for the evening.

TUESDAY — COOK-OFF DAY

Forty mini-kitchens had been set up in the hotel's chandeliered ball-

210

room. After a short inspirational program on the beachfront lawn, finalists clad in official contest aprons literally paraded to our work stations.
There we prepared our recipes twice, once for the judges, the other for
photography.

Cameras popped, food editors scooped, and TV camera crews added
their equipment to the astonishing atmosphere. All of this amidst live
musical entertainment! Whew... that evening's event, a relaxed dinner
and night club show at the hotel, dispelled the day's exhilarating tense-
ness.

WEDNESDAY

A day of touring the Dole pineapple cannery and Del Monte Plantation
and lunch at Kemoo Farms was followed by reveling in yet another
tropical sunset aboard an enormous catamaran for the evening's cocktail
and dinner cruise.

THURSDAY

The BIG day — night, actually. After a day at leisure, finalists, guests,
hosts, food editors, and the media en masse — with representatives
from every finalist's hometown — assembled once again on the Royal
Hawaiian Hotel's beachfront lawn for the festive Awards Ceremony
followed by an elaborate banquet.

Little by little the suspense was broken as the four $2,500 Second Place
prizewinners were announced, the four $10,000 First Place winners
accepted their awards, and finally the $25,000 Best of Contest recipe
and Grand Prize winner was proclaimed. "Pineapple Meringue Cake"
took top honors, an updated and revised heirloom recipe that had been
in the winner's family for many years. Prior to this, the winner had
entered only one other recipe in a contest, and that ten years earlier.

FRIDAY

Return to reality with luggage full of memories and a case of four fresh
golden pineapples after a fantasy week of adventure in paradise.

I still believe I was the Grand Prize winner... I had to pinch myself on
the return flight home. As one veteran recipe contest winner has put it
so well:

"There's no other experience like being a contestant. It turns the
average person into a star for a short time. The sponsors treat you
royally, all expenses are paid, and you get to meet interesting people."

Confessions Of A Recipe Contest Hobbyist

After this experience I was hooked on recipe contesting as a hobby. I have entered many contests and collected the winning recipes from cooking contest newsletters, magazines, newspapers, and from the sponsors themselves.

Since the trip to Hawaii I've entered a myriad of recipe contests without a win. But despite all the misses, and near misses, it's been almost as much fun collecting prizewinning recipes — seeing what's cooking in other kitchens and experiencing the fun vicariously through many other winners who've had a chance to show their stuff.

I conclude that I'm really a much better collector of prizewinning recipes than a winner of recipe contests. The consolation prize is that prizewinning recipes always add a unique dimension to entertaining. Guests are intrigued when I mention that the main course won $50,000 or the dessert they are about to enjoy won a Caribbean cruise. It is then that good meals become memorable meals.

Memorable meals — that's what AS GOOD AS GOLD is all about.

Want To Know More ???

The following cooking contest newsletter Editors would love to add new members to the vast club of contesters:

Karen Martis, Editor and Publisher
COOKING CONTEST CHRONICLE
P.O.Box 10792
Merrillville, Indiana 46411-0792

Joyce G. Campagna, Editor and Publisher
THE COOKING CONTEST NEWSLETTER
P.O.Box 339
Summerville, South Carolina 29484

Sadly, the Blue Ribbon Cooks' Newsletter has not been published since the sudden, unexpected death of its beloved Editor, Hanna Foxe, in October, 1992. Those of us who knew her through her newsletter miss her very much indeed.

Photo by Forest Wells

Linda Davis-O'Brien Receives Cookbook's First Place National Award
The Boathouse, Central Park, New York City

From left, McIlhenny Company Vice President Paul McIlhenny, Cookbook Chairman Linda Davis-O'Brien, Chesapeake Bay Maritime Museum Executive Director John Valliant, and McIlhenny Company President Ned Simmons.

ABOUT THE AUTHOR

Linda Davis-O'Brien's first cookbook, FROM A LIGHTHOUSE WINDOW, benefitted the Chesapeake Bay Maritime Museum in St. Michaels, Maryland. It was selected as the First Place winner in the 1990 National Tabasco® Community Cookbook Awards competition.

Linda's recipe contest credits include:

* Finalist, 1973 Seagram's V.O. & GOURMET® MAGAZINE'S International Hors d'Oeuvre Recipe Contest, San Francisco, California

* Finalist, the Pineapple Growers Association of Hawaii's 1977 National Pineapple Cooking Classic, Honolulu, Hawaii

* Semi-Finalist, 1991 Newman's Own & GOOD HOUSEKEEPING's Spicy Diavolo Sauce Recipe Contest

* Selected as a Semi-Finalist for the State of Maryland, 1993 National Beef Cook-Off

Linda's plans for the future include producing a Second Edition of AS GOOD AS GOLD; her dreams are to be a judge in a chocolate contest — or recipe contests of any kind; and her aspiration is to design the ultimate His-'n'-Hers-'n'-Friends kitchen because that's where all the fun is.

INDEX

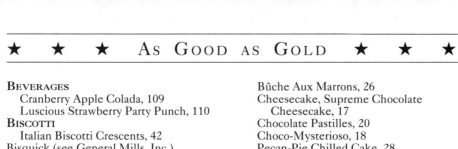

★ ★ ★ As Good as Gold ★ ★ ★

P.O. Box 768
St. Michaels, Maryland 21663

Ship To: (PLEASE PRINT)

Name _____

Address _____

City _____ State _____ Zip _____

Daytime Phone Number _____

_____ copies of AS GOOD AS GOLD @ $16.95 each $ _____

Postage and handling @ $ 2.50 each $ _____

Tax — Maryland Residents Only — $ .85 per book $ _____

TOTAL ENCLOSED $ _____

Make check or money order payable to AS GOOD AS GOLD and enclose with order. Please do not send cash. Sorry, no C.O.D.'s.

★ ★ ★ As Good as Gold ★ ★ ★

P.O. Box 768
St. Michaels, Maryland 21663

Ship To: (PLEASE PRINT)

Name _____

Address _____

City _____ State _____ Zip _____

Daytime Phone Number _____

_____ copies of AS GOOD AS GOLD @ $16.95 each $ _____

Postage and handling @ $ 2.50 each $ _____

Tax — Maryland Residents Only — $ .85 per book $ _____

TOTAL ENCLOSED $ _____

Make check or money order payable to AS GOOD AS GOLD and enclose with order. Please do not send cash. Sorry, no C.O.D.'s.